When God Calls a Woman

When God Calls a Woman

The Struggle of a Woman Pastor in France and Algeria

Elisabeth Schmidt

Translated, with notes, by Allen Hackett

The Pilgrim Press
New York

Originally published in French as *Quand Dieu Appelle des Femmes: le combat d'une femme pasteur* by Elisabeth Schmidt; © 1978 by Les Éditions du Cerf, 29, bd. Latour-Maubourg, Paris; and as *En ces temps de malheur (1958-1962) J'Étais Pasteur en Algérie* by Elisabeth Schmidt; © 1976 by Les Éditions du Cerf, 29, bd. Latour-Maubourg, Paris. Translated, with notes, by Allen Hackett.

Library of Congress Cataloging in Publication Data

Schmidt, Elisabeth, 1908-
    When God calls a woman.

    Translation of: Quand Dieu appelle des femmes.
    Includes bibliographical references.
    1. Schmidt, Elisabeth, 1980-   . 2. Reformed
Church—Clergy—Biography. 3. Clergy—France—Biography.
4. Clergy—Algeria—Biography. I. Title.
BX9459.S35A3613   284'.23 [B]   81-12009
ISBN 0-8298-0430-7 (pbk.)   AACR2

The Pilgrim Press, 132 West 31 Street, New York, N.Y. 10001

Contents

Preface

You know best how it happens that you have this book in your hands, but I want to tell you how it came to exist in this form. In so doing, I wish to thank the four women who made it possible.

First, my gratitude goes out to our Swiss Quaker friend Nelly Haywood. She chanced to see Elisabeth Schmidt on a television program focusing on her then recent book, *Quand Dieu Appelle des Femmes, le Combat d'une Femme Pasteur* (1978). Nelly Haywood was impressed with the author's quiet authority and deep compassion. She bought the book and read it. Then, remembering my lively interest in the French Protestant movement, she sent her copy to me with the cryptic note: *To Allen, hopefully of interest, Nelly.*

The book captivated me also, and I sent for its companion volume, Elisabeth Schmidt's earlier book, *En ces Temps de Malheur (1958-1963), J'Étais Pasteur en Algérie.* It became clear to me that the two books made one rounded whole and that they told the story of a brave and significant ministry. Because Elisabeth Schmidt was the first woman to be ordained in the French Reformed Church, and because her "combat" (or struggle) had wider implications, I entertained the idea of making a translation combining the two accounts that could be published in the United States.

I broached the idea in a letter to Elisabeth Schmidt, to whom I am indebted on four major counts:

- For "the living of these days"—her blend of fiery zeal and judgment and her forthright way of sharing her experiences and feelings;
- For her venture of faith in allowing me to interpret her words and to negotiate with her French publishers, Les Éditions du Cerf, in Paris;
- For her careful responses to my many queries, responses embodied in the notes, which are designed to diminish the strangeness of the French milieu; and
- For her willingness to come to Strasbourg from the south of France, with her physician sister, Simone, so that we might meet and work out "clarifications" in the translation, particularly in relation to Algeria. (Dorothy and I were in Europe in July 1980 to attend our granddaughter's wedding in Germany.) During our work sessions, after which we entertained one another at tea, we deepened our friendship and achieved a real sense of spiritual communion.

My litany of gratitude goes on to include my wife, Dorothy Shuman Hackett. She has shared fully in my ministries in parishes and as an area minister. Our partnership goes on in my retirement vocation—studying and interpreting our Reformation heritage as it is expressed in France. Dorothy typed draft after draft of the translation and made many helpful editorial suggestions.

I am also indebted to Marion M. Meyer, senior editor of The Pilgrim Press. Because we had worked together some years ago, I sent the manuscript of the translation to her, when it was well along, with a letter outlining the rest. She felt that the book would contribute to the dialogue concerning women's ministries and has followed it through the channels of publication with her customary good workmanship and enthusiasm. Thus we join in repeating Nelly Haywood's words: "Hopefully of interest!"

Allen Hackett

Introduction

You will find in these pages the autobiography of a French-woman, born in 1908 and now in her retirement. This is the honest account of a remarkable spiritual, geographical, and historical pilgrimage. Elisabeth Schmidt is a woman pastor, unique in France in her time. She was the first woman to be ordained in the French Reformed Church, the ordination coming just before the midpoint of her career. This fact, in itself, suggests the struggle she refers to in the title.

It was a struggle on many fronts: women's rights, church-manship, theology, and race relations. She was a participant in some of the major movements of our century, in the church and in her nation: she remembers her father's call to the colors in World War I and the victory parade up the Champs-Élysées; she knew the Student Christian Movement in its heyday between the wars; she was saddened by France's capitulation to Germany in World War II and the anti-Semitism which she helped to combat; she shared in the struggle for Algeria's independence and nationhood; she was pastor in a university city in May 1968, when students and workers brought France to a standstill. She shared in the gradual strengthening of ecumenical relationships with the Roman Catholic Church.

Elisabeth Schmidt's parents were intellectual atheists who never mentioned God, the Bible, or the church to their two daughters. Her father was a deputy from the Vosges, her mother, a teacher. In this "advanced" household, women were never considered "the weaker sex," unfit to manage large affairs or to perform the major jobs in society. It was assumed that Elisabeth would go into teaching, preferably in science, the field her father had abandoned for politics.

Elisabeth Schmidt resembled her parents in their independence of mind, but her course took her in a new direction. When Madame Schmidt's serious illness sent mother and children to Switzerland, Elisabeth, forbidden to attend the school course in Christian education, listened from the back of the room and, back in Paris, got her mother's permission to go to Sunday school. Finding the parish a warm and welcoming community, she requested baptism and united with the church.

At the Sorbonne and through the World's Student Christian Federation, Elisabeth Schmidt found a camaraderie which largely effaced the loneliness of her childhood. Here too she experienced an imperious and undeniable call to offer herself in full-time Christian service, a call which took precedence over an attractive offer of marriage and her virtually certain success as a teacher of philosophy. She did not attempt to determine the form of her ministry but embarked, in Geneva, on the finest theological training then available to her. Convinced that when women enter a field which men have kept as their private preserve, the women ought to excel, she went to the head of her class, won the preaching prize, and got the longest ovation at commencement.

In the summer of 1935 Elisabeth Schmidt, now twenty-seven, offered herself for service, "no matter where." She was ready for the church, but the church was not ready for her. One church official, embarrassed to meet a woman looking for a pastorate, offered her the work of a pastor at the salary of an evangelist—an offer she firmly refused. Finally, she was sent to a parish deep in the Cévennes mountains for a "probationary year," at the end of which, although a man would have been ordained if he had proved himself in the ministry, Elisabeth Schmidt received only a "pastoral delegation." This enabled her to do the work of a pastor without official standing.

In 1940 France was invaded by the Nazis and cut in half. A friend from student days needed help at an internment camp near the Pyrénées, so Elisabeth Schmidt went to Gurs, where, teamed with a trained social worker, she was part of CIMADE, the nonviolent resistance movement which sought to thwart the anti-Semitism of the Nazis and the collaborationists. Still unordained, she was the only pastor in a camp of 25,000 detainees until typhoid fever cut short her service there and sent her to the hospital. Her pastoral career was at a standstill.

In 1942 she was called as pastor of the important church in Sète, on the Mediterranean coast, although her credentials were still limited to a "pastoral delegation," renewed from year to year. At Sète, with her congregation, she experienced the German conquest and the American liberation and helped to shape the city's postwar reconstruction. Here, in 1945, the local presbyterial council, without her knowledge, wrote to the national church leaders requesting her ordination. Four years later, in 1949, the National Synod, by a vote of 62 to 18, granted the Sète church's request "as an exception."

Over these long years, the question of "feminine ministries" had become more than a question of ecclesiastical discipline and church policy. It was also the locus of a theological inquiry. What happens "when God calls a woman" and she says, "I come"? Can men say that she may not? This would be presumption, denying God's freedom to call anyone. Thus what begins as a problem of ecclesiology becomes a study in theology.

Elisabeth Schmidt's theology is grounded in the Word of God, "the only infallible rule of faith and practice." Well-meaning delegates to the National Synod repeated Paul's injunction that "the women should keep silence in the churches [1 Cor. 14:34]"; recognizing that those particular women, in that particularly boisterous church, may have let their new freedom in Christ go to their heads and merited silencing, she insisted on the words of the same apostle Paul, writing to the Galatians (3:28): "There is neither Jew nor Greek, there is neither slave nor free, there is neither male nor female; for you are all one in Christ Jesus."

The ministry in Sète continued until 1958, when Elisabeth Schmidt was called to Blida and Medea in Algeria, where her parishioners—French officials, air force officers and men, merchants, teachers, seamstresses, and, at a great distance, scattered plantation owners—were fast disappearing back to France on the eve of Algerian independence. In the midst of terrorism, she put out feelers of understanding toward the Algerian Muslims, untouched by Christian churches, and stayed on during the first year of Algerian nationhood, holding Sunday services and teaching at the boys' lycée.

Long after her male counterparts had received calls to churches in France, a lifeline was thrown to Elisabeth Schmidt in the form of an invitation to join a team ministry in Nancy, the capital of Lorraine. Here, she found a parish "on the march." At the side of three colleagues, she first experienced a collegial ministry, sharing the preaching and the administrative responsibilities in turn, and was "officer in charge" in May 1968, when the student-worker protest movement rocked all France.

During those years, Elisabeth Schmidt was more and more drawn into regional and national church life. She was moderator of her regional synod, a member of the National Synod, and, finally, just before her retirement in 1972, vice moderator of the National Synod.

To withstand the strains of those thirty-seven years; to minister in such diverse parishes and in the nonchurch at the internment camp—all this took a heavy toll of physical and spiritual strength. What resources could she draw on? The book reveals a woman of prayer. She finds in the Bible not only guidance but sustenance. She is a faithful friend, a generous hostess, and a welcome guest. The children of her colleagues call her "Tante Elisabeth" or "Taty." She is a true and patriotic Frenchwoman, ashamed of the Vichyites but proud of the fact that her Alsatian grandfathers had opted for France in 1870, during the Franco-Prussian War.

Elisabeth Schmidt neither obtrudes nor hides her feelings. You will taste the salt of her tears and laugh quietly with her at some of the foibles of our human condition. In the words of a "niece by affection," a music student in Boston, "She is SOMEONE."

Allen Hackett

When God Calls a Woman

1

Some Landmarks—
Childhood and Adolescence

I HAD BEEN GIVEN PERMISSION to stay later than usual in the garden.

My parents had just left Paris—where I had been born three years ago, on May 31, 1908—and settled in a villa at Meudon, after the birth of their second daughter, Simone. Today I have few mental pictures of our apartment in one of the houses built by the architect Hector Guimard in the 16th arrondissement.

On this lovely evening at the beginning of July 1911, I was seated on my father's knee, looking at the stars which seemed to be lighting themselves; in Paris you don't see the immense sky so well, and I was asking about those distant lights.

The Godless Universe of My Early Childhood

My father took the opportunity to give me a course on universal gravitation. I tried to follow his explanations, which intrigued me, adding more questions after each answer until we came to questions without answer. I have kept, saved from all sorting of papers, a composition written when I was about thirteen, in the third form of the lycée, on the subject "Some Memories from Childhood." From it I can repeat this conversation with my father.

"You are sure that the stars never get off their tracks?" I asked him. "Perhaps a star will hit the earth and that will be terrible!" In spite of my father's reassuring explanations I added, "And nobody looks after them?"

"Of course not!" he answered.

My father, Henri Schmidt, was then a deputy[1] from the Vosges, a radical socialist, and a Freemason. He had abandoned the preparation of a thesis on mycology and thrown himself, as a young man, into politics. At his marriage in 1905, he had held out against the pressures of his milieu and had refused any religious ceremony. This was a crushing disappointment to his parents, who were deeply convinced Protestants.

My mother, Angèle Kilbourg, had not even been baptized. My grandfather Kilbourg was a Voltairean. After sound university studies in France and in Germany, my mother had been appointed German professor at the Girls' College in Saint-Dié. It was there she met my father. My parents had agreed to give their children an education from which all religious influences would be removed; the words "God," "religion," and "church" did not come to my ears. In the notebook where my mother wrote down my first childish questions, there is no mention of these words. I wonder today how they answered my question, "Where does thought come from when I think?"

My grandfather Schmidt and my grandmother (even when she was left a widow) had scrupulously respected the wishes of my parents: to say nothing contrary to a Godless education. I did not know where my grandmother went when she went to church on Sunday mornings. Then why did I have for this grandmother a special preference? Children perceive what does not need to be expressed. There were mysterious harmonies between the deep faith of the ancestor and the unconscious search of the granddaughter. The pastor of Saint-Dié, when he was a refugee in the south of France during the war, felt that he could share with me a confidence from my grandmother: "I pray God every day that he will bring back to himself my granddaughters, who are being brought up in atheism. I can say nothing, do nothing. But I know that God can act in a way we cannot foresee."

The memories of my early childhood are peopled with faces which are somewhat blurred in my mind today: friends, relations, members of parliament, artists in the Third Republic; children of some of them were my playmates. I also had friends among the residents of the villas near our own. The one garden that I could not enter was that of Jacques Maritain, the only neighbor with whom my parents had no dealings.

I heard a lot of talk about "the Chamber," and about "ministries falling." It was a bit mysterious, but my parents let me ask questions. My mother even took me to visit the Chamber of Deputies one day during recess, and the sergeant-at-arms showed me my father's place. I was quite let down because the deputies had desks and inkwells, just like schoolchildren!

During summer vacations we went to my grandmother's home in Saint-Dié. Learning to take long walks on the trails in the Vosges forests was part of my education. I also recall happy afternoons spent at the chalet of the Ferry family. I did not like the portrait of the man with side whiskers hanging in my father's study (a portrait of Jules Ferry),[2] but I liked Madame Ferry. She kept me from being punished by my mother when I showed, in the Ferry house, some claims to independence in the name of freedom.

In the narrowly anticlerical climate of the beginning of the century, my father must have believed, like so many others, that in voting for the Law of Separation of Church and State he was signing the death warrant of the churches. He had given me a big red book carrying in gold letters the title *Republican Catechism*. It had to do with the mistakes in the Bible. Since I had never heard the Bible mentioned, I didn't understand it at all. But I admired my father a great deal.

Without being well informed about his social ideals and his different activities (interventions, speeches and reports in the Chamber, public lectures), I knew that his electoral platform included a stand against alcoholism. Even today, few people in France dare to attack alcohol!

I was brought up with a certain austerity. Simply clothed, I was reprimanded for any evidence of coquetry. My parents demanded that I work hard in school, spoke of my future university studies, and held Madame Curie up before me as an example. I realize today that their education was advanced for the time.

In spite of everything I received from my family, I was not a happy little girl. I was missing something, but I did not know what.

Trials and Searchings

It was certainly under the gnawing of adversity that I began to seek the sense and the why of the things of life. Then came 1914: war! It seemed to me that a foul beast had attacked the universe where I lived. My parents, although nourished on the humanitarian aspirations of Romain Rolland, were still the children of Alsatians and Lorrainers and shared their spirit of vengeance. The whole need for the absolute which God puts in our hearts was oriented toward the Fatherland. By this I was led badly astray!

In 1917 my mother had surgery; I understood that she was expected to die. My father was called up for military service. Suffering deepened in me an unfathomable gulf, where I was alone. No one could answer all the questions which were reeling around in my head.

In Switzerland I began to find a little light and peace. My mother was sent there to follow a course of sun therapy at Leysin, under the supervision of Dr. Charles Rollier. Our maid, Juliette, agreed to go too, to take care of my sister and me. In this time of war a frontier would separate her from her four brothers, who had been called up for service.

Thanks to her devotion, my sister and I could accompany our mother to Leysin.

Dr. Rollier, a fine Christian doctor, had inspired the creation of a private school where the pupils took the sun cure during class time. He had enough prestige and authority to convince my mother to send us there, but it was clearly understood that I would not follow the course in sacred history. In a corner of the classroom, grappling with an insoluble problem, I listened to this forbidden course. Through stories totally new to me, I gathered that a Mover hides behind the characters: God. But what is God? I remember my astonishment at the story of Joseph's pardoning his brothers (in Genesis 45). The whole class recited this summary: "God has changed into good this evil which you have done." "That is still more beautiful," I told myself, "than supervising the stars."

The teacher of the course got permission from my mother to take me to the Christmas tree at the church in Leysin village. What did I hear through the songs or the words of the pastor in this place of worship which I entered for the first time? I have only one clear memory, that of a great emotion. I felt good among these people who seemed to love one another. My mother also allowed me to visit a French-woman, a very sick person, bedridden ever since she was fifteen. In spite of her suffering, she never complained but gave affectionate attention to my childish tales. I guessed that what she never talked about was her Catholic faith.

How can we know if God exists? And whom can we ask? Will we ever fully assess the anxiety and the questing of children for whom time seems longer than it does for adults? One day I told myself that if there were a God, he might perhaps be present within me. I took a bold resolution: to speak to God and ask him. It would no longer be a matter of imagining because Another might be there. It was very hard, but I made this leap. I asked God to tell me if he existed by giving me what I called "a proof."

At the end of the year 1918 my mother's health was

considerably better. She could then leave her hospital room while continuing Dr. Rollier's treatment. It was decided that we would all four live in a furnished apartment with a big balcony for the sun cures which Leysin offers to convalescents. While Juliette was busy getting our new home ready for us, Mother sent us for ten days to a child-care center. I do not know today why the stay in this center was so painful to me then, at ten years of age. I felt very unhappy there among young people who were rehearsing Christmas carols. My eyes filled with tears as I heard them singing for a joy which I did not share; I felt shut out from an unknown world, ill thought of by the headmistress and unable to tell anyone my worries.

Neither my education nor my nature led me to ask for any spectacular evidence of God's existence, such as a vision or a voice. I chose for my "sign" an ordinary fact of life. Juliette was to come get us in the early afternoon of December 24 to take us to our temporary home in Leysin. If she came earlier than the agreed-on time, that would prove there was a God. My childish feeling attached great importance to my deliverance from that child-care center. And the "proof" I wanted was more precious for being my secret. Juliette came to get us in the early afternoon of December 22! That was the sign I had been asking for.

In the spring of 1919 we left Leysin. A severe ordeal awaited Simone and me on our return: the definite separation of our parents. I no longer knew myself when I faced my father. My whole confidence and my admiration were crumbling. I defied him and harried him with questions, among them: "Why didn't you tell me about Christ?" He gave me a pocket-sized book. On the yellow cover I read, Ernest Renan, *The Life of Jesus.*

Many of the pages seemed difficult for me, but I continued reading avidly; even if I didn't understand it all, the beauty of the message of "the Galilean" moved me. I cried as I read the last pages on the story of the crucifixion and the tribute Renan pays to Christ.

At Meudon I no longer found the world of my childhood. I was astonished at the distancing of so many "friends" whom our house had previously welcomed, and at the aloneness of a sick woman in the process of divorce while her husband went his own way. It was surely at this sad time that I began to be concerned about the place given to women in society; I learned the precariousness of opportunistic friendships and the fragility of political ties. This experience gave me a rather somber view of the world, saving me for the rest of my life from naive illusions about the natural goodness of humankind. Still today I keep a sharp, critical sense in my outlook on politicians of all parties.

I had stealthily gotten hold of a Catholic catechism of the Diocese of Versailles. The abstract definitions of the catechism, without reference to the biblical stories, let me down completely. I visited a Catholic church in Paris and found there nothing of what I expected from it. Then I remembered my Protestant friends from Leysin and my grandmother in Saint-Dié, and I asked my mother for permission to follow a course of Protestant religious instruction. But we had to wait until the divorce was final and custody officially entrusted to my mother. As soon as it was possible, she agreed to write to Monsieur C, the pastor of Sèvres-Bellevue-Meudon.

Baptism and Joining the Church

Pastor C, after a long visit with my mother, invited Simone and me to Sunday school.

Before passing through the door of a Protestant church for the second time in my life, I was seized by a sort of panic and wanted to turn back. My sister, calm and smiling, would have none of it, and we went ahead. I was certainly aware that I was then voluntarily taking a decisive step on a new path. Fortunately, the inside of the small church struck me as welcoming, with wooden wainscoting six feet high lining the light walls and an olive-green velour carpet covering the center aisle and the floor of the choir.

Since I was a student in the lycée at Sèvres, Pastor C asked me to join the catechumens of that school, whom he gathered in his home after the Wednesday classes. My third-form classmates and I, seated around the dining room table, used to ask questions freely. I had no feeling of being under pressure. New Testament in hand, the pastor led us to listen to the scriptures and to discover the message of the Christ.

I was like a person parched with thirst who finally finds a spring, like a confused child trying to find the way at night who finds a light. The Gospels were truly "good news" for me. Not only had they never been proclaimed to me, they had even been hidden. This Jesus, whom Renan had described as a great man, became mysteriously present and alive. Everything that I had been searching for, in my anxiety and my ordeal, I seemed to find in Christ.

In visiting the Louvre, I had stopped in front of the Rembrandt painting "Pilgrims of Emmaus" (Luke 24:13-35); the only light emanates from Christ, and it illuminates the travelers who do not know and have not yet understood. In some ways that was what I was feeling. The "Come unto me" of Christ had for me, who so much loved to dispute, the force of an indisputable authority, yet all the warmth of a love which ignores the imperfections of human affections.

In the spring of 1923 I made a big decision, that of answering the call of Christ; I asked for baptism. I was baptized on April 28, 1923 in the church of Meudon-Bellevue. I had not followed the usual program of religious instruction in the Protestant churches—Sunday school and two years of catechism—but Pastor C did not impose on me any further delay before I could share in the Lord's Supper.

I had heard my Catholic schoolmates in grade school and at the lycée speaking of "first communion." At the time this expression was empty of meaning for me. Going to the

Sunday service, I had been present at a Protestant observance of the Lord's Supper. The breaking of bread, the cup passing around the little circle[3] had made an extraordinary impression on me. The same gestures have been repeated ever since the first Supper "in remembrance of him" across all the centuries; time is wiped out; the living Christ welcomes us to his table. As I joined the circle of believers around the communion table, I too entered little by little into the sociological reality of a church. I found, among the members of this welcoming community, an atmosphere of affection which for me was sweet and helpful. I had the impression that the believers shared a secret with me, that of the love of God, which I had just discovered, like the treasure hidden in a field which the gospel tells us about.

Even so, rather soon I experienced some difficulty in adapting to the habits of my new spiritual family, when it came to the form of witness we should give to unbelievers or the shape which our service in the world ought to take. Pastor C had asked me to be a Sunday school teacher and then to give my Thursday afternoons to some young adults and some women and to a group of children who would have been running the streets had it not been for us. I questioned the style of this activity as too paternalistic and proposed in vain some innovations in the biblical studies.

My years at the lycée came to a close. I was excited by philosophy. Encouraged by the philosopher Louis Lavelle, I decided to be a teacher, to study for the Licence[4] in philosophy at the beginning of the university's fall term —this in spite of the keen disappointment of my parents, each of whom had been hoping that I would begin studies in science.

2

University Studies and Call

COLLEGE YEARS LEAVE UNFORGETTABLE MEMORIES. In the old buildings of Richelieu's Sorbonne I found a renewed joy in studying and a freedom which was dear to me: the freedom to organize my own work in spite of the light constraint of the programs, the freedom to read and to make all kinds of discoveries. I very much loved my years at the university. I loved the atmosphere of the libraries, where, lifting my eyes from the page of the open book, I saw innumerable volumes lining the walls. I loved the hours of discussion after class in the buzzing corridors. (Among the groups which formed I had noticed one in particular; a young brunette often wearing a red corsage, whom the students called "the virgin of the Kremlin," seemed to be the center of it—Simone Weil. Her name was always at the top of the list of examination grades. In reading *Heaviness and Grace* [*La Pesanteur et la Grâce*] in 1949 I really came to know the person who was for three years my fellow student.) I liked the long walks on the sidewalks of the Boulevard Saint-Michel, alone or in deep conversation with other students even when the fine rain of Paris was falling, filtering the lights of the storefronts and the cafés.

I wanted to keep my independence, and I did not want to be enrolled in any group. Therefore it was with great hesitation that I agreed one day to go with another Protestant student to a meeting which she assured me was different. It was held at 11 rue Jean-de-Beauvais, a street in old Paris which, in their own time, two other students must have walked, students named John Calvin and Ignatius Loyola.

The Fédé and God's Call

I climbed an uncarpeted wooden stairway in an old and cheerless house and came into a big room where a lot of students had already gathered. The president of the World's Student Christian Federation was making a speaking trip through Europe. He was introduced by Pastor Marc Boegner and interpreted by a woman everybody called Suzanne. The woman's face seemed radiant, like those of the saints in some pictures; it was Suzanne de Dietrich. Since that day I have often climbed the old stairs. I found in the "Fédé" a Christian group of students which met my aspirations. This was because of its spirit of free inquiry, its openness to the problems of the world, and at the same time its concern for the spiritual life and for service. The general secretaries were Pastor Charles Westphal and Mlle. Claire Jullien, whose names I write with gratitude. Bonds of friendship tied me to those whom I met in the rue Jean-de-Beauvais. Time has not broken the bonds after half a century. I was quite surprised when the general secretaries asked me to be co-president of the Paris group, along with Charles Bonzon (who later became director of the Paris Missionary Society). However, I accepted.

At the university, along with the required courses, I studied under Étienne Gilson, Jean Baruzi, and Raoul Allier. They all familiarized me with the Christian culture of past centuries. I studied St. Theresa of Avila, St. Francis of Assisi, St. Bernard of Clairvaux. I wrote an article on Bernard of Clairvaux for the magazine *Foi et Vie*. Little by little I was shedding a certain number of a prioris about medieval Catholicism and discovering at the same time the spiritual riches of contemporary Catholicism. In this I was helped by the climate of the Fédé, ecumenical before its time.[1]

Philosophy always fascinated me, but I did not realize at first that work for my diploma was leading me into theological questions. My topic was "Freedom According to Malebranche: Its Relations to Grace." Federation activities took a larger and larger place in my life; one day I came to the point of asking myself whether teaching really would answer all my aspirations.

As a student in Paris, I met with my father in a climate which had gradually changed. Why was it to him that I confided the problem which had been troubling me? One of my good friends in the Fédé had just revealed his love for me and was asking me to marry him. Why did my father have such a categorical word? "Don't commit yourself at your age." I was then twenty-one. "Wait until twenty-five to get married. Unless you wait, your whole career will be broken." Why did I hear those words as a message coming from on high? I would only understand later.

I had taken part in the annual meeting of the Student Christian Federation at Easter 1930. It was held in a YWCA vacation center, "The Bluebird." The range of lectures and their quality left unforgettable memories with many of the participants. We were initiated into Karl Barth's theology by W.A. Visser t'Hooft, who was still unknown in France, and by Pastor Pierre Maury. Pierre Maury was to bring out in 1933 *Parole de Dieu et Parole Humaine* (*The Word of God and the Word of Man*).[2] Meanwhile Adolph Keller, the missionary, was opening up to us our responsibility as Christians toward the whole world, inviting us to listen to the voices of the colonized peoples.

It was while I was following one of Pastor Maury's lectures that I experienced the certitude that God was calling me into Christian service. If I had heard a voice or seen a light, I would not have failed to do an elementary psychological critique of these perceptions. But it was a call to the very depth of my being, beyond expression in language. It was at once imperious and loving, a compelling call which required complete availability and thus the abandonment of my teaching career. I didn't ask whether I had understood correctly, because the choice of life which God was deciding for me had all the weight and evidence of truth. I did not dispute it. I did not balk. I did not calculate. I did not think of the difficulties and the sacrifices. This call was a grace so overflowing the present instant that there was no question of disobeying it.

I came back from the meeting at the Bluebird as though traumatized. I needed time to understand what had happened to me and what decisions were to be taken. It was clear to me that I was not called to be a foreign missionary or a deaconess. The path which had been indicated by this inexplicable and indisputable inner certainty was leading toward the church in France. What function would I fulfill in it? Nothing was very precise at this time except that I should have a theological preparation.

In the education I had received from my parents, there had never been any talk of the subordination of woman, or of woman's mediocre intellectual faculties, or of woman's incapacity to fill important posts. Upon becoming a Christian, I had not found in the gospel a single word of Christ which ran counter to the idea I had formed of the role of woman in society. I rejoiced to read in the Acts of the Apostles and in the letters of Paul that women had shared in proclaiming the gospel. Priscilla taught; the apostle mentions her name before that of her husband, Aquila (Romans 16:3; Acts 18:2-3, 26). Women prophesied (Acts 21:9). Phoebe had a ministry at Cenchreae (Romans 16:1). And Paul proclaimed "there is neither male nor female [Gal. 3:28]." As for the Old Testament, even in the midst of a patriarchal civilization, Deborah was a prophetess and judge in Israel (Judges 4—5). The passage in the Epistle to the Corinthians (which I was to hear so often later on) had not troubled me: "The women should keep silence in the churches [1 Cor. 14:34]." I imagined that some women, excited by their recent experience of Christian freedom, needed to be called back to order, in the same way that certain feminists who are too agitated end up by doing a disservice to a just cause.

Thus the pastoral ministry seemed to me possible for a woman, as professions such as medicine and the law had become possible. Would I be led toward this ministry? I had no idea as yet. In any case, I could not have imagined all the obstacles and oppositions that I was to discover some years later.

I asked for an appointment with Pastor Boegner,[3] to consult him. Right away he spoke of a possible pastoral ministry after my theological studies. Thus he seemed to envisage the possibility that the pastoral ministry would someday be granted to women in France, as it was in Alsace. But he insisted that so far as women were concerned, the exercise of the pastoral ministry was incompatible with the state of marriage—this with a somewhat stinging humor.

Then Monsieur Boegner advised me to study theology under good conditions (I had thought of doing it by correspondence while occupying the post of a philosophy professor). He assured me that I could get a scholarship at the Geneva seminary; these scholarships were much more substantial than those in the French seminaries, and there was parity of diplomas between the Genevan seminary and those in France.

When I announced my decision to my mother, she was very much concerned by it. For myself, I understood her anxieties very well; I was going to give up the material security which a functionary's post procures. She saw me turning toward uncertainties, risks, and poverty. I accepted the verification of my calling which she required: that before beginning my theological studies I should work for a year toward the *agrégation*. (This is a very difficult competitive examination, distinctive to France, to be taken after completing the Licence and the Diplôme d'Études Supérieures.) In the fall I went back to the Sorbonne and gave myself entirely to my university work.

During that year I attended mass several times at the Benedictine abbey in the rue Monsieur. I did not go out of literary snobbery, to observe Isabelle Rivière[4] kneeling in a corner of the chapel. (She came every day to pray there with her Benedictine daughter, whose voice she could not pick out from the other voices which came through a dark curtain.) The Benedictine choir had an extraordinary unity and purity; it made the presence of God very real and helped me to pray. I thought about these nuns. I understood the wholeness and the absoluteness of their consecration to the Savior. They had left family, love, and fortune, but this great separation for the sake of faith had brought them into a framework of discipline and service, where obedience to God expressed itself by obedience to a rule, to a hierarchy. However deep my communion in Christ with these invisible sisters had been, in their chapel God gave me the certitude that my path was not theirs.

In October I left for Geneva. A group of Fédé friends came to see me off at the station. While I was at the window of my third-class compartment, a bouquet of flowers in my hand, my friends began to sing "It's Only Au Revoir" (to the tune of "Auld Lang Syne"). Was there a feminist meeting the next day in Geneva? Some men passed several times in front of my car, shouting slogans against women's suffrage. In spite of the emotion, we all laughed a lot as the train gently rumbled off.

Theological Studies in Geneva

I was warmly welcomed in Geneva, both by the professors and by the students. In the bright amphitheater, one single Genevan woman was taking a full theological course. However, a group of girls called "women ministers" were taking half the course. In 1917, at the request of Prof. Eugène Choisy, the Consistory of Geneva had created the Institute of Feminine Ministries. This institute gave young women who had their *baccalauréat* two years of courses to prepare them to fill a ministry in the church. Once the diploma of the institute was obtained, these students did an internship and then could hold posts as parish assistants, recognized and salaried by the Geneva church.

I had three years of studies, rich in experiences, in the city of Geneva, whose lake and mountains I so loved. At the theological seminary, future pastors received a specialized intellectual training. Exegesis of the Old Testament in the Hebrew text and of the New Testament in the Greek text made me discover a sum of research and science which the Sorbonne had not led me to suspect!

It was also under the direction of our professors that my comrades and I came up against our first experiments in ministry. To begin with there were the tests of our first sermons in the country churches. One winter Sunday in Divonne, I was much troubled by the reflection of one woman after the service: "How you moved me! I thought that you were Joan of Arc!" Had the French Protestants come to that?

More formidable and decisive were the periods of student summer service in the parishes. I did my first probationary period[5] at Fives-Lille with Pastor Henri Nick, considered in the north as a saint.. He assigned me to conducting the Sunday worship at Tourcoing. There the congregation, which was composed primarily of proselytes, sang with conviction and sustained me. The concierge invited me to lunch; she told me, as she cut for me a large piece of bread which she spread with salted butter, "Little girl, keep it up! You may not know it, but my husband is deaf. Well, he heard you!" In encouraging me this way, the Protestants of Tourcoing seemed truly of the twentieth century.

The next year, I substituted for Madame Bourquin in the post at Quiévrechain. Madame Bourquin, née de Coullon, was a native of the canton of Neuchâtel in Switzerland. She was a licenciate in letters and had done several years of theology. Her husband, a Swiss pastor, had enlisted in the French army and been killed at the front. One week after his death, she had come to live in the middle of the heaps of ruins in this corner of the north. Lodging in a kind of trailer, visiting those who were still living in the basements of their destroyed houses, she had little by little gathered together a community and then seen to the building of a church, whose stained-glass windows she had designed. She had set up a church[6] according to Calvin's expression and had pastoral charge of it. She conducted worship and preached, but on festival occasions it was a neighboring pastor who came to celebrate the Lord's Supper at Quiévrechain after the service was over in his own parish. Madame Bourquin had never had "pastoral delegation."[7]

I was within sight of the end of my theological studies and the "final examinations," as they were then called. I was bent on being first in these final tests. When very few women accede to a discipline which is considered more than any other the preserve of men, it seemed to me that they should take the prizes. Actually I was first in my class.

Urged on by my professors, I had competed for two university prizes. I shared a prize in philosophy with a male student in the Faculty of Letters. I won the preaching prize; the jury for this last (composed of theologians and lay people) was chaired by a colonel in the Swiss army. And how surprised I was to hear applause, more solid and longer than the rest, when the preaching prize was awarded to me at the *Dies Academicus* in the great amphitheater of the university. The militant feminists of Geneva had come to give me an ovation!

A Door Opens

Leaving Geneva, my male French fellow students went to fulfill their military service; on their return the church would entrust them with a parish where they would do a probationary year before being ordained as pastors.

For me the future remained unknown, but I did not doubt God's call; it had been confirmed to me in many ways. I never forgot the words of Prof. A. Gampert, the dean of the theological seminary: "It seems certain to me that God has called you to the pastoral ministry. Therefore God will open the door for you, don't doubt it now. In the march of faith and obedience, never forget that the Savior does not trace out the path for us in advance. He makes it clear to us from day to day."

I wrote to the presidents of the two unions of churches,[8] Pastor M. Rohr for the Evangelical Reformed Churches and Pastor A.N. Bertrand for the Reformed Churches. I offered my services, saying that I was ready to accept "no matter what form of ministry, and no matter where."

Pastor M. Rohr, both in a letter of response and in the course of our two conversations, always seemed very ill at ease. I came out of his office, after our first meeting, sad and revolted. He had considered entrusting me with a small parish. "Since this parish has financial difficulties," he said, "you would have there a pastor's work and an evangelist's salary." At our second meeting, he told me flatly, "No, our Evangelical Reformed Churches have no work to entrust to you."

I have quite a different memory of the meeting with Pastor A.N. Bertrand when I went to the appointment he had given me in the rue de l'Oratoire. His office was on the top floor of the building, like an upper room, the walls lined with dark bookcases overcharged with books. Pastor Bertrand did not stay behind his desk while we talked but sat on a chair not far from me. This gesture was very meaningful to me and overcame some of my anxieties. Right away I experienced the impression of being before a strong personality, in whom the administrative rules of the church would not stifle the pastoral and human interest. I guessed that he was sensitive to my anxieties and at the same time open to the question of the future. He treated me as a candidate for the ministry, spoke to me about a job in Rouen with his son-in-law, Pastor Henri Manen, and asked me to come back the following week.

A week later he said to me, "After thinking it over, I'm going to send you to the Cévennes, to a village that has been without a pastor for six months; it is a church that needs to be wakened up. There are only six or seven people at worship at Sainte-Croix-Vallée-Française. But I am sure that you will find there some live embers under the ashes." After he had given me some background information, he told me that I would find again in the Cévennes some of my fellow students from the Geneva seminary. Then, like a man who knows how to take the risks of leadership, he added, "As president, I am taking the responsibility of entrusting a parish to you; but the National Synod[9] alone can decide if the church will admit women to the pastoral ministry and be willing to ordain them. I can put your foot in the stirrup, but it is for you to show how you handle yourself in the saddle."

Thus God opened a door for me.

3

The Decisive Years—
Ministry in the Cévennes

IN THE BEGINNING OF SEPTEMBER I went to the post which had been entrusted to me: Sainte-Croix-Vallée-Française. I liked the name of this village, "The Holy Cross in a French Valley." "You can't get lost in such a deserted spot," several friends said to me. "There's no railroad station and only one telephone subscriber."

On my way there, I was to go first to the ordination of one of my Geneva comrades, Roger Campiche, in his parish, le Collet-de-Dèze, on September 4, 1935. After the night on the train from Paris, I took the autorail which links Sainte-Cécile d'Andorge to le Collet. Thinking especially of the afternoon ceremony, I took time to look at the rolling hills and the little valleys and wondered at the light on this beautiful September morning, as I went quickly to the *presbytère* (parsonage).

Someone was greeting the various guests of the parsonage with a firm and smiling authority. It was Lydia Campiche, a young woman with an energetic and luminous face, reflecting her happiness. One could easily tell that she was closely associated with her husband's ministry. The church of le Collet, the children, and the youth movements of the parish were to benefit from her pedagogical gifts. At that time everybody found it quite natural that a wife should give up her profession when she married a pastor. I was happy, later on, to see Lydia Campiche resume a teaching responsibility in Geneva and then become the director of the famous Brechbühl School.

One thing was on my mind: What would be the attitude of the Cévennes pastors toward me after one or two years in the ministry? In the student world you are scarcely aware of the way a given occupation warps your mind. But the smile and the warm handshake of Roger Campiche reassured me. Nor did I perceive any masculine pride in several other young colleagues who were present at this ordination. I was expecting some astonishment, discreetly veiled, or even a secret disapproval on the part of the older pastors. But they were all very cordial, welcoming me to the Cévennes as you welcome any newcomer.

The ordination service was led by one of our former professors from Geneva, August Lemaître. When I went into the church, I was struck by the large number of people who were already in the pews, even in the balcony. Dark clothes predominated in this congregation, which kept a grave and respectful silence.

Built in 1646, this building (along with the Vialas church) was one of the only two Reformed church buildings which escaped the systematic destruction ordered by the Sun King. Thus it is a precious testimony to Protestant architecture in the seventeenth century. Inside the unsculptured wooden door, the rectangular building gives you an impression of solidity and grandeur. A round arch thirty feet high cuts its width in the middle and rests on two rough-hewn stone blocks. The exposed timbering, with its beams and rafters, adds an original character to the sober beauty of the place.

This was the first time that I had been present at a pastoral ordination. Everything struck me as simple and true. This ceremony, which is controversial today, did not have the institutional appearance whose weight and rigidity people like to denounce. And when my friend and brother, after having taken the pastoral vows, said, "May God be my helper," it was not a vain ritualism to me. I saw only the sign of continuity from apostolic times: the Savior, as always calling people to serve him; the presence of the people of God gathered together, welcoming the pastor, at the same time recognizing the ministry with which this brother is charged.

The second stop arranged for me was at Saint-Germain-de-Calberte. Pastor Marc Doret drove me to the parsonage in his old Mathis. Evening was falling, and the mauve heather hillsides were drowned in light as the sky turned flame-colored.

Marc Doret had been my fellow student at the Geneva seminary; he and his wife wanted to share with me the difficulties and the joys of their ministry and to give me some advice. One of their warnings struck me particularly. Marc repeated it as he took me to the autorail which was going to take me to Florac: "Don't forget that in this country each new pastor is sized up by the whole village at the first funeral service which he or she conducts."

At Florac with Pastor André

At Florac I saw Pastor Frédéric André, the president of our region,[1] waiting for me on the platform. I found him, as I had earlier at le Collet, a man of somewhat antiquated politeness, but cordial without paternalism. When we came to an old small square of which his house formed the corner, he told me, "The door is always open, as you see. Just knock and come in!" Madame André greeted me with the perfect ease of a woman who is used to having the most diverse kinds of people coming through the open door of her house. She told me that she had spent most of her life in Florac. I can still see her, seated on a low chair in front of an old worktable in a room whose carpet was flowered in faded colors, whose garnet velour armchairs and small white curtains at the windows created a decor from the end of the last century. No, nothing about her reminded me of the pastors' wives in English novels. She had spunk and personality and was in no way dominated by her husband.

As we were finishing the meal at the big table in the dining room, the Andrés each took half of the fruit the other one had chosen. "We've been doing this since our wedding," they told me. Had this gesture become a vain ritual, or did it remain a meaningful gesture? The daughter of divorced parents, I was always moved when I met old couples whose marriage seemed to be a success.

It was probably hard for Madame André, the daughter and the wife of ministers, to understand what my progress must have been from the atheistic milieu of my childhood toward faith, and, even more, what problems my situation as a "woman pastor on trial" could raise for me. She too had probably had to surmount struggles and sufferings, but in the tight-lipped way of her time. Pastor André belonged to that generation of pastors who had lived through the financial difficulties which followed the Law of Separation of Church and State, but without opposing the law. (In general, Protestants were in favor of it.) His wife, in later conversations, sometimes alluded to that period, and I understood how firmly she must have sustained her husband in his trials. One day she also brought up the death of their daughter, with serenity and restraint, adding, "I said to my husband, 'My friend, why do you want us to be spared?' " *Mon ami,* were words which often came to her lips, full of confidence, of intimacy. It seemed to me to express, in the Florac manse, the spiritual equality of husband and wife. I have always remained grateful to Madame André for not having shown any negative reaction to the idea of a pastoral ministry for women. I have so often met it among others of my sex.

Arrival and First Service at Sainte-Croix

Pastor André took me to the bus which links Florac with Saint-Jean-du-Gard and serves Sainte-Croix. I was in a hurry to arrive, and the trip seemed to me interminable. The bus climbed slowly to the long village of Barre-des-Cévennes. Everybody seemed to know one another. They chattered in a patois which I did not understand, but in which, even so, I caught on the wing some Latin roots. I had to find another rhythm of living: that of the country.

After Barre, the bus descended by a small twisting road with sheer drops. The valley got more and more narrow. Finally the bus passed the brick buildings of one of the rare spinning mills that were still working, then a blue sign with white letters saying "Sainte-Croix-Vallée-Française"!

Getting down from the bus, I had the impression of arriving in a lost country. I was looking for a village as you imagine it: a central square with some houses, a church, the mayor's office. I saw none of that. At the bottom of this narrow valley was the bed of an almost waterless creek,[2] straddled by a one-lane bridge. Two roads followed the creek bed, one on each side. Houses with slate roofs and gray walls backed up to the mountainside. Other houses were hooked on to steep slopes without any visible access road. Everything seemed to me somber and sad in spite of the brightness of the sky. How would I manage to live here? Looking for pastures or cultivated fields, I experienced a kind of suffocation in the narrowness of this valley. How many inhabitants lived in this desert so poor and so austere?

There was no parsonage at Sainte-Croix, so the presbyterial council[3] had been obliged to find lodgings for me. I understand better today the embarrassment of the council members, all of whom were men. Houses for rent are very rare in these little villages. I imagine that they may have been saying to themselves, "Should we get involved with a landlord and sign a lease when they are sending us a woman pastor from Paris? Perhaps the experiment will not last." Therefore these gentlemen had reserved a room for me in the one existing small hotel. The presbyterial councilors had explained to me that the village had had electricity for some years, but there was no question yet of running water. They added, trying to make life as agreeable as possible for me, "You can take your meals at the hotel, where the food is very good. In that way you won't have any worry about cooking." I did not tell them that this arrangement, dreamed up by men, was most disagreeable to me. All my life I would observe that men do not imagine that a single professional woman might need a hearth (no matter how small) with her personal affairs arranged according to her taste and the chance to do her own cooking.

Thus on the evening of my arrival I found myself in a second-floor room looking out on the backyard of the hotel, that is to say on the vegetable garden. The view consisted of the chicken coop and the toilets at the far end of the garden. The wallpaper in the room was of an old vintage, with silver designs, almost completely invisible, on a black background. "This was for several months the room of the pastor who came as an interim," the charming daughter of my hosts told me. "This is where he died." The room struck me as dismal. A big spider ogled me from the ceiling. I wrote my first sermon here.

The next day some of the church officers briefed me about the parish. They confirmed the figure on church attendance which Pastor Bertrand had given me: "Yes, hardly more than seven. But," they added right away, "you will be warmly welcomed everywhere."

In 1935 at Sainte-Croix, only a tenth of the population was Catholic. A priest was in residence, living in an old house next to a Romanesque chapel clinging to the side of the mountain. In this village he had no authority and took no initiative. He and I never had any real encounter for five years. Besides my status as a heretic, there was the fact that I was a woman charged with pastoral responsibilities. That upset all the Catholic dogma and traditions!

The communal cemetery was empty of Protestant tombs; I would never go there with a funeral cortège during my five years of ministry. Excluded from the "holy ground" of the cemeteries for two centuries, country Protestants had buried their dead on their own lands and continued to do it; it was a tolerance granted by the law in regard to a secular custom. At the far end of the field they dug a grave; the very small luxury which the richest allowed themselves was to surround the family burial plot with a low grille. But three yew trees planted nearby threw their slim silhouettes against the sky and announced to the traveler that Protestants lived there.

On Sunday morning I was quite surprised to find fifty people gathered for worship at the church. The building, built in 1840 in rectangular shape, seemed huge to me. High windows with rounded arches lighted white walls. A gallery ran around three sides. In my pastor's gown, I slowly climbed the stairs which led to the pulpit at the far end of the church.

At the door some people had said to me, "Will you get used to it? It's a far cry from Paris! At least you will not languish here?" The singing accent of the Cévenol mingles warmth and spontaneity with great politeness. Stepping apart from the groups, an elderly man introduced himself as Pastor Arnal. I learned later that he was the founder and president of the Cévenol Club.[4] He ended his considerate questions by expressing the hidden feeling of humiliation which was then felt by the rural world in relation to city people: "These people are thinking, What do you expect? As far as we are concerned, she will be just a shooting star who will not stay long here in our mountains." So these Protestants were afraid I wouldn't stay with them, while I was wondering if they would accept *me!*

I hadn't noticed at first the absence of a stove in the church, but I had observed that the building as a whole gave the impression of neglect, with dirty windows and worm-eaten and broken pews. On the second Sunday—from the height of the pulpit—I called on the village to put the building back into better condition. I got no immediate reaction. But one morning, at the first equinoctial rain, I saw women coming, armed with brooms, pails, and aprons, telling me that today they could begin cleanup. Some men followed them with the necessary tools. The work went on joyously with more and more volunteers; in two and a half days the little team finished the first round of repairs. These days gave me the feeling that I was beginning to belong to the village. Another proof was given to me; the presbyterial council searched for a house to rent and found one.

Discovery of the Parish

My parish included several communes. First of all was Gabriac, which I found by climbing a cart track on the side of the mountain about two miles from Sainte-Croix. It had a church like that of Sainte-Croix, but smaller. While waiting to find the door to my parishioners' hearts, I had to find the doors to their houses! In the middle of different groups of buildings, stables, coach houses, rearing houses (for silk-worms), I had to search out the living quarters. The entrance was marked by a door framed in white.

I also ministered to the commune of Moissac, which begins below Sainte-Croix on the national road which leads from Barre-des-Cévennes to Saint-Jean-du-Gard. A Romanesque chapel, classified as a historical monument, stands in the middle of an overgrown plot of land several yards above the road. An apse with no side chapels, built of very dark stone, with an unsculptured door, its heavy buttresses have kept it standing through the long centuries. Old tradition puts its building back to the tenth century. It is called Notre-Dame-de-Valfrancesque and was probably built to celebrate the victory of the Franks over the Saracens. Across the valley, on a promontory, are the lacy ruins of a feudal château. Two nearby farms on the other side of the valley are called Fez Begon and Fez Roland. Do these names go back to the period of Charles Martel? No one could tell me exactly how long this abandoned chapel had been designated for Protestant worship, and I did not undertake any search of the archives.

When I entered it for the first time on Sunday afternoon, it took me only a few seconds to realize that a stone had fallen out of the vaulting. Big blobs of green mildew formed strange designs on the white and rose plaster with which the black stone had been daubed. I was able to convince the presbyterial council to prepare a repair application for submission to the prefecture in Mende. Alas, when I left in 1941, mildew continued to cover the walls with nonrepresentational pictures.[5]

Beginning in October, the shutters and the doors of some houses of Sainte-Croix were closed until the next vacations. The students who wanted to follow their studies beyond the certificate were boarders in Alès or Nîmes. Emptied of some of its summer residents and adolescents, the village became quieter and little by little took up the rhythm of winter life.

I knew that after the chestnut harvest I would more often find my parishioners at home. Therefore I began to visit the ones farthest out, those whose houses I saw on the heights, those who lived in the narrow valleys called "flumes," opening up into the Vallée Française. Each one of these properties had a name, sometimes a name in patois like *Escuto se ploou* ("Listen to it rain," or "Listen to see if it is raining"). Sometimes it was a surprising name like "Babylon" (perhaps because Babylon was mentioned in the Bible?).

In 1878 Robert Louis Stevenson traveled with a donkey, wandering about the Cévennes.[6] Forty years before my arrival, a pastor in Vallée Française had also chosen this mount on which to visit his flock. I found another solution: to go on foot with mountain shoes and a pointed walking stick. I informed myself as exactly as possible about the route to follow to arrive at this or that farm. The explanations were always the same: Leave the paved road at such a place and follow the path (made by the steps of the inhabitants or the postman). The schist glistened in the sun between the heather, the broom, or the scrub oak. Sometimes, in detouring around a ravine, I lost sight of the house and its yew trees and only the path itself kept me from getting lost on the steep slopes. Some paths simply vanished. I sometimes had to search, with a certain anxiety, for the place where the path took up again. And I understood better the meaning of the picture which Jesus chose to express what he could be in our lives: "I am the Way [John 14:6]."

I was always warmly welcomed in these isolated houses; the traditions of hospitality remained very much alive. "Come in! Sit down and relax!"[7] This is the way I was invited to sit on the cane chair or in the armchair in front of the large fireplace. Yes, "put yourself together" from the fatigue of the climb or the heat or the cold of the season. The man stirred up the fire, threw some vine stalks on the embers, and brought a big log which he wedged in the back of the hearth. The woman prepared coffee with quasi-ritual gestures. There must have been very little change since the eighteenth century in the big kitchen where the old clock counted the hours.

I felt that I intrigued them a little: "A Parisienne, coming to *this* place?" I found almost everywhere the same questions, tactfully put, on the matter of my family, but always also the traditional "You're not discouraged here after Paris?"[8] How could I make them understand that you don't *get* discouraged in the service of Christ?

On my way back I would think of the solitude of those whom I had just left. How did they spend these long winter nights? With their dreams, their fantasies, or the richness of an inner life nourished by the scriptures? How speak of the beauty of the Cévennes to those who experienced each day the poverty of the earth and the trials of isolation?

During my rounds of visits, I sometimes met shepherdesses sitting on rocks, sheltered from the scouring wind, watching over some animals, goats or sheep; I had seen some of them reading small-format New Testaments, which they would slip into the large pockets of their smocks. When I came at the time when the flocks go in, what joy I felt in hearing the shepherdess speak to her sheep, calling each one by a different name! In the serene beauty of the Cévenol evenings, it called up the pictures in the first verses of the tenth chapter of John. The shepherdess lighted up the Gospel for me.

Discovering Synods

The regional synod[9] took place each year in November, when the beautiful days were over and white frost covered the lands near the ravines. Each parish was represented there by two delegates: the pastor and one of the members of the presbyterial council. I therefore went to the meeting with Monsieur B. It was something of an event for the parish whose turn it was to entertain the synod. I noted sadly that the lay delegates were, with one exception, all men. The men sat and deliberated; women busied themselves with feeding them. That gave a rather queer vision of the church. However, women voted for the election of presbyterial councilors when they had not yet received the right to vote in civil government!

At the beginning, after the roll call of the delegates, the president of the region, Pastor André, asked the synod to give me the voting privilege. Without objection or demand for explanation, the synod gave it to me unanimously. Was such a decision in accord with the church discipline? It didn't worry me very much. The Cévenols were rather suspicious about anything which smacked of canon law and authoritarian hierarchies. The synod vote doubtless seemed perfectly legitimate to them. As for me, it proved that, in the eyes of the church in this region—for pastors and lay people—I was accepted as a full pastor.

Christmas came, preceded by all the preparations for worship services and Christmas trees. I had been able to move to my new house, a building of modest dimensions, without a cellar, whose back wall abutted the mountainside, so that the two ground-floor rooms were quite humid. I preferred to live on the second floor, in my study and my bedroom. Two adjoining rooms on the third floor, accessible only from the outside, became a parish center, particularly for meetings of young people.

In the springtime I received a letter which surprised me a little. Monsieur and Madame Charles Latune wrote me that they were planning to take a trip to the Cévennes and wanted to meet me, since I was a friend of their pastor son. The name Latune sounded familiar to me as one of those you see among the board members of churches and church-related organizations.[10] I also knew that Madame Latune Sr. was a relative of Pastor Boegner.

They came for the service at Sainte-Croix and spent the night under my roof. Simple, used to the inconveniences of pastors' homes, they were interested in the life of the Cévenol churches and attentive to what I told them about my parish. The idea that the Latunes might have been charged with an investigation of my ministry never occurred to me at the time. However, their observations and those of my colleagues were added to the report which the president of my region, Pastor André, was to prepare. This personal file also constituted the dossier on the pastoral ministry of women, since I was still the only woman pastor "on trial."

At first I sometimes experienced the rather painful impression that I was in an irregular situation. I had spoken about it with the president of the region and with colleagues and friends. In our *pastorale*,[11] in the organization of our common work, there was never an indication that I was not a pastor by the same right that they were; in the practice of the ministry, in leading worship, on calls, and at meetings, the painful impression left me completely. But the twelve months of ministry seemed to me too short a time to take the grave decision of asking for pastoral ordination. I didn't do it. I still needed to reassure myself that I was not misled about the form my service ought to take.

The National Synod of the Reformed Churches Grants Me a "Pastoral Delegation"

The National Synod of the French Reformed Churches was held June 23-25, 1936 at Agen (halfway between Bordeaux and Toulouse). It was the first National Synod which had to take a decision concerning a concrete case, on the pastoral ministry of women. In his report, Pastor A.N. Bertrand told how "he had taken the personal responsibility" of having me do a year of "probationary service." He summarized the favorable judgments which had been gathered concerning my ministry. Finally, deeming it necessary to postpone a decision in principle until the reunion of the two Unions of Churches (which would take place in 1938), he proposed that "a pastoral delegation be granted" to me.[12] Pastor Boegner wrote me an affectionate letter to inform me about it, adding, "The Synod requested that its gratitude to you should be expressed" and concluding, "A little patience is still necessary."

The discussions of the Synod were not reported to me. (When it is a matter of persons, the Synod meets in executive session.) Our Protestant regional paper for July 1936, *Le Soc* ("The Plowshare"), recalled "a morning of very spirited debate." I enjoy today rereading the description which Pastor Frank Salles, with his alert and humorous pen, gave concerning the deputies at the Synod of Agen: "They had the air of 'senators.' . . . I counted thirteen domes of the most beautiful ivory, thirteen covered with the most beautiful snow, and then a whole forest of scalps, none of which had stayed blond. In the middle of this Areopagus, you saw three or four unhappy little boys of thirty-five or forty years who were being kept on their best behavior."

It must have been the Holy Spirit that inspired these older men to arrive at the point of granting "pastoral delegation" to a woman. In spite of the structure of the society in which they had lived from childhood, they voted like sons of the Reformation.

The Protestant press was very restrained. As for the big papers, this decision was unknown to them (or else they had not caught its interest). The notorious feminists, men and women who were preoccupied with the promotion of womanhood, did not care what took place in Synod meetings and were not looking for victories in Christian milieus—even Protestant! On reflection, this silence seemed preferable to having my case seized upon by feminist leagues. The Synod delegates, all of them men, could have been annoyed by it, and the deeper meaning of the question which I was posing to the church would have been falsified. Thus for the moment I was solaced and grateful for the decision of the National Synod at Agen.

The next year the National Synod of the Reformed Churches, held at Castres April 13-15, renewed my pastoral delegation on the same terms.[13] The commissions and the Synod always brought up the question of my ordination, even when I had not asked for it. Every organization has its structures. Since I had done my probationary year, the Synod was looking to the stage which normally follows it: ordination.

My Ministry Is Not Geographically Limited

My extended internship did not impose any restriction on me; I could carry out my ministry not only at Sainte-Croix but in the whole region and beyond. My colleagues and I arranged pulpit exchanges. I think I conducted worship at least once and often twice in all the churches of the region, not forgetting Florac, the parish of the president of our region. I remember a service at Barre-des-Cévennes on a Sunday after Christmas. It was cold at this altitude, and the cattle had not gone out. During the whole service we heard the bleating of sheep in the nearby stable. The congregation seemed to remain indifferent to it, but for me the shepherds in the Gospel of Luke (2:8-20) became more concrete. We organized youth rallies called Rural Courses in the different valleys of the Cévennes (Vallée Longue, Vallée Borgne, Vallée Française). We also conducted revivals.

Not only did I have this great privilege of being part of a pastoral team which had accepted me, I also found at the hearths of my colleagues a refreshing stop and a warm friendship. Their children called me "Taty" or "Aunt Elisabeth." (Today it is the grandchildren of some of them who call me "Aunt Elisabeth.") One day Monsieur Boegner observed, "You have lots of friends in the church."

From 1936 on I was even called on to come out of my mountains. A YWCA "group conference" held at Alès asked me to address its members and to hold two open forums, in the evenings, in the large church in the city.

In April 1937, while the leaders of the two unions of churches (Reformed and Evangelical Reformed) were working to restore the unity of French Protestantism, a meeting drew together the pastors of the two unions who lived in the Cévenol valleys. My colleagues asked me to lead them in a study of the burning question, "The Authority of Scripture."

In November of that same year, 1937, a great encouragement was given me: The president of the region asked me to lead the devotions at the regional synod which would be held that year at Vialas. I felt myself crushed by the difficulty, and at the same time grateful for the confidence that had been shown me. The synod worship service took place in the evening in the sanctuary, which was like a twelfth-century chapel. An electrical failure had blacked out the village. The old kerosene lamps lighted the congregation very little, and I saw only white blots of faces emerging from holes of darkness. I was then concerned with the scant attention which the churches of this area were paying to the dangers of Nazism. Preaching in the shadows in this church, where the Word alone could bring light, I developed the reproaches of the prophet Ezekiel against his people: "You have not gone up into the breaches [Ezek. 13:5]." It was after the synod at Vialas that I felt truly integrated into the church of the Cévennes.

We also held a special meeting of the synod of the Reformed Churches of our region to vote on the entrance of our churches into the French Reformed Church. It only lasted a few hours and took place at Sainte-Croix. Monsieur Boegner announced his coming and expressed the wish to be my guest. At the time when the sessions were over it was broad daylight. Monsieur Boegner and I set out for a walk on the road which climbs from Sainte-Croix to Saint-Martin-de-Lansuscle. After several sharp turns the horizon grows wider. You can look from the ruins of the Moissac château to the houses of Gabriac on the side of the mountain and follow the straight line of the road built by Bâville[14] just under the crest of the mountains that dominate Vallée Française. "What solitude!" Monsieur Boegner said to me. "And what silence!" We kept on a little while longer on the rocky road. Then, stopping and putting his hand on my shoulder, Monsieur Boegner asked me, "But after all, Elisabeth, isn't this solitude too hard on you?" I don't remember my exact response. It called up the joys of the ministry and quoted the words of St. Augustine, "God gives what he orders."

Monsieur Boegner asked me to draw up for the National Council a short memorandum summarizing my experiences and my reflections on my ministry. I never got around to it. It did not seem to me that the time had yet come. I ran the risk of seeming to express the final conclusion of my research. I also ran the risk of having my words badly misquoted and twisted.

The wisdom of the Cévenol peasants and the silence which

enfolds the valleys helped me to make the decision (which I have never regretted) to write nothing on the pastoral ministry of women and to refuse to speak about it. I had to be a pastor; that was the only thing which mattered. To show the reality of movement by walking was no longer a philosophical discussion for me.

The French Reformed Church Renews My Pastoral Delegation

At the National Synod of the French Reformed Church (finally reconstituted in 1938), two decisions were taken concerning the pastoral ministry of women. This Synod was held at Bordeaux, May 9-11, 1939. Right at the outset it was voted to defer until later the question of principle. Then it was decided to grant a pastoral delegation to two women: Denise Hourticq and me. Denise Hourticq, who herself had a slight motor disability, was carrying on a pastoral ministry with the patients at the sanitarium in Berck (a small town on the English channel near Calais).

But how cautiously these decisions were drawn up! "The Synod neither prejudges nor promises." It was clearly stated that the "pastoral delegation" which had been given did not bind the Synods to grant ordination later on! The Synod minutes continue, "This last question [i.e., the ordination of women] is to be considered in depth at the Synod of 1941."[15] In the ecclesiastical vocabulary, how well these things are stated! I came to the conclusion that the delegates from the former Union of Evangelical Reformed Churches must have swelled the number of those opposing the pastoral ministry of women in the National Synods of the French Reformed Church.

I discovered little by little that traditions weighed more heavily in the French Reformed Church than I had imagined. From this I experienced a great letdown. The real situation of the church seemed to me two-faced. One face was that of my pastoral ministry at Sainte-Croix, which was accepted by my colleagues and by the region; the other was that of the soft-pedaled reticences of the ecclesiastical government. We would say today that I perceived the reality of the gap between the base and the summit.

Why had the faithful in the Cévenol churches accepted me as pastor? Did the women in the Cévennes have a privileged situation compared with their lot in the rest of France? Woman's life was hard in the comfortless houses and harder still on the farms isolated on the mountainside. The men gave scarcely a thought to making the women's work easier. On the farms that were farthest away, on the heights, only the men sat at table; the women served them. I noticed that my presence at their special occasions seemed to upset this tradition; when I was invited to the table of a family in the village, I often heard the head of the family say to his wife, "Come now, come sit down," as though he were discovering for the first time that she had been standing all along. And being made the confidante of many sufferings and kept informed of known or hidden dramas, I met the habitual severity in regard to the woman who had "slipped" and the usual indulgence toward her partner.

The Cévenol women did not express their claims brazenly. However, they affirmed by their bearing a spiritual freedom; their Protestant education had freed them from submission to an ecclesiastical hierarchy. The past was often brought to mind, and no one forgot the Cévenol prophetesses or the part played by women in the resistance in the prisons of the Sun King or in the Camisard underground.[16] This past had helped somewhat in sweeping away the theology of submission to men.

The Occult

On a day of hard rain I saw a man approaching, a man of no particular age, perhaps fifty years old. He had come a long way from the farm where he lived alone with his daughter. Monsieur M left his big umbrella outside and took off his wide-brimmed felt hat with a gesture full of nobility. He asked me to come right away to his house to calm down his daughter, who was chasing him with a knife. Through his mixed-up explanations I gathered that his daughter must be a mental patient in crisis, and I advised him rather to call the doctor. "No," the man said to me as he remained standing, "the doctor can't do anything for her. It's the pastor we need." He only consented to sit down when I told him that I would go with him. We climbed through a rain which transformed the path into a stream.

A little before arriving at his farm, Monsieur M confided to me, "My daughter reads books. Oh, such books! You know, the bad books which are sold by the people who pass through the mountains like that." It couldn't be a question of pornographic books, because their devotees were more common in the city than in this desert. "Then, are they books of sorcery?" The word frightened him, but it was the right one.

Mlle. M received us politely, with the traditional gestures of a hostess who welcomes drenched travelers, poking the fire and preparing a hot drink. The father left the two of us alone by the fireside. She was calm. I asked her to bring me the Bible and told her it was the best book. I read her a passage from the Epistle to the Romans affirming that nothing "will be able to separate us from the love of God [Rom. 8:31-39]." Put at her ease, Mlle. M spoke to me of other books in somewhat enigmatic terms. I thought for a moment that she was going to show them to me, since I had asked her to. But she pulled back as though she were closing a door giving access to an underground secret. Thus I never laid my hands on these sorcery books, and I will never know how they had come to trouble this unhappy woman. The solitude of the isolated farms favored or aggravated all kinds of imbalance, and at a time when the remedies were still far behind what they can be today. Mlle. M had no more seizures, so far as I know. From this I concluded that no more salesmen for sorcery books had further disturbed her fragile psyche.

In the village of Sainte-Croix there was someone who raised other problems for me by the strangeness of his behavior. Monsieur R had a name whose gravelly sounds brought to mind scrubby undergrowth in the sun. Tall and thin, with a face like a knife blade and shining black eyes, he strode along the mountain paths in seven-league boots, clad in a ridiculous costume. He was the "village idiot," saying out loud what others were thinking silently. There was something of Don Quixote in him. For many years he had given a talented performance. The village accepted it with a kind of complicity, as the court accepted the king's jester. Nobody could get him to give up playing this part. But his twelve-year-old son had to be rescued. His mother had absolutely no power over him. He tried to imitate his father and played the idiot who refuses to obey anybody at all.

With the mayor, the teacher, and the doctor, it was easy to draw up an application for the John Bost Foundation in Laforce.[17] But how many hours I spent trying to get the parents to admit that for their son's own good they ought to separate themselves from him!

At last the boy was entrusted to the John Bost Foundation. A year later he came back to Sainte-Croix to spend several weeks of vacation at home. To the amazement of the village, he was suitably clothed, polite, and talking about the trade he was going to learn. He was the unexpected sign which put a question to us all: "Is there any limit to what inventive Christian love can do for the rejects of society who are suffering from mental deficiencies?"

Then what place did the occult hold in the Cévennes? Was the bonesetter, who worked quite openly, considered as having some "power"? The enlightened minds said, "He has a science." Everyone said of another such person that he "had the gift" for burns. Even the faithful assimilated this gift with the gifts of the Spirit spoken of in Paul's letters. As for the practices of sorcery, the bewitchments, I was certainly the last person to be informed. People of God and sorcerers have been fighting each other in most civilizations. The occult remains the secret of night, the kingdom of the Prince of Darkness.

The Cévenol Mentality Before 1940

Some pagan superstitions which had come down from the depths of the ages, some traces of sorcery among the feebleminded, in no way characterized the Cévenol mentality. It was the past, that of the Camisard war, which marked the people. The Cévenols talked about it in season and out of season. For the poorest farmers, this past was their nobility. For the best educated, it was an example from which to draw a political and social message. Some liked to recall to me the role which was played by the son of a pastor of the wilderness, Rabaut-Saint-Étienne, at the time of the vote on the Declaration of the Rights of the Man and of the Citizen in August 1789.[18]

I remember the story an old woman told me; wrinkles had not altered the symmetry of her face, and her beautiful brown eyes shone with vivacity. She spoke slowly with old words and many verbs in the simple past.[19] She told, as if she herself had been a witness of it, how a wilderness service was going to be held in the dale near her house. The king's dragoons had been warned of it by traitors, but the "watchers" saw them climbing the valley soon enough for the Protestants to scatter to escape arrest and the galleys. I had not yet gotten used to the noises of the farms, the creaking of wood, the animals shifting in the stable while the fire crackles. I discovered what an intense life of its own an oral tradition can have. When I turned my head, I imagined that I could almost see, through the window slit behind me, the king's dragoons arriving!

This past served as an excuse to those who were the farthest separated from the church; it was enough for them to have had ancestors who were loyal to their faith to the point of martyrdom. How many times I have heard men who never came to worship say, "If they closed the church, I would go get my gun!" You find hypocrisies or ambiguities even in the use of the past.

This Camisard war (1702-1704) had been made into a legendary epic, a saga of the mountains; it gathered up, in a way, all religious wars, even the whole history of France. A thirty-year-old man with little more than a grade-school education explained to me the origin of the name given to a farm near the church in Moissac: "The Fez Roland," he told me. "That comes from the Camisard chief, you know, this Roland who sounded his horn at Roncevaux."[20]

What we often forget, when we want to utilize the Cévenol past politically, is the fact that this Protestant community was educated by the Bible. Their ancestors had learned to read in order to study the Word of God. I was often astounded to meet so much finesse, so much spiritual intelligence on the part of my parishioners. They had a culture which they owed as much to the scriptures as to their schools. In these far-off valleys the churches had been the "open universities" that people were looking for elsewhere. And still today the Christian faith forges personalities and the gospel gives nobility of heart.

Another slice of history, that of a more recent past, had marked the spirit of a certain number of Cévenols. Speaking with Protestants who "did not frequent the holy assemblies" and rather ridiculed those who went, I was surprised to recognize in their statements political slogans of the Third Republic, anticlerical and in the spirit of Freemasonry. The influence of Sébastien Faure, the "atheistic preacher" whose eloquence had seduced big audiences in the South, had operated even in these mountains. I saw myself brought back to the time of the "Republican catechism"! Since the end of the 1914-18 war, anticlericalism had lost some of its virulence. Had it evolved more slowly in this corner of the Cévennes?

Women, very little politicized, seemed to have been less influenced by the wave of atheism at the beginning of the century. They followed carefully the cottage meetings which were organized during the winter in the different areas—the "freshets." One year in one of the "freshets" there were even meetings exclusively for the men! They all came —except the one whom I met on my way home. He was coming back from the café, swaying on his legs; in spite of his condition, he recognized me. Then, with the clumsy and ridiculous gestures of an alcoholic, he took off his hat and bowed very low before me, like a grandee of Spain, in this wild streambed at midnight in the moonlight.

We were no longer in the days of the Combes ministry.[21] Events were running ahead in the rhythm of our modern times. How would these people of the Cévennes, where so many had abandoned the Christ, meet the dramas which were in preparation?

In spite of the Munich agreements and their deceptive illusions, a certain disarray took possession of people's minds. I then prepared a little brochure as a supplement to our regional paper, *Le Soc*. I passed around some books in the smaller circle of the presbyterial councilors, especially *Le Village sur la Montagne,* which tells of the arrest of a German pastor by the Gestapo.

The War Begins

And it was war! . . .

In this withdrawn valley I felt myself far from any danger, and I had offered my services to the National Council of the French Reformed Church as a replacement for any pastor near the German border who had been called up for military service. Monsieur Boegner told me to stay at my post. In the depths of the Cévenol valleys, the solitude was terrible for the wives and mothers who were wearing themselves out on their lands. So the realities of the war remained distant until the day when the gendarmes asked me to go with them to a family where they had to take the official announcement of the death of the young father.

Young pastors had been called up. Elders conducted some services but refused to officiate at funerals. This clericalism seemed regrettable to me, but I had to go and take the place of absent colleagues. The means of transport grew fewer. I remember one funeral which was arranged for the time when the baker came to replenish the supplies of the hamlet four miles from Saint-Germain-de-Calberte. On the way I had to sit on the coffin, which the delivery van was also carrying, in the middle of all those round loaves of bread.

The days following the armistice (after the fall of Paris and the North) were terrible for me. I sank into a kind of despair, with the impression that my presence at Sainte-Croix was useless. I had a premonition of all the misfortunes which were about to flood over the occupied peoples: repression, concentration camps. . . . A visit to the Maurys, who were at their Anduze house, comforted me. I got the letter sent by Karl Barth to some French pastors. It lighted up what I was still seeing in a confused way, confirmed me in the attitude that I believed right, and brought hope back to me.

During this first winter of 1940-41 the valley was peopled by some refugees, families who were abandoning the city and settling in their summer homes. High school students ran the risk of losing a school year. I was therefore asked to give some lessons. I did it with joy. It was thus that I gave the first Greek lessons to a boy who later became a pastor and succeeded me at Sète in 1958. I also gave philosophy lessons to a young Polish nobleman whose father had served under Sikorski's command in 1939. The de S family was living modestly in a dilapidated manor house which had belonged to the family of Madame de S. My "pupil" had just caused a scandal at the Catholic church of Sainte-Croix: when the curé had, in the course of his homily, preached submission to Marshal Pétain, the young man had left the church, slamming the door. He was going through a crisis of revolt, very much alone in this valley.

That winter was rugged. Big snowstorms knocked down pylons, and we were without electricity for a week right at Christmas. A parishioner made me a gift of a quart of kerosene. She said to me, "At this Christmastime you have many preparations to make. You have to be able to work, so here is some oil for your lamp. We would miss it if we did not see your window lighted at night."

As all pastors do, I had asked people to make sure that isolated folk and refugees got invited to spend Christmas day with families in the parish. The little group which had charge of assigning the "guests" came to discuss with me the questions which members of the de S family were raising for them: "Polish nobles, Catholics, coming from Paris! Nobody dared invite them!" I don't know how things worked out, but the de S family asked me to give them the pleasure of coming to spend the close of Christmas day with them. I went for the first time to their small manor house. It held for me all the mystery of old houses, while one single kerosene lamp threw a cone of light on the table where we shared a wartime meal. In spite of all the diversities of our experiences and of our lives, we were experiencing a real communion in adversity. I was later able to put the young de S in contact with a Dominican father who was not a Pétainist!

Quick Departure at the Call of CIMADE

Country houses were worth a little bit more since city people had been fleeing from the food scarcities in the cities. This was the moment that the owner of my house chose to sell it. In spite of the uncertainties of the times, I involved the presbyterial council in building a manse.

The village still had no running water. But since we had to plan for the future, I asked the architect to provide for a bathroom. This news spread through the village. Some people who did not want to be left behind in the matter of household conveniences followed suit. Thus Sainte-Croix would have five bathrooms before it had running water. This thought pleased me. Sainte-Croix was becoming an avant-garde village!

While the workmen were beginning to dig the foundations, Madeleine Barot announced her arrival. We had known each other since our years at the Sorbonne. I knew that since May 10, 1940, after her return from Rome, where she was librarian at the Farnèse Palace, she had devoted herself to the refugees, becoming general secretary of CIMADE.[22] I also knew that she had managed to implant a CIMADE team in the internment camp at Gurs.

Coming on the evening bus, she told me about her ministry among the refugees and about what could be done within the living conditions of the camp, without hiding the risks which the team members were running. She told me of her hope of placing CIMADE teams in other refugee camps (the figure officially admitted by the Vichy services was 400,000 "internees"). At the end she told me the purpose of her visit; she importuned me to come to the camp at Gurs, which she was going to leave, and that posthaste—in a week's time at the outside.

Madeleine's demand did not surprise me, but I was troubled by the short notice she was allowing me for leaving Sainte-Croix. She swept this obstacle away at a stroke: "Any pastor at all can take your place here, but at Gurs I need *you!* Besides, when I came through Nîmes I saw Pastor Boegner. I bring you his words: 'I have no right to tell Elisabeth to go to Gurs. But if she decides to answer your appeal, she will go with my full approval!' "

Madeleine took the 6:00 A.M. bus, having barely slept. I promised to answer her in forty-eight hours. With very little hesitation I recognized in the call from CIMADE a call from God. I tried to picture to myself the difficulties, the sufferings which a pastoral ministry behind barbed wire might entail. It is at each new stage in our lives that we ought to "count the cost," as Jesus invited us to do. Who does not balk before obeying? (Moses himself did.) But to accept an order and get yourself moving brings a kind of liberation. I felt myself freed from all fear, rich in all the promises of God, as newly attested by God's Spirit. Therefore I sent Madeleine Barot the promised telegram with my acceptance.

The parishioners were summoned to an emergency meeting the following day, in the course of which I planned to say au revoir to them. I felt people's disturbance. My precipitate departure upset all the habits and customs of parish procedure. Without being able to spell it out for them, I was asking my parish to go without a pastor for a while at Sainte-Croix itself, so that others, plucked up from their homes and their country and living within barbed-wire fences, might have a Christian presence beside them.

As I climbed into the taxi which was taking me to the first stop on the way to Gurs, I realized what a sad uprooting this departure was for me, how many ties had been spun between this parish, which had been entrusted to me, and myself. I wanted to look forward, to put off until later the review of all that I had learned and received during these six years. But, hidden in the depths of the car, I could not hold back my tears.

4

The Camp at Gurs, 1941

At the end of the afternoon on a beautiful July day in 1941, I reported to the camp at Gurs. On the day before, I had had to secure the authorization necessary to enter the camp, which we had previously requested. Madeleine Barot introduced me to the prefect of Pau, and I received from his office a little wine-colored card which had only some typewritten notations. I was designated as a "social worker" and my place of work as the "Gurs Camp Reception Center." Priests and pastors could not take up residence in the camp. They were only allowed short visits to hold services. The police hadn't yet heard about women pastors. Therefore I could enter the camp and live there.

Arriving at the camp, I was not surprised to see a geometrical arrangement of chestnut-gray wooden barracks with tarpaper roofs, surrounded by barbed wire and watchtowers and stretching two miles in one direction and just over a quarter of a mile across. From the way Madeleine Barot had described it to me, I had pictured the camp much as it was. But the reality gave me a shock. Right away I was choked by an unbearable stench (an indefinable smell of latrines, decay, lice, and death). The smell grew stronger as we followed the central passageway to reach the Protestant barracks at the other end. Later, when I left Gurs to go to the hospital, this smell followed me, clinging to my hair and embedded in my skin.

The forest surrounds the camp. The eye cannot discern any village, although Gurs is only six miles away and Navarrenx is only four miles. The impressive wall of the Pyrénées closes the horizon toward the south. If the July heat accents the stink, at least it dries the soil, which the heavy rains turn into dangerous mud.

Who Were the Internees?

On this clay plateau the barbed wire imprisoned 25,000 people. Who were they? Members of the International Brigade from the Spanish Civil War who had not been able to go back to their own countries did the camp chores. There were also anti-Nazi foreigners who had fled to France before the war, at a time when no distinction was made between Jews and non-Jews; they were counting on the protection of France. There were foreign Jews who had come into the southern (unoccupied) zone, believing they would be safe there. These internees were for the most part intellectuals —college graduates, doctors, artists—representing the whole range of an intelligentsia which had quickly opposed National Socialism. Finally, there were 7,200 people who had come at the end of October 1940 in sealed boxcars from Baden and the Palatinate. This convoy was destined to be sent to the ghetto in Warsaw. To this day no one knows why it was detoured to France.

The CIMADE barracks, once used by the police but left unoccupied, had sheltered the suitcases of those who died in camp. The barracks had a rare comfort—a floor and a roof which were nearly tight. There I found Jeanne Merle d'Aubigné, with whom I was to be teamed. She had come to work with Madeleine Barot beginning in January 1941. She was an authentic social worker, whose devotion and experience, together with her natural distinction and her white hair, inspired confidence and respect. At the entrance of our barracks there was a corridor leading to two small rooms, one of which served as an office. Next there were two others, one fitted up as a kitchen and the other as a library. The rest of the barracks made a big room warmed by an old cylindrical stove left over from World War I.

How well I remember that first night at Gurs! I scarcely slept on the military cot, which also dated from 1914. I was still to learn the realities of camp life; the lice, the vivid light of big bulbs which lit up the camp and pierced the mica windows, the noise of the rhythmic steps of the security patrols, and the conversation of the guards heard through thin wooden partitions. I was beginning to find out the conditions of life which were imposed on these men and women right in my own country. This camp was run by Frenchmen; each morning the "foreign workers" hoisted the tricolor.

I experienced a strange sense of relief at no longer being in the shelter of a remote valley in the "Nono Zone,"[1] but rather next to the men and women who were the forgotten victims of the war and of the armistice. They were not only forgotten but ignored. Neither the inhabitants of the nearby villages nor the guards had any idea who these men and women were, parked there and under surveillance. No doubt their identity was written on the police blotter in the director's office, but once they were within the barbed wire around the camp and the barbed wire around their section (an island of barracks designated by a letter of the alphabet), these internees were depersonalized. They had been plucked from their native soil, their country, their family. The members of a single family, arrested together, were scattered in different camps and no longer knew anything about one another. (One woman only learned several months after her husband's death that he had also been in the camp at Gurs.) They were deprived of their profession, their milieu of work—in short, of everything which helps a human being to discover and to develop himself or herself. And having lost their freedom, they found themselves gathered, with terrible promiscuity, among other unknowns suffering these same conditions of detention. Who, then, had any care for them? It was better not to raise any questions if you lived near this camp—or any of the others! French people at that time had a good many other things on their minds!

Yes! Our being there, in a barracks next to the other barracks, had a clear meaning. First of all, our presence gave a signal that these detainees were not completely forgotten. Again, it showed that a certain number of French people disapproved of the conditions of the armistice. Our coming to these internees, whom we met on the main street (which they christened "Ugly Alley"), or in the barracks, and our listening to them as they told us about their lives "before," could help them keep their personalities.

I remember that November evening when I went to see Monsieur K. He was an anti-Nazi Czech who spoke six languages and held several doctorates. The camp was already floodlit, but I could hardly see in the barracks because the one light bulb had not yet been turned on. (It would only be lighted for a short time at nightfall.) In a few minutes or tomorrow the rain would begin to fall through the cracks in the roof, and big rats would run around in the dark. The clothes, hung above the bedsteads to keep them away from the rats, looked in the semidarkness like a sinister vision of bodies hanging.

Impelled by the love which Christ inspires, could our presence bring a little light into the shadows and despair of those whom we were visiting? How could we not feel overwhelmed by the immensity of the misery which we were trying to assuage, and the little that we could do?

Hunger Relief

One of our major concerns was nourishing these hunger-stricken detainees. Their weakened condition, together with their other hardships and anxieties, made them prey to every kind of epidemic. When I arrived at Gurs, several relief organizations were already at work. Swiss Aid, particularly aimed at children, was installed in the barracks next to ours. The Quakers had also been authorized to come into the camp; twice a month they received tons of merchandise, allowing them to distribute 2,000 food supplements per day.[2] The YMCA, which had carried on such a helpful program in soldiers' canteens and prisoner-of-war camps in World War I, had not been allowed to come into Gurs. CIMADE took their place. The International Red Cross sent large convoys of food, tons of rice, at the time when the dysentery epidemic was growing worse. A team of internee doctors, led by Dr. Heinrich Mayer, drew up a list of men and women for whom malnutrition would lead to serious illnesses and who should have priority in receiving emergency rations.

The president of the International Red Cross, Dr. Alec Cramer, father of Pastor Cramer, a seminary friend from Geneva, had visited the camp at Gurs. It was on the small table in my room that he had written his report. As a Frenchwoman, I was ashamed of what Dr. Cramer might include in it. CIMADE, with Dr. Cramer's help, calculated the cost of the food distributed each day to each detainee— 3.50 francs at the outside. The Vichy government had allocated 11 francs a day for each "guest" at the camp. Even adding to the cost of food the overhead expense of salaries and maintenance, the figure of 11 francs per day, multiplied by such a large number of detainees, allowed for a large amount of graft. Who was getting the profit from it? Only God knew, and some of those who lived in the camp. But in the climate of that France, humbled and muzzled, was anyone going to scrutinize the accounts of the functionaries in the matter of defenseless detainees? It was not that spectacular cruelties were noticed. Rather it was the hypocritical and sordid exploitation of those who are without defense. What words can you find to describe those who enrich themselves while they are starving to death those whom they are supposed to be guarding?

Bertha Lenel said to me, "Look at this cemetery!" Bertha was a German deaconess nurse who administered a hospital in her own country. One day a special police control had come to arrest her because she was considered a Jew; two of her grandparents were Jewish. The fact that her father, a German officer, was killed in the last war had carried no weight in comparison with this heavy heredity of Jewish blood! Bertha had been one of those who arrived at Gurs in a sealed freight car in the convoy from Baden in October 1940. Tall and thin, always wearing her deaconess uniform, she managed to remain impeccably clean with her stiff collar, her little white cap, and her nurse's apron. With her competence and her devotion she continued, in the circumstances imposed on her, to care as best she could for all the patients whom the internee doctors turned over to her.

"Yes, look at this cemetery," she repeated to me, while I looked in the direction where her finger pointed. Outside the first barbed-wire fence, a large space of freshly turned earth was pushing back the grass of the meadow. From a distance you saw no gravestones, no crosses. Some days thirty new graves were dug there. She added, "This growing plot of ground is an accusing witness." I kept silent.

In my turn I had to accompany a convoy to the cemetery. It was that of an Austrian who, during the Spanish war, had been a major in the International Brigade. I had visited him a few days before his death. The food supplements had not saved his broken-down system. Stretched out on his bedstead, his legs swollen by the edema of hunger, he seemed lucid. He spoke perfect French and wanted to recite Verlaine[3] to me. Never had the poet's verses had as much meaning for me, or as much musical beauty. Several of the Austrian's barrack mates followed the wooden coffin with me. Its light boards bent under the weight of this man who had died of hunger. The rabbi followed another coffin and our pitiful cortège walked along, surrounded by armed guards. I shall always hear the noise which the two bodies made as they were let down into the graves and fell into the brackish water which oozed out three feet under the ground. The rabbi recited the psalms in Hebrew. Perhaps they were the same psalms I read in French. I tried in the few minutes which were allowed us to affirm the Christian hope to the detainees who were present and to make myself understood by the guards, dressed in rough dark blue, who were in a hurry to see their chore finished up.[4]

Worship in the "Protestant Barracks"

In the big room of our barracks, a worship service was held every Sunday morning. It brought together a large proportion of the Protestants in camp, coming from diverse traditions and countries. A former organist in the Strasbourg cathedral provided the music. He managed to let us hear on our mediocre piano the admirable fugues and chorales of J.S. Bach. He was not a Jew himself but had wanted to follow his Jewish wife. The reverence at these services was of an exceptional quality. For the weakest, the effort made to take part in them was too much. Almost every Sunday one of them fainted. Every preparation had been made; taken to one of our beds, the patient was cared for by a doctor or a nurse and given a little food. No one was surprised by such an incident. I think that I was the most disturbed.

These men and women were hungry for the Word of God and wanted to slake their thirst at the springs of living water which the gospel helps us to discover. In this universe of desolation we all understood better that God had chosen to come to us through him who was the Man of Sorrows.

The internees absolutely insisted on giving some of their meager bread rations for the communion services. The words "the breaking of the bread" took on a new meaning there. To serve the wine of the Lord's Supper we had only the glasses from the canteen. I had written to the Cévennes to ask for the two goblets which belonged to the temple at Saint-Roman-de-Tousque (a branch of the Sainte-Croix parish). These two eighteenth-century pewter cups had served in the "wilderness" in the clandestine assemblies of the persecuted Protestants. It seemed to me that they could have the honor of serving, in another extraordinary time, in a "church behind barbed wire."

The first Sunday after my arrival, I had asked the pastor who then had permission to come into the camp to hold Protestant services to preach again on that day. I had just discovered the conditions of life in the camp. Certain images followed me even in my sleep. Did I have the right to preach to the detainees? It was true that I had come to them of my own free will and taken certain risks. But as for me, I was free. I could go out of the camp, leave it when I wished. Thus I did not truly share their misery. In all my life I have never trembled as much before a sermon as when I was getting ready for the first one I was to preach at Gurs. Little by little the bonds of friendship and spiritual communion which grew up between us, and the evidences of confidence and gratitude which were given to me, freed me from this question: "Have I the right to preach to detainees?"

This question also must have arisen for the rare visitors who had permission to come into the camp. Thus Pastor Marc Boegner came to Gurs to visit the CIMADE post (he was the national president). He received red-carpet treatment from the director of the camp and was awaited with emotion by the Protestants, for whom he represented a living symbol of the universal church. The internees were following anxiously the evolution of the situation in Europe and in France. They saw the anti-Semitic laws of the Vichy regions coming, one after the other, and guessed where they were leading. The crematory furnaces loomed on the horizon. The detainees knew what courageous protests had been registered by the National Council of our French Reformed

Church and the difficult and repeated démarches of Pastor Marc Boegner. They knew of his letters, of which the best known is the one he addressed to the Chief Rabbi of France in March 1941.[5]

From the entrance our famous visitor ran his eye over the camp as a whole: the miserable barracks lined up straight, the watchtowers, the strangely built latrines, which stood near the periphery of the barbed wire, so inaccessible to the detainees going there that some stuck in the mud and died or died of the cold after slipping on the ice. Then Jeanne led him to the barracks which the director would have wanted to hide from him, where men whose weakened systems could not resist typhoid were agonizing.

I had always seen Marc Boegner the master of himself in any circumstance. I had seen him taking the floor in the most varied circumstances with perfect ease. But on that day he could not hide his emotion. Our room was full. When he came in, there was a long silence in which he must have felt the expectation of so many distresses. He sat behind a little table facing this gathering, so different from those whom you meet on the other side of the barbed wire. His face hidden in his hands, he did not break the silence but murmured, "No, I can't speak. . . . Elisabeth, you say something." Had the internees heard him? I don't know. But I launched into an improvisation whose words I have forgotten. I wanted to express the reality of the bonds uniting those who suffered under the detention with those who, presently free, were fighting to give back freedom to the captives and to solace their sufferings. I was so moved that the words came from my heart, which was finally freed from any scruple about speaking to the internees at Gurs.

Our Barracks As "Culture Barracks"

We did not want our barracks to welcome only Protestants. We had no idea of trying to create a sort of Protestant ghetto in the midst of the other detainees. Together with the staff members of the other relief agencies of our community, CIMADE created a library open to all. The light shelves, hastily installed in a small room in our barracks, bent under the weight of the books which were sent by the YMCA. Covered with lime-green paper, the books were carefully cataloged by internee librarians. The inventory ran up to 5,000 books, most of which were out. Doctors, engineers, historians expressed the desire to read specialized works, and we requested them from the Geneva committee of the YMCA, which sent them to us as quickly as possible. When I went into a barracks, I could see the light lime-green spots of our book covers in the hands of detainees or on their bedsteads. One day one of the detainees said to me, lifting his book, "These books! They are our salvation!"

There were among the internees many music lovers and professional musicians. These last were deeply affected by being deprived of their instruments. They wasted away in spite of emergency food rations. To put a violin back into the hands of a man who had been the first violinist of the Vienna Philharmonic was to snatch him from death. CIMADE, thanks to gifts from the YMCA, rented musical instruments and bought sheet music. Ten musicians made up a small orchestra. In spite of all the obstacles which camp life imposed on practice time and rehearsals, they set to work. They found a reason for living in preparing for real concerts, and they succeeded in offering us an hour of classical music every week.

Each Sunday—concert day—Jeanne Merle d'Aubigné and I went to the barracks which was at the disposal of the musicians. We brought folding chairs to sit on for the musicale, and those in charge led us to a corner which they called the "box" reserved for CIMADE. Actually they were concerned to keep us a little away from the mass of those who were gathering and might have shared more parasites with us.

Each time I was surprised to hear these ten musicians

managing to interpret so magnificently, with second-rate instruments, pieces by Mozart, Beethoven, Schumann. And I looked at the listeners. They were dressed in threadbare clothing with washed-out colors, or else in brown or beige outfits which internee tailors had cut from camp blankets. They sat huddled together on backless benches. Most of them listened with their eyes closed, their faces expressing joy or ecstasy. The power of music! Where were they? With Mozart in the baroque decor of a hall in Salzburg? In the living rooms of their own homes, where they had in other times heard "A Little Night Music"? And then at the last chord their eyes opened and they found again the bleakness of the barracks, having forgotten for a moment their hunger and all the misery of the present. Perhaps they had understood better how the liveliness of Mozart is a victory, and how fully J.S. Bach imparts to us hope and peace.

Some of those who frequented our library had baptized our Protestant barracks "culture barracks." Thinking of this name, I suggested to Jeanne Merle d'Aubigné and to the Protestant group that we might give some lectures to which we would invite all the internees and the camp authorities. I would be responsible for studies in literature. The Protestants whom we consulted expressed the desire to know modern authors better. But I wanted first to offer them Navarre, where they were—its geography and some phases of its history. Without lingering over Henry IV, I sketched personalities from this old kingdom: Marguerite d'Angoulême, Queen of Navarre, who, waiting for the return of the sun, one time when she and her entourage were bogged down (perhaps here on the plateau of Gurs), had dictated some of the novellas which make up the *Heptameron*; Jeanne d'Albret, her daughter, who several times mounted the pulpit at Oloron. In a cycle of one lecture every two weeks, I discussed Charles Péguy, Ernest Psichari, François Mauriac, and, of course, Paul Verlaine, on whom they had particularly asked me to speak. How attentively the detainees listened to passages from these authors! It was as if they were finding again the real France, the France they had once asked for asylum. How moved they were to hear the words of the poet who wrote from his prison, with a twig dipped in ink, "The sky is over the roof!" I was so happy to help them forget for a moment the France which was keeping them behind barbed wire that I forgot a representative of "General Intelligence," of the Vichy police, or of the Gestapo, lost among the audience, was probably spying on my words. The library, the concerts, the lectures brought many internees (of all races and of all convictions) into our barracks, giving us many contacts.

Camp Tragedies

In the camp the tragedies of our time assailed us every day without respite: each day the despairing faces, the stiffened corpses picked up in the morning at the dysentery barracks.

Anti-Semitism revealed there its most absurd, not to say burlesque aspects. A strange telegram reached the camp director when I had been there about a month: The German authorities ordered that Madame X should be brought back to Kehl and that a nurse should accompany her during the trip. Madame X was one of the old ladies who had come in the convoy from Baden; she was Jewish, but the widow of an Aryan. Her daughter, although half Jewish (like Bertha Lenel) had not been deported with her mother because she had married an officer, an important personage at that time in Himmler's entourage. The officer, giving in to his wife's entreaties (she was rightly fearful over her mother's fate) had succeeded in having his Jewish mother-in-law considered an "honorary Aryan."

The old lady, somewhat exhausted and mentally limited, showed an infantile pleasure in getting ready for her departure, a joy which her fellow captives hardly shared! Not having understood her departure from Germany any more than her liberation from Gurs, she suddenly resumed the imperious tone of a grand dame and demanded perfumed soap for her trip. (I couldn't help telling her that she would find in Germany all the soap they had captured in France.) Having arrived like a vicious beast shut up in a sealed freight car, she went back first-class, accompanied by the attentions of a registered nurse. This departure aroused many comments. It could only accentuate the tensions between the political internees (whether Jewish or not) and the Jews of the Baden convoy.

I discovered at Gurs how little I knew about Jewish piety, despite my theological studies. The way in which the Jewish believers were going through their present sufferings could only impress Christians. Some rabbis were revered like saints. (It was after the war that the series of Jewish studies appeared in *Foi et Vie,* a magazine then edited by Charles Westphal. The first Jewish-Christian meetings were also organized at that time.) I shall always keep the mental picture of a group of Jews praying at the corner of one of the men's "islands," their hands held out in a gesture of supplication and their eyes turned toward Jerusalem. From these emaciated faces with their gray cast, from the rhythmic words of their prayer, there emanated a mysterious force which the barbed wire could not contain. Until that time I had not fully grasped why, and how often, God is referred to in the psalms as "my deliverer." (Cf. Psalm 40:17.)

Finally we were no longer able to ignore—or pretend to forget—the clause in the armistice agreement which obliged us to turn over to Germany the political refugees to whom France had given asylum. This clause was recalled to us in a brutal and intolerable way.

On a gray fall morning the CIMADE team was informed that Madame N was going to be taken away. Madame N was a member of our community. She was Aryan according to the categories of the Third Reich, but she opposed Hitler's policies. She had had to seek asylum in France and had given wartime France some information, the nature and importance of which is, of course, unknown to me. Claimed by the occupying authorities "in the name of the armistice honorably signed," she was being sought out on that day to be turned over to the Germans. Leaving our barracks quickly, I noted that mounted police had surrounded the camp. All sections were encircled. With my card, I could go through the barriers and get to the barracks, surrounded by guards, where I would find Madame N.

Madame N was an asthmatic. She had a sharp attack at the time when she realized that Hitler had not forgotten to reclaim her. The guards were willing to wait a little before seizing her. When she had taken her medicine and the bronchial spasm had subsided, she was able to distribute some of her things to her fellow captives. I clasped her in my arms and embraced her, slipping her a little sugar and some money. She said "Thank you," almost imperceptibly. Then, lifting her head with a sort of pride, she let herself be led away, saying in a louder voice, "Adieu." More than a hundred armed men to arrest this weakened woman already behind barbed wire! Did this deployment of troops underline the importance of the services she had rendered to France and to the allies?

The Problems of Ministry Behind Barbed Wires

Present in the middle of the camp, CIMADE was at the outposts of Christian service. Perhaps there it was manifesting new forms of ministry and there coming up against questions which the traditional church was still refusing to put to itself. The Protestants gathered in our Gurs community had been shaped and taught in the traditions of their country and their church. But they were no longer in that world. In the apocalyptic urbanism of a camp, no specific tradition could carry any weight. Thus, paradoxically, the pastoral ministry of a woman could be practiced quite freely in this place of detention. I never had at Sainte-Croix the impression that the Cévenols considered me as a religious functionary whose stock-in-trade was to preach. I sometimes felt it at Sète, after 1949, and at Nancy. But at Gurs I was quite free from this misconception. To be sure, in the church at Gurs we found the normal variety of ministerial activities: the administration of the sacraments; preaching; the diaconate, with many kinds of relief work; and teaching. The permanent importance of these functions was affirmed here, as it had been across the centuries, in Europe and more recently in mission lands. But the usual problems in the practice of the ministry presented themselves to us from a different angle of vision.

Some of the Jews came to ask for instruction with a view to baptism. Their motives were complex, but it was hard to rule out the possibility that these Jews were looking on baptism as a kind of security (quite illusory, of course). There was no question of taking advantage of an exceptional situation to proselytize—and this at a time when other Jews were affirming with so much courage and nobility their solidarity with their brothers and sisters in race and faith. In any case, the delay of the two years of religious instruction required by the French Reformed Church protected us from any undue haste! In these circumstances the request for baptism obliged me to make theological reflection, a reflection which the parishes in old Europe had neglected, but which they would take up again after the war.

Quite unexpectedly, the question of religious marriage was put to us. Two internees asked me one day for a "benediction on their union." She was single. He had been married at the time of his arrest; he knew nothing about his wife and thought she was dead. Could I really understand what they were asking of me? Was it any surprise that some women had prostituted themselves to get a little food? Was it any surprise that there had been liaisons and clandestine meetings (with complicity) in this topsy-turvy and lonely climate, where all previous bonds seemed to belong to a world forever left behind? But for these two, the question was different. They had met in "Ugly Alley," and love had been born between them. This love was to them a gift of God which helped them live and which they believed to be durable and profound. I found it improbable and beautiful, in such a setting, to see the happy smile of love on the faces of these detainees. They could not be married by a civil ceremony. But a French pastor cannot officiate at a wedding until after the civil ceremony. That's what I told them right away. The argument surprised them. "But," they said to me, "what about the Protestants who were secretly married in the wilderness with the blessing of the pastor, although in the eyes of the kingdom they were living in concubinage?" It was hard to explain to them that their situation was very different from that of the Protestants under Louis XIV. It was sad to remind them that they were not going to found a home in a camp where married couples were in separate barracks and could only meet on the central alley between their respective islands. The whole sociological conditioning which surrounds "nuptial benediction" (to use the expression of marriage announcements) was as though pulverized by the realities of imprisonment. The theology of the couple, the theology of sexuality, needed to be deepened and the churches would only turn to this task very slowly.

Yes, the church in camp was made up of all these questions and many more. It was the full richness of human encounters in this setting of misery and poverty. It was the special quality of friendships knitted between us. It was the reality of our spiritual communion. How can I conjure up the testimonies of those men and women who manifested the presence of Christ in their life at Gurs? I am thinking of the slight man, humble and self-effacing, who, from Sunday to Sunday, grew weaker and thinner. His name was not on the list of the detainees who needed food relief because he was getting packages from friends in France. We learned that he was giving all his food packages to his barrack mates and keeping nothing for himself.

In later sermons at Sète and at Blida I quoted my conversation with Madame P. I had gone with her down "Ugly Alley," toward Island M, to which she was returning before nightfall. She told me about her pilgrimage toward God, how she had discovered the truth of the gospel. She stopped a moment. Her slender silhouette, her feet shod in wooden shoes, her clothes made of blankets floating around her, stood out against the horizon of the barracks. She held me with her clear look and continued, "In Vienna I lived in a splendid house. My husband was an influential man. We entertained many friends and had interesting relationships. Yes, I was rich with many of the riches of this world. I have been completely stripped of them." There was a silence of several seconds between us and then she resumed, in a tone of deep conviction, "Here I have found another kind of riches, those which no one can take away and which are worth more than all the others. Saint Paul said it, didn't he?"

Dr. Heinrich Mayer could write, a long while after the war, "I would not want to relive those years for anything in the world. But they led me to become more of a believer than I had ever been. They gave me that something that makes a man unshakable, so that nothing can take away his faith. Christ would not be what he is for us without his suffering and death."[6]

No doubt we were sharply separated from those who lived on the other side of the barbed wire. It was impossible to write to friends because the mail at Gurs and even at Pau was heavily censored. But in spite of the isolation, in spite of the difficulties of communication, we felt ourselves upheld by those who were sharing our work through their gifts. We were surrounded by prayers. And in this closed universe of the camp, the universal church became more real and closer than in traditional parishes.

Typhoid and Departure from the Camp

One December evening I went to bed shivering with
fever, knowing that I was very sick. Was it typhoid or
typhus? I asked myself. (Several times I had found body lice
in my clothing.) Dr. Mayer diagnosed it as typhoid, which
seemed to me somewhat reassuring. I did not want to have
myself cared for by the French camp doctor. His inhumanity
toward the detainees was insupportable. He could not use
the scarcity of beds and medicines in the little hospital as a
pretext. He contented himself with signing death certifi-
cates. Since he wanted to be correct toward me, I saw him
appear on my doorstep two days later. He asked me if I was
satisfied with the care I was receiving. I answered that I had
complete confidence in Dr. Mayer and that I certainly had
typhoid. "No, you have the grippe. Take aspirin."

Dr. Mayer had a blood sample taken, but the flask never
left camp. They did not want it known outside that there was
a typhoid epidemic. At night a young assistant nurse came,
sent she told me by the camp doctor, to spend the night at
my bedside. I could not stay in the Protestant barracks. I was
an embarrassment and could be an additional cause of
contagion. I left by ambulance for a hospital in Pau. Outside
impressions came to me through a sort of fog in which I was
floating somewhat euphorically. But when I saw along the
central alley the internees who, behind the barbed wire of
their islands, were waving me good-bye, I understood
despairingly that I was leaving them for good. I was to learn
some time later that the members of my family, the officers
of the French Reformed Church, and other friends had been
busy on the telephone. Pastor Boegner had wired Pastor
Nouvelon in Pau, asking him to arrange for my hospitalization in their excellent clinic. Pastor Nouvelon's wife came in
the ambulance which extracted me from the camp.

As soon as I could leave the hospital, my sister took me to
her home in Montauban. Some people visited me, asking

solicitously about my health. But no one asked questions about the camp from which I had come back. A kind of fear began to insinuate itself into the cities. People were suspicious of one another. My friend Madame S, with whom I had lodged in Geneva when I was a student, invited me to come and finish my convalescence at her house. The Geneva government allowed me a month's visit, providing that my friends would feed me with their personal food rations.

As my strength came back to me I returned to the concern which gripped me by the heart; the acceptance by my church of the pastoral ministry of women. Completely absorbed in the sufferings of the internees at the camp, I had repressed this question, pushing it into the background. I also felt that Jeanne Merle d'Aubigné was very reticent, and I had not spoken of it with her. Nothing had been decided in the Synods except to give me a pastoral delegation, the recognition of a ministry with a time limit. Was my pastoral delegation for the parish at Sainte-Croix automatically valid at Gurs? I had not worried about it except to know if the internees would accept me as pastor. I had left one parish at the call of CIMADE, and I had no assurance that another would be entrusted to me. Would this first experiment made by the French Reformed Church be without a sequel—the experiment of confiding a parish to a woman, the experiment of granting me a pastoral delegation by a decision of successive National Synods? It did not seem to me possible that it was a dead-end street! I remembered some words of Dean A. Gampert[7]: "To walk by faith is not to see the whole way ahead of time, but to discover it day by day, with unforeseen detours and to keep the certainty that God is leading us."

I tried to banish the bitterness which can rise in a woman's heart when she realizes that the situation of a man would be different; a male pastor would surely be called to another parish.

The Hospice of "The Flowery Hillside"[8]

The last weeks of convalescence seemed to me interminable. Then an unforeseen appeal reached me; Madeleine Barot asked me to come as pastor-chaplain to help the director of "The Flowery Hillside" at Le-Chambon-sur-Lignon. I answered the call immediately and went to the Haute-Loire. The Flowery Hillside was a hotel a few miles from Le Chambon. CIMADE had rented it as soon as a few internees were allowed to leave the camps, on condition that they were under an authorized organization and under police surveillance. There, as at the "Mas du Diable" near Tarascon and at the "Foyer Marie Durand" in Marseille, CIMADE gathered together families which had been dispersed in different camps.

These establishments imposed a heavy financial load. Madeleine Barot had accomplished the tour de force of persuading the Vichy authorities to allow Princess Bernadotte of Sweden to go into the camp at Gurs. She came there in her capacity as vice-president of the board of the World's YWCA, which had previously brought its help to women in prison during World War I. Once past the barbed wire, the princess was immediately convinced of the necessity of augmenting the gifts made by her committee and by the Swedish Lutheran churches.

How moved I was to see dear Dr. Mayer, Sister Bertha Lenel,[9] and several parishioners from Gurs getting off the autorail at the stop just below the hotel! What a joy to see them settled in a real house with beds, sheets, and food which, in spite of the difficulty of those times, was adequate and well prepared! In the good air of the plateau, almost 3,000 feet high, facing a horizon of mountains with gentle contours, everyone got back strength and a little hope. A young girl among the boarders at The Flowery Hillside, seeing a little bird in a cage, asked, "Tell me, Mama, why is the little bird in a barracks?" The memory of the barracks was still so close!

In July I received a letter from Pastor Gall in Florac. He had succeeded Pastor André as president of the region of the Cévennes. He asked me to substitute for him during the month of August. He also spoke rather vaguely of the possibility of my being called as the second pastor at Florac. This letter brought me the providential sign that the experiment would go on, and that God was tracing out a new stretch of road for me.

My health strengthened by this stay in the mountains. I was happy to rediscover a parish ministry, but not without scruples at leaving The Flowery Hillside just when the situation of its guests was worsening. The plan for deporting Jews was being perfected, and we noted with shame and sadness the zeal of some French people to have it put into execution. Pastor Marc Donadille was able to take my place, and I left at once for Florac. This friend had to meet all the difficulties from the wave of arrests in August 1942. I learned later that, thanks to his sangfroid and that of some of the people at the establishment, and thanks to the devoted complicity of the villagers in Le Chambon-sur-Lignon, all the guests of The Flowery Hillside had found hiding places in deserted barns, with the exception of one young girl. Saved from arrest, they were finally taken to Switzerland.

5

Interlude in Florac

THUS I GOT TO FLORAC IN MIDSUMMER, 1942. I found once more the towering cliff of Rochefort, the little old square, the noise of the torrent passing under the old bridge, the bowling green[1] and its shade trees. The streets were enlivened by summer residents spending the summer in their family houses, and by city people who had come in search of foodstuffs that could not be found in the big cities.

I had a lot of things to think through: the experience at Gurs; my anxiety over the fate of the internees in the camps, which I could not talk about. All these things made it hard to readjust to the life of a traditional parish in the nonoccupied zone.

After one of the services, two of the presbyterial councilors asked to speak to me in confidence. I had met them several times at meetings or synods. "Mlle. Schmidt," they said, "you should know that two years ago we asked to have you as pastor at Florac. We were then told that you had not yet spent five years in Sainte-Croix, and that it would be better for that parish if you should stay on there for some years more." (I had known nothing of this request.) They went on, "Now we know that your coming as a second pastor to Florac is being considered. The present intern, Monsieur L, would be sent somewhere else. But we think that it would be better for him to stay on at Florac."

They assured me all over again that they felt it was a shame I had not come to Florac two years before.

The following day I visited a very sick parishioner who was the mother-in-law of the intern, Monsieur L. She was very feeble, but she said to me right away, "I know that I can trust you; let me tell you not to come to Florac. René would like to stay here. If you accept the pastorate at Florac, he will have to give way to you."

The night before, I had been able to say to the councilors, while thanking them for their frankness, that nothing had been decided about my coming to Florac. But before the sad face of a dying woman, I did not have the time either to investigate or to think and to meditate. Without looking for any diplomatic formula, I answered, "Madame, under these circumstances, I will not come to Florac." The lines of the sick woman's face relaxed. "You have relieved me of my last worry before leaving this world. Thank you, oh! thank you." Thus, by this promise made to an agonizing woman, I had closed again the door which I had thought I saw opening— the door to a continuing pastoral ministry.

Immediately I wrote to Pastor Gall, to Pastor Boegner, and to several friends, including Marc Donadille. And when my substitute work was over, I went back to Montauban, to my sister's house. Her hearth has always been a haven to me in the midst of life's tempests.

My friend Marc Donadille answered my letter right away. I could imagine the dramatic days lived out by the guests at The Flowery Hillside when I read, "I've just had some hard days, and you ought to know the reason for our worries: We were expecting a raid." He wanted to give me some news and also some advice about my own future. He had recently seen Pastor Boegner. The latter considered that "the National Council is less and less favorable to the pastoral ministry of women." He went on to wonder whether the National Council would give me another assignment. Marc Donadille thought best to give me, in all friendship, some advice, as I dreamed of the future: "Don't get too revved up: make a show of great submission and humility . . . weigh the pros and cons. . . . Before pressing forward, you must watch out for your natural violence."

Today I reread with emotion this letter which at that time had so affected and revolted me. Coming back from Gurs, I was learning that "the National Council is less and less favorable to the pastoral ministry of women"—outside the barbed wire! Nothing is more exasperating for us, as women, than the duality of men's attitudes toward us: on the one hand, this solicitude by which they show their love of neighbor; on the other, this refusal to admit us to the places they have saved for themselves, and always without daring to say so frankly.

I didn't understand very well what could have been the attitude of the National Council. My first years in the Cévennes, the pastoral delegation granted at the end of my first year of probation and renewed later—all these had nourished some of my illusions. I was only beginning to discover what power, what weight of tradition and custom I was hurling myself against when I raised the question of the pastoral ministry of women. "Watch out for your natural violence"? The violence of my indignation, and of all the anticlericalism it was so dangerously feeding!

Jewish raids began at Montauban, as in the rest of France. I met once more, in another setting, all the distresses and questions of this time of testing. Thinking of so many men and women who were living in the tragic uncertainty of tomorrow, I forgot my own uncertainties and all the theological, sociological, and historic questions which I could turn and turn over again in my head.

Like so many others, I had to accept suffering at the hands of the church. That is part of the "pruning" of which the Gospel of John gives the secret: "I am the true vine, and my Father is the vinedresser. Every branch of mine that bears no fruit, he takes away, and every branch that does bear

fruit he prunes, that it may bear more fruit [John 15:1-2]."
I was being brought back to the essential thing: to seek the
will of God in an unconditional way. In this sort of night I
could not take any decision. I weighed each day how fragile
is our hope, but also how strong it can be. God alone could
open a breach through all these stones, gathered in such
good Christian conscience to erect the fortress of human
traditions in the matter of the place of woman in the church.

My Path Becomes Clear

Shortly after my return to Montauban, I had a telephone
call from Monsieur Bouteiller. As an elder in the church at
Sète, he told me that he was looking for preachers for the
summer Sundays and asked if I could take the next service. I
accepted, very glad to spend a few days with friends who had
already welcomed me several times in their big house.

I had no knowledge of the thoughts and the investigations
which the Sète parish had undertaken. It was a strong
parish, though the number of families did not quite come up
to the figure which would warrant creating a second pastoral
post. During its meeting on July 4, 1942 the presbyterial
council had decided to call a deaconess to help the incumbent in the post, Pastor Franck Balfet. Monsieur Bouteiller
had talked to the various members of the council about me.
They had the idea of calling me as an assistant pastor rather
than as a deaconess. But before they went any farther they
wanted to get acquainted with me and hear me preach,
without my knowing about their plans. Hence the telephoned request.

After church on Sunday morning, a man who seemed to
me very old (I was young!) asked me to come to his house
that afternoon to meet the members of the presbyterial
council. In the parlor of a big apartment whose windows
looked out on the quay, facing the sea, I took my seat in the
circle of the members of the council, all of whom were men.

After several friendly words about what they had heard of my ministry in the Cévennes and about my sermon in the morning, the vice-president asked me if I would accept coming to help Pastor Balfet; that is to say, to alternate with him in leading the worship, to share with him in confirmation classes and in the Sunday school work, and to take charge of the youth movements. "Of course, you would not do funerals or marriages," the vice-president[2] said to me.

I accepted this program without any objection, with the submission and the humility becoming to women!—not without noticing that in their eyes the sacraments did not seem to be excluded from a woman's pastoral ministry. Next I heard, with a surprise which I hid very badly, the treasurer's question: "What salary are you asking?" I answered, "Why, naturally, the salary of a single pastor as it is determined by the National Synod."

I was very much surprised by this call, without any previous letter from the president of the regional council. Pierre Bouteiller remained very reticent, saying only that "President Boegner had given the green light." I waited a quarter of a century to hear about the conversation which Pierre Bouteiller had with the president of the National Council. Monsieur Boegner, surprised at the question which the elder from Sète was asking him, began by saying, "Elisabeth to Sète? But that's impossible!" Did this initiative on the part of an elder seem dangerous to him? In any case, the discussion was long. In the end: "You want her? Very well, take her. But in three months you will come asking me to take her back. Au revoir, cher ami!" My friend Monsieur Bouteiller told me this and added, "That's how he dismissed me, in a tone of voice like an admiral's."

At the presbyterial council of September 19, 1942 the decision on my coming was taken officially. (There had been no meeting since the one on July 4.) The minutes state, "Mlle. Schmidt will be invited to come to Sète on September 23 or 24 if possible, to conclude a definite understanding with Pastor Balfet. Thereupon the council will decide and ratify whatever agreement has been reached." The council meeting on September 25 "puts on record" that Monsieur Balfet and I have divided the work. The council decided to give me the salary of a single pastor in the French Reformed Church and to find me a lodging "in which I could settle definitely among my furniture." In the meantime I would stay temporarily in half of a small house belonging to a prisoner of war.

Once again I found myself in a delicate situation. The formalities had been respected in the minutes of the presbyterial council. But, in fact, my coming to Sète had been decided by the presbyterial council while Pastor Franck Balfet was on a long leave of absence to allow him to rest. The experience in Florac was recent and it helped me. Since I was a woman, I had to accept winding roads! I remain grateful to my colleague, Monsieur Franck Balfet, for having accepted me as he did.

6

Ministry in Sète

At the end of September 1942 I settled temporarily (a "temporary" arrangement which lasted until 1946) in several rooms of a newly built, clean house with a little garden, situated at 1 rue de la Convention.

For some people Sète calls up first of all the name of Paul Valéry, who sang of the "Sea Cemetery," and the names of artists who fixed on canvas the "Sète Tournaments" in the splendor of July. One of them was Couderc, who became curator of the museum. The personality of Jean Vilar, the actor and director, is associated in my memories with Sète, because I followed and admired his creations at Avignon and because ties had been woven between his family and myself.

Sète offers many aspects which it takes a certain time to discover, with its canals which crisscross the city, the bridges which span them and which you see rearing themselves up, immense, during the time that it takes to let the boats go by on their way from the sea to the lagoon. Sète, a peninsula between two bodies of water, is neither Venice nor Rotterdam: you will find there no old neighborhoods. Actually, it is the most recent of the great French ports. Its construction began in 1666. (A first attempt made under Henri IV had been abandoned.)

The city has grown slowly. It barely topped 10,000 inhabitants in 1830, remaining too long a "sea city," or a "maritime suburb" of Montpellier. The people of Sète had to claim their independence, first in relation to the tutelage of the Bishop of Agde, and even more in relation to the metropolis. The rich burghers of Montpellier handled the bulk of the port business, and the people of Sète complained of their imperialism. In spite of the founding of the Chamber of Commerce in 1872, which marked the economic independence of Sète, a certain antagonism between the two cities continued, under the most varied forms. I even discerned it several times in the relationships between the churches of Sète and those in Montpellier.

The Protestant Community of Sète

It was only in the eighteenth century that there was any thought of a reformed church in Sète or that any note was taken of the names or the presence of preachers. The port of Sète witnessed numerous clandestine embarkations of hounded Protestants, arriving from the cities or from the Cévennes. (We should mention the name of Squire Saurin, a lawyer, who left with his wife and his two children. The younger one was nine years old and became the famous preacher Jacques Saurin.) After the law of Germinal X (1802),[1] the church in Sète had a pastor, Louis Marion.

The Protestant community which I found on coming to Sète was very different from that of the Vallée Française. It had no unity of origin or of social milieu. The Protestants were found among the small businessmen and the lower echelons of government functionaries. They often came from the Cévennes or the Tarn. Their proportion was more significant among the liberal professions and especially the big merchants. Three of the four firms of maritime brokers were in the hands of Protestant families, and during the sixteen years of my ministry in Sète the successive presidents of the Commercial Court were active members of our presbyterial council.

Why had I had the impression, when I first entered the

church at Sète, that it was luxurious? Was it because of the stained-glass windows lighting up the vast edifice, almost square in shape? Still, they were subdued. Was it because of the dark wood of the pews, arranged to allow two lateral aisles? Was it because of the pulpit, clinging against the back wall, accessible only through the sacristy? (There were some of these "surprise pulpits" in Montpellier and Nîmes.) No, it was rather because of the organ (the gift of a music-mad parishioner), placed in a gallery above the pulpit. It was luxurious, especially in comparison with the poverty of the Cévennes.

Yes, a long time had gone by since the Protestants of the city of Sète (Cette)[2] sent a request to the Count of Saint-Priest, intendant of Languedoc. They asked for a place of worship in the city itself, since "the Protestants are possessors of only a poor cabin on the shore of the lagoon." This church had been consecrated on August 1, 1872 in the presence of eighteen pastors, during the ministry of Monsieur Lucien Benoît. It surely expressed the need of Protestants to affirm themselves as present in the city, at the same time that it expressed the joy of being free to profess their faith.

The church at Sète had one notable distinction: The Law of Separation of Church and State, which was well received in general by Protestants, was greeted with enthusiasm by the pastor of the church at Sète. Lucien Benoît saw in it the means of "bringing the Christian church back to its origins." The Protestants also saw in it the chance to show their independence. The church at Sète did not join either of the two unions of churches. While promising to support them with its gifts, it kept its financial independence.

Pastor Camille Leenhardt, coming to occupy the post of pastor in 1922, got the church to join the Union of Evangelical Reformed Churches, but it insisted on keeping its financial independence. It retained its independence but became a parish of the French Reformed Church after 1938.

It was this autonomy which had allowed the church to hire me without having to debate about finances with the ecclesiastical authorities.

The Occupation of the City

I had barely had time to get acquainted with some of the parishioners when the situation changed. On November 10, 1942, after Bible study, I was seeing a girl scout leader home toward eleven o'clock when motorbikes, going full tilt, went by us with a deafening noise. They were the first outriders of the army of occupation which was arriving on this Mediterranean shore. Wearing the green uniforms of the land army, the blue uniforms of the navy, or the sand-colored uniforms of the men who had fought in the desert, the Germans became masters of the port. The lighthouse became blind and the coast was cemented with blockhouses. But can a people become servile in front of the vast sea?

I remember the parishioner who, meeting me on the Noel-Guignon quay, said to me as he introduced himself, "As for me, there is only one savior, one chief, one leader, that we have to follow, and that is the Marshal."

"Oh," I answered him, "since you call yourself a Protestant, I was thinking that you were going to say 'Jesus Christ.'" What was intolerable was the alienation of the intelligence, the abandonment by Protestants of any critical spirit, of all individual thought. This was the most dangerous of the victories of Nazism.

Such aberrations were rare. There was only a small group who regretted the National Council's protests or Pastor Boegner's interventions, at the time of the roundup of Jews, or when political refugees who had been welcomed by France before 1939 were surrendered to the Germans.[3] The majority of Protestants kept a sort of nimble neutrality. No one asked me questions about the camp at Gurs. They preferred not to know. But some rare and authentic resistants, who had understood the meaning of my presence at Gurs, spoke to me confidently. I never had any difficulty with my colleague on this question, and I am very grateful to him for that.

One morning in October I saw, coming to my house, a blond twelve-year-old boy with an intelligent and serious face. "Can anybody hear us?" he asked as he sat down in my study. Reassured, and knowing that I was alone in the house, he began, "I know that you were at Gurs, so I can confide in you." His whole family had been able to escape the Jewish raids, and his father and mother had been maintained in the Montpellier hospital, thanks to a doctor. His sister had been hiding in a barn since the arrival of the Germans in the southern zone. But the situation could not be prolonged. "Come see her, that will give her courage; then you will find a way to send her elsewhere."

After all necessary precautions had been taken, the brave Frenchmen who were hiding her took me to her. She did not have the fate of Anne Frank. With the help of one of the elders, who thought it was more prudent to take her to a way station for a night train, I told her to go to the Cévennes to my friends, the Marc Donadilles, who were now at Saint-Privat-de-Vallongue. She got there without difficulty and my friends welcomed her, having her play the role of a *jeune fille au pair*.[4] The people of the countryside believed it, or pretended to. Her parents succeeded in joining her and occupied a small abandoned house on the mountain nearby. The boy, with books furnished by Pastor Donadille and with his help, prepared for the *baccalauréat*. He passed it in 1945. Today the whole family lives in the United States.

In this case, as in others which followed, a kind of clandestine complicity grew up between some of my parishioners and myself. Helping people in danger has always been part of the tradition of the Christian church. These circumstances gave this help a very special character.

At Gurs we had been awaiting the defeat of Nazi Germany in complete unanimity. At Sète, I had to be the pastor of all and to guard against becoming "partisan." My horror of Nazism and of those who were servile to it must not destroy the love of neighbor even if he or she had been alienated from what I believed by the ideology of the day.

Very quickly, in the presbyterial council, everyone seemed to forget the first restriction which had been placed upon me: not to perform marriages or funeral services. I officiated at a first wedding at the beginning of December 1942. A leading citizen of the city asked on his deathbed that I conduct his funeral service. I did it. There was no further restriction on the exercise of my ministry.

Beginning in May 1943 Pastor Balfet announced his approaching departure. In October, he was going to be pastor at Vésinet, near Paris. Pastor Cadier, the president of the region, declared the post of Sète vacant. He seemed to want an incumbent named without delay. He had several conversations with the presbyterial council in my absence. Some names figure in the minutes of the meeting of the presbyterial council on July 2, 1943. One of the elders told me that Pastor Cadier had come to tell them that Pastor X was applying for the post at Sète but would not move to the parish until after the war. The rumor was going around that the city would soon be evacuated and would become a "war zone." One of the elders took offense at this candidature by Pastor X: "You are proposing to us this 'Jean-Foutre,'[5] who won't come until after the war! Very well, let him stay where he is! Now Mlle. Schmidt, she has the courage to keep on being our pastor amid these dangers. We don't need any other!" Thus I remained as the sole resident pastor at Sète beginning with the opening of school in October 1943. A colleague evacuated from Alsace, Pastor Van der Perck, a refugee in Montpellier, conducted two services a month and some other services for more than a year.

The Germans excavated the hill of Sète to install ammunition and food depots and an underground hospital. It became almost certain that "Sète Mountain" would be a stronghold like Royan and that the city would be evacuated.

You saw more and more moving vans on the streets. Even those who were staying put their furniture, their linen, and their silver in storage outside of Sète and camped in their houses.

These months of testing and waiting woke up the sleepy Christians. A little group of them began to reflect on their responsibilities after the war on such matters as environment, employment, and public health. Another group undertook very concretely to find places of refuge for older people and children. I proposed to both groups the study of the Apostles' Creed to illuminate their research and their action.

Partial Evacuation and Bombardment

In the spring of 1944 the occupation authorities ordered the evacuation of part of the city. New identity cards were distributed to the only ones who would have the right to live in the city and receive food rationing coupons. I was one of 7,000 to 8,000 classified as "useful"; about 1,500 were classed as "indispensable." The grade schools and lycées closed, as did some hospital services. You no longer met older people or children on the street—they had all gone. What a sad city it was!

At the same time that they evacuated the city, the Germans required the remaining population to abandon all dwelling units along the canals. Trenches filled with explosives and linked by a fuse were dug every sixty feet along the quays by the occupying forces. The "useful" and the "indispensable" people had to settle in a small perimeter called the "restricted zone"; my house was there.

I had written in the February 1944 issue of *Le Lien Protestant* (*The Protestant Link*), the little parish bulletin, of which I had become the sole editor:

> I am well aware that our anxious hearts would like to have the certitude that we shall be spared, that the horrors of war

will pass us by. . . . Nevertheless, when so many beings are suffering, we have to ask not "Why am I being tested?" but "Why should I be spared?" Why should we not take our part in the sufferings of war? So many others have already had to leave hearths, and that a long time ago. Now it is our turn also. "This doesn't seem possible," we say. But "this" has been possible for our compatriots, our fellow believers. It is only egotism which has allowed us to distance ourselves from the reality of their suffering. We are beginning to learn the meaning of a word that has been used a great deal during this war: the word "refugee."

At the same time I published in our house organ the end of a letter which Pastor Roland de Pury wrote to his parish in Lyon from Switzerland, where he had regained his freedom thanks to an exchange of political prisoners. I left out the author's name because of the censorship.[6]

Keep on praying as you have done until now. For there are all those who remain behind the closed door. There are all the prisoners in the world. There are all the cells in the world, and no one can imagine the despair which fills them. May God give you his own compassion, his infinite pity for the captives. We have to be free and to free every creature. It is the only problem of our life. And you know it: Liberating is serving. We can only serve or enslave our neighbor.[7]

I embrace you in my heart and in my joy,

Your pastor and your friend

The group of Protestants who met at worship on Sundays kept on shrinking. We no longer had an organist. The singing was dominated by men's voices, since more men than women stayed on in the city. The vice-president of the council left Sète, taking with him the parish records to put them in safekeeping in his country house. Some of the elders who remained had suggested the possibility of dismantling the organ! But the work would have been long and costly, and that idea was dropped.

On June 25 at nine thirty in the morning, the wailing of a

siren tore in shreds the calm of this beautiful summer day. Into the shallow shelter dug in my garden (at Sète the water seeps in. fast) my neighbor came to join me. I wore a saucepan on my head—the supply of helmets had given out. For fifty long minutes the deafening roar of airplanes, the whistling and the bursting of bombs, as thirteen waves of American planes attacked our German-held port city . . . then a strange silence. A first bird began to sing, then others. My neighbor and I came out of the shelter. She and I were astonished to find the houses still standing.

I wanted to go to the hospital. Wishing to enroll in a Red Cross training course, I had chosen, on the advice of officials, to join the "Emergency Teams," as giving me more freedom of movement. I went into the women's surgery room, where the nursing sister asked me to stay and wash the minor wounds of the casualties whom other Red Cross teams were slowly bringing in. My mind a little dulled by the ether, breathed for two hours on end, I was not surprised to be the only volunteer in this room. I left quickly for the decommissioned church of "the Penitents," where the dead were to be brought.

My Red Cross arm band (stamped by the German commandant) allowed me to pass the barrier of the church turned morgue. The Little Sisters of the Poor were finishing the task of making the mangled bodies "presentable" to the families and were arranging the personal effects in little rubber bags which they were pinning to their clothing. Fifty-two bodies were spread out under the vaults, protected from the burning June sun by the thick walls. When the relatives were allowed to come in, the church rang with the sobs and lamentations of all those who were searching for their relatives. One woman addressed a nursing sister: "At least you must have found his pocketbook. He had fifty-three francs in it." She had a dry eye and an evil look. Then she resumed her ritual moaning.

I had offered my services in case the hospital did not have

enough nurses. Not only did the Mother Superior accept them for the night, she asked me, if possible, to bring someone else! At nine o'clock the men's surgery was turned over to me, with thirty postoperative cases, three of them dying. The smell of the room, which was dimly lighted by a blue night light, was unfamiliar to me and to the friend who had come with me. She fainted toward two o'clock in the morning. The night watchman kept the calm of old troopers; he quietly ate his midnight meal. And the wives of the three dying men, although they were allowed to stay beside their husbands, were out of their element and quickly left us alone.

I had the intern on duty called for one of the wounded. He was surprised to find me changed into a nurse. He explained to me that no new operation could take place before morning. I was indignant, totally lacking the submission of a nurse toward a doctor. The administrator of the hospital put in a brief appearance in the room and hid his annoyance at finding me there by saying many kind words to me.

I went home on the Monday morning broken with fatigue and filled with indignation at the incurable improvidence of the French. It seemed incredible that one or two teams of nurses had not been provided to back up the hospital personnel in case of a bombardment! It was also incredible that the old antagonism between Montpellier and Sète had lasted even in these circumstances and prevented calling on the Montpellier doctors for help. I learned later that a surgical team from Montpellier had been waiting quite close to the Sète hospital. What should be done so that a similar mistake would not be made at the next bombardment? Who would take the responsibility of a protest? I decided to write a letter to the competent authorities of the prefecture and wrote to the prefect. I would give a copy to the doctor and the hospital superintendent.

But before preparing this letter, I had to take care of the funeral services of the victims of the bombardment, which would take place on Tuesday, June 27. I went to see the mayor about the organization of the religious services. He looked embarrassed. He hadn't thought about the Protestants. I insisted. "There were three Protestants killed, and one is a Swiss. The port had preferential arrangements with Switzerland." (Sète was a "Swiss port.") His only answer was, "Go work things out with Curé X." Curé X was even more surprised than the mayor by my visit. These Protestants certainly were obnoxious! I learned that the bodies would not be moved, that there would be a simple service of general absolution at "the Penitents," then a cortège to the cemetery. The Catholics being in the majority, I left it to the priest to choose (with the bishop, who might come) which service would begin on the balcony of the old church, now turned morgue, and which service would close at the cemetery.

According to an understanding with the bishop's office, it was agreed that the short Protestant service would take place before the Catholic absolution, and at the cemetery the pastor would close. Catholic friends who were part of the Red Cross team explained to me that they were charged with the logistics and that they would make sure "that the Protestant service was not skipped." The bishop was astounded to see members of the Red Cross awaiting his arrival on the steps as a signal for the pastor to begin—and that this pastor was a woman!

While I was walking with the grieving families, behind the camions carrying fifty-two coffins, one covered with a Swiss flag, I learned that the bishop was going to address a message to the people before going back to Montpellier. This would take place where the cortège was going to disband, with only the families going to the cemetery. When the procession stopped I came to the microphone. "Are you through, Monsignor?" I asked, taking the microphone. The current was cut off. (By whom? I don't know.) But I had a good voice, and the silence was complete. The Bishop had protested against the "unforgivable Anglo-American bomb-ings." I called, in the name of Christ, "the only Leader who can be followed unconditionally," for building tomorrow a juster and more fraternal world. At the cemetery no one left before I finished slowly reciting the Apostles' Creed.

It was very sad for me to feel no communion between the Roman Catholic clergy and myself. This bishop must have been a Pétainist and he must not have read *Témoignage Chrétien*.[8] No doubt it was still sadder for the several Catholic lay people who had had real ecumenical attitudes.

The Evacuation of August 15, 1944

On the evening of August 14, Monsieur V and his wife came to camp at my house; they had stayed in hiding up until that time in their apartment on the waterfront. On that evening, radio messages from London were interminable; we were listening to them anxiously, receiving them well in spite of the jamming. "It is for tonight," Monsieur V said to me, "but not on this side of the Rhône." The night was magnificent, with many shooting stars at this season; togeth-er we wondered at the beauty of creation, and the words of the psalm flowed from our hearts: "The heavens are telling the glory of God [Ps. 19]." We all slept lightly. Far-off sounds of explosions came to us in the course of the night.

The next morning, after a first alert, a sound truck announced that the city had to be evacuated before nine o'clock that night. Only those who had cards as "indispens-able" would be authorized to remain. Everyone found in the city without that card would be shot. Should I leave? Or obtain a card as "indispensable"? At the mayor's office the French, crumpled up and impotent, referred me to the Germans: "This is a war zone! We are no longer in charge!" The Germans told me to "go take a walk." I had reached the vice-president of the council by telephone. He was Professor Mourgue-Molines. He said to me, "If the Americans arrive, they will have their own chaplains and they will have no need of you. So follow your parishioners!"

I said to myself, "Isn't leaving, fleeing from danger, the same as deserting?" In the end it was theology which cut through the question for me. I answered myself: "The church is neither a place nor a building but a *people*. Therefore, I will follow my parishioners."

I went to the railroad station with a pack on my back and a suitcase in my hand to join the three trains of cattle cars that were going to take the Sétois who had not left on their own. For a week I lodged at the house of the vice-president of the regional council of our church, spending my days with small groups of Sétois "refugees." The explosions at the port of Sète had been heard in Montpellier. From the roof of the hospital the doctors thought they had seen Sète in flames.

The German troops, in cars, in hearses, by bicycle, or on foot, camouflaged by branches which withered in the August sun, were leaving the Mediterranean shore. The road being open from then on, I took the first car which was taking six or seven functionaries to Sète. We were stopped at La Peyrade. The commandant of the liberated city and of the port was not authorizing our reentry until certain precautions had been taken, in particular, verifying whether the water supply had been poisoned. A little group of Protestants, therefore, lived for several days in community in the Bouteiller house, and services took place in a classroom at Frontignan.

The city quays were riddled with holes after the explosion of the mines which had been planted. The stones from the quays, thrown violently on the roofs, had broken the tiles and sometimes pierced the ceilings. Not a single pane of glass had held up against the concussion; an impalpable gray dust covered the whole city, filtering in everywhere. To my great surprise, the temple was unharmed. We had been right in leaving the organ there. Only the young people's rooms had been damaged.

The Difficult Regrouping of Communities in the Postwar Years

Sète and its region had been liberated from the Germans, even if the war continued in the East. It was rather extraordinary to see one power tumble and another power spring up from the shadow. I was in no way surprised, I was expecting it. Furthermore, during the transition period, the military commandant of the Sète sector was a member of the presbyterial council. We were living through the experience proclaimed by scripture: "The form of this world is passing away [1 Cor. 7:31]," the great image, its feet partly of iron and partly of clay, was broken in pieces (Daniel 2:31-35), but "The word of our God will stand for ever [Isa. 40:8b]." (I remember now that these three scripture passages came together in my mind one time when I was called upon, impromptu.)

The resistance movements invited me to a big meeting in the city theater. From the stage, where I was seated with six or seven fellow citizens, including a priest, I saw 1,800 people jammed in from the orchestra seats to the peanut gallery, despite the fact that the majority of the people of Sète had not yet come back to their city. I shared in the great élan of joy which buoyed up the crowd, the joy of the Liberation! I would need the tongue of a Michelet to express its richness. But I also knew the power of evil, and I had no illusion about the inevitable relapses after these heroic thrusts.

When it was my turn to speak, I recalled my experiences at Gurs, stating the necessary conditions so that the postwar years should make clear the defeat of Nazism. For us, the victors, this would require that we not confuse justice with vengeance. This touched off some whistles, and I addressed the hecklers: "We owe this respect to the numberless victims—not to repeat the errors of their torturers." I have the impression that it was the genuine members of the Resistance who broke into applause.

Thus, turning aside from saying what could have pleased the crowd, I reenacted, at mid-century, what Pastor Médard had done in the same theater at the beginning of this century. Sébastien Faure was closing a lecture on "The Crimes of God," defying anyone to answer him among this crowd, whipped up by his eloquence. The pastor of Sète got up and, coming to the stage, said simply, "Now I shall speak to you of the goodness of God."

The city only filled up again very slowly. There were not enough workmen to repair the roofs and replace all the broken glass. Sète continued to lack water, habitable housing, and enough food supplies. But the opposition of minds was harder to surmount than material difficulties. There had been too many resentments and too much bad blood between some and others. Christians cannot find spiritual communion in lying and self-satisfaction. In *Le Lien Protestant* for November 1944 I wrote:

> Alas, there is only egoism which puts gulfs between us. Will you allow me to be frank, since from now on we can express ourselves without constraint? There is also the insufficient love of justice. When our Reformed Church protested during these years of oppression against the great iniquities of which we were witnesses—the massacre of one part of humanity in the name of racist theories, reprisals and methods of torture, forced deportation of men treated like merchandise for the industrial productivity of the enemy—at that time there was a small minority of Christians who regretted that "the church was taking sides." . . . They wished to dissociate themselves from the acts or the words of the National Council. We should then have been unanimous. It is not now a matter of agreeing out of political opportunism. That is not the question. Let us remain strictly on the ground of the requirements of the Christian faith. In all loyalty, let those who would have liked to see the church keep quiet, ask themselves if there was not, ahead of the concern for justice, a political preference or simply a too great attachment to material goods,

which Christ condemns so severely. . . . Let them humble themselves before God. Let the errors of the past serve us all. Quite likely tomorrow Christians as individuals or the church itself may be obliged to protest against this or that injustice. May we then be able to do it truly all together, with faithfulness, and in unanimous obedience!

Without waiting for the return of the citizens of Sète and the resumption of regular meetings, I busied myself with seeing how we could prolong the contacts between Protestants and Catholics which had been established during the years of hardship. In *Le Lien Protestant* of June 1944 I had published some of the notes from a young man of the parish, condemned to forced labor in Germany. He was a simple person without much education, but he knew how to express, with simplicity and with his deep faith, his ecumenical experience:

> From about two to three o'clock in the afternoon I had a short religious conversation with a Dominican seminary student, a very beautiful conversation. Here is a brother in Christ who is alone. No parents, it is almost six months that he has been in Germany without having news from his relatives and he doesn't know where they are. So I invited him to come and meditate with me and read the Bible —which he accepted with pleasure.

The little group which shared this ecumenical concern was hoping that we could form at Sète a Committee for Christian Civic Action (CCCA) as in other cities. We had set a date for an initial meeting in early December 1944. Alas! One day I saw coming to my study an older man, belonging to the Catholic bourgeoisie of the city. He told me of his great embarrassment and his sense of letdown: the priest with whom I had had a first conversation—and whom I believed to be open to this undertaking—was opposed to the creation of this CCCA. I could not needle these brothers and sisters into disobeying their hierarchies. I was further stung by the fact that the great majority of the presbyterial councilors, learning of the opposition of Abbé C to the meeting on

December 4, considered that I was harboring too many illusions about the evolution of the Roman Church.

The Presbyterial Council Requests My Ordination

At the meeting of the presbyterial council on January 24, 1945, I found out about the letter which this council had sent on January 1—after having met in a special meeting without me—to the President of the National Council of our church, Pastor Marc Boegner:

Dear Pastor;

The Presbyterial Council of the Church of Sète, meeting January 1, 1945 under the chairmanship of Monsieur L. Buchel, vice-president, reviewing the two years in which Mlle. Schmidt has been carrying on her ministry in our church, concludes that it can only congratulate itself on her activity.

Her preaching, clear, direct, and incisive, has never departed from a high spiritual tone and a high oratorical quality.

Her study groups have put within the range of the faithful her theological learning and have rounded out and deepened her preaching. Her religious instruction has brought new souls to the church among the youth.

Her social activity has had a bearing, first, on our diaconal program, which she has awakened from a long sleep. While, by her methodical visits, she has uncovered sufferings which had been ignored, she has at the same time known how to tap the necessary resources to assuage the suffering.

The lectures which she has inspired, under the aegis of the Family Associations, have been seminal in developing a true parish life, whose development was held back by the necessary evacuation of the city of Sète. This has placed Mlle. Schmidt before new tasks which she knew perfectly how to fulfill, finding host families for all the children, refuges for the older people, and lodging for whole families.

After having spent herself untiringly in this task and after having brought it to fruition in spite of all the material and administrative difficulties, she insisted on remaining at her post. This was in spite of the extremely painful life caused by the nearly total evacuation, with its attendant lack of water and the difficulty of securing food. She only left her parish for a few days and a few miles, this under the strict orders of the authorities.

During the bombardment of the city she gave succor to the wounded and herself filled the role of a nurse in a disorganized hospital through a night of terror. This did not prevent her the next day from authoritatively representing the Protestant Church, stepping up to give her public testimony at the time of the solemn obsequies of the forty [?] victims in spite of the obstacles which were raised before her on purpose or by accident.

Considering that nothing in these two years has revealed in their pastor any inferiority or lack in the accomplishment of a particularly difficult ministry, as much from the physical as from the spiritual point of view, the presbyterial council of the church at Sète requests that, without waiting for a final decision to be taken on the question of feminine ministry, Mlle. Schmidt should receive full pastoral ordination.

The council believes that to refuse her this formal consecration any longer, after ten years of a completely consecrated ministry, would be to contradict a demonstrated fact and finally to run the danger of injuring a vocation in depriving her of the spiritual sustenance which the church accords to all its pastors. The council hopes that the National Council will take the necessary measures to bring these desires rapidly to pass.

Please receive, Mr. President, the expression of our profound respect.

> The Councilors: L. Buchel, G. Bonfils, H. Roux, P. Bouteiller, Dr. Démontes, Vincent, Planchon, Gantet

If its laudatory style did not please me, nevertheless this letter gave me great encouragement. For one thing, it affirmed that you cannot deny a plain fact: the reality of the pastoral ministry of a woman. Furthermore, the council put its finger on the spiritual sustenance which the church owes to its pastors. But, learning the same day of Pastor Boegner's answer to the council, I noted sadly that nothing had changed since 1938. He said that it would be necessary to wait for the question to be treated by a National Synod. However, he confirmed that "Mlle. Schmidt will remain at Sète so long as you and she believe that her place is in your midst."

I wrote the following day to Monsieur Boegner to tell him that I had in no way asked the council to write to him. His response to my letter contained one sharp distinction, which he had not written to the presbyterial council in Sète:

> I think I know that you do not want your case to be treated outside of a doctrinal examination of the ordination to be granted or refused to women Bachelors of Theology. But I have to conclude that the National Synod, as it is presently constituted, does not appear to me likely to authorize the pastoral ordination of women. I doubt that the National Council[9] would by a majority be favorable to any proposition of this kind. On the other hand, I am practically certain that it would be ready, bowing before an interior evidence, to give its consent to yours.

Would the National Council really have changed its mind? Pastor Boegner, certainly. He had moved from his opinion of 1942: "Elisabeth to Sète? But that's impossible!" Since the Liberation, women had the right to vote in civic matters. Trained as a lawyer, Monsieur Boegner had always seemed to be sensitive to the sociological conditions in which the church had to announce the gospel.

Continuing my reflections or my exchange of views with friends, I had come by the year 1945 to the point of saying to myself, If I *did* decide to request ordination for myself (which I had not yet done), it would not be a claim on my own behalf (feminist in the eyes of some), since the local church was attesting that I had in fact been performing a pastoral ministry in its midst.

The Church at Sète Abandons Its
Financial Independence

The first regional synod after the Liberation met at Montpellier at an unaccustomed time, February 27–28, 1945. At the presbyterial council which preceded it, on February 23, we had finally taken a decision on the question brought up and discussed so many times during a period of over twenty years by the pastors who had succeeded each other since 1922: that of the financial independence of the parish. The council voted to abandon this independence, but not unanimously: there were three dissenting votes.

At the regional synod (where I was happy to see two women as lay delegates) the report of the regional president, Pastor Cadier, recalled that the presbyterial council of the parish of Sète "requests that Mlle. Schmidt be confirmed in her role as the incumbent pastor in the church at Sète and that no other provision be made for replacing Monsieur Balfet. Still concerning the church at Sète, we are happy to welcome it into the synod, upon its recent abandonment of its financial autonomy." Here, the minutes record, "on motion by Pastor Cadier, the synod welcomed the Sète church with a standing ovation."

Some people might have been surprised that I wanted to see the church at Sète give up its financial independence, which had been maintained in spite of all the efforts of my predecessors. It seemed to me that it was time to bind ourselves again in full communion with the other churches, this solidarity having always been one of the claims of Protestants.

In this city in process of reconstruction, our parish organized, during the spring, a series of addresses open to the public, in a neutral hall, the Trianon moving picture theater. The lectures were given by Pastors Cadier, Lauriol, and myself. (I can still hear Monsieur Lauriol picturing [favorably] "those who turned their coats inside out, all the seams showing.") My address was on the camp at Gurs and the work of CIMADE. We drew large and attentive audiences. It was clear that the anticlerical reflex had less play when it came to the Protestants.

The youth movements were looking for new structures. The Protestant Council on Youth (the national PCY) called on me to take the presidency (today we would say the "animation") of the regional youth council. No one has ever refused women the right to busy themselves with youth movements!

But to climb up to one of the Montpellier pulpits was, in the little Protestant world of the South, an honor that no one thought to see offered a woman. First of all, Pastor Genet, of the parish of Montpellier Maguelone, asked me to conduct the service. This parish, before 1938, was in the Union of the Reformed Churches—which had taken the responsibility of entrusting a parish to a woman and had for the first time given pastoral delegation to a woman. Then, in November 1946, Pastor Roger Chapal made the same request to me for the parish of Brueys which, before 1938, belonged to the Union of Evangelical Reformed Churches. So here I, a woman, had preached in Montpellier! And afterward I was to do it each year at Maguelone and just about every other year at Brueys!

The Regional Synod of Quissac, 1947

Finally the synods put on their agendas the pastoral ministry of women! These were the regional synods of November 1947, which were to study this question before the National Synod decided it in the spring of 1948.

The regional synod took place at Quissac from November 10–12, 1947. Of the little city itself, I have no memory. I stayed with an old lady who was far removed from the parliamentary and synodical jousts. At breakfast she talked to me about her vegetable garden. The bedside rug on which

I had just knelt, like everything else in the room, spoke of the poverty of her life. But she had nobility in her hospitality and a great deal of tact, since she hadn't spoken to me about the subject of our work.

Pastor Berton, recently called as the president of our region, had asked me, on behalf of the regional council, to be the reporter on the pastoral ministry of women. It quite surprised me, and I was afraid of falling into some kind of a trap. But I had accepted and gone to work.

For the exegetical part of my report I had made full use of a study which I had asked from my former professor of New Testament at Geneva, Pastor Franz Leenhardt. This study was to appear in the theological quarterly of Montpellier, *Études Théologiques et Religieuses*. It concluded, "New Testament study gives us no decisive argument for rejecting the pastoral ministry of the women whom God calls to it." This affirmation seemed fairly bold in the French Reformed Church in "interior France."[10] (In Alsace-Lorraine there have been women pastors since 1922.)

I submitted my report, which concluded with the request for my ordination. I added, "I have never asked for it in the twelve years in which parishes have been entrusted to me. I have refused to write or publicly debate on this question. I have imposed these twelve years of silence on myself, asking God to keep me from all error and to lead me. Today, I believe that the hour has come for breaking this silence. I have not been able to shed God's call, nor to avoid the charge to minister which he has entrusted to me. And I feel constrained to put this question to the church."

My report was listened to with special attention. I felt the tenseness of the assembly in the long silence which followed it. I knew that I would not disarm my opponents by my several exegetical notes; would they perhaps be less aggressive for having noted my concern to be prudent, and to suggest exacting standards for future women pastors?[11]

The discussion was long, terribly painful for me. As in all deliberative assemblies, there was a little confusion, but I believe that by following the official minutes in the regional archives and my own notes I can give an outline of the debate. President Berton expressed his emotion at having heard the conclusion of my report. Pastor H. Bosc[12] felt it necessary to speak eloquently in praise of my ministry. Then there were those who refused to link an experience which Pastor Pellegrin called "prophetic" and Dean Leenhardt called "personal," to a general rule.

I heard astounding things in this synod: Pastor Roger Chapal declared that "the ministry of parish assistant corresponds better to the destiny of a woman"—that is to say, a place of subordination. Pastor C. Conord, general secretary of the French Reformed Church, very much opposed to the pastoral ministry of women, had chosen to come to our regional synod, doubtless because I was a pastor in this region. He said to us, "In presiding over a hearth, a woman seems to give her maximum." A certain image of womanhood weighed upon the synodical decisions. Then, as always happens in the case of a clear skidding off the track, a reversal took place.

In spite of the influence of the dean of the seminary, the holder of three doctorates; in spite of the ties of the president with the synod in his region; in spite of the new and grave threat brandished by Pastor Conord—"The ministry has been entrusted to Mlle. Schmidt, but reserving the decision in principle"—the synod took another direction. The proponents of the pastoral ministry of women advised me to ask first for a vote on the motion proposed by the regional president, assuring me that it would be rejected. This motion began by affirming that women could not be ordained to the pastoral ministry; then it admitted exceptions, regretting that we are not Anglo-Saxons to accept this pragmatism.

The president's motion was rejected and in the end, after amendments, mine was voted.[13] This text, rather badly drawn because of the successive changes, filled me with joy;

it affirmed first of all the question of principle. It had avoided dissociating the principle from the personal case. I knew that the unanimous vote on paragraph 3, together with the number of votes obtained on paragraph 1, meant that everyone wished for my ordination.

I waited, doubtless with too many illusions, for the National Synod of spring 1948. Pastor Boegner had advised me to go there without being a delegate; thus, he said, the Synod could question me and ask for some clarifications. I received an invitation as an accredited visitor.

Two days before my departure I received a letter from Monsieur Boegner saying, "I am tempted to advise you not to make the journey to Grenoble." Members of the National Council were thinking that my presence could antagonize certain members of the Synod. His tone was embarrassed. "Obviously, you are still free to come to Grenoble," the letter continued. It ended thus, in a very Boegnerian style: "I have a great desire to obtain as large a majority as possible in favor of your ordination. It must not happen that any reticence or hesitation should be induced by a presence which might give some the impression that you are coming to sustain your own cause."

Astonished and hurt by this letter, I consulted Pastor Cadier, who was a member of the National Council, by telephone. He told me that at a regional synod he had himself asked for me to be heard at the National Synod. The illogicality of these gentlemen seemed to me disconcerting; nevertheless, I decided to go. I wrote Monsieur Boegner, "If there are some troubled spirits whom the very sight of me will prejudice, a larger number could be surprised by my absence and find that I take so lightly the decisions of the National Synod that I won't stir myself at such a time!" And I added, "I shall take most seriously everything that you say. I shall keep from all conversation . . . and I will only be present at the sessions . . . quiet behind a post, like the tax collector in the parable [Luke 18:9–14]."

The Synod That Said "No!"

Arriving at the last minute at the temple of Grenoble, I actually did sit behind a pillar. They make a rather imposing sight, more so than a regional synod, these men in dark clothes, pastors and laymen in equal numbers. It reminded me of sixteenth-century Protestant engravings. But if there was no woman at the First National Synod in 1559, I was surprised to find none at that of 1948 (she would have had to be a laywoman, naturally!). Thus, in a Reformed Church, where women elect the presbyterial councilors, none of them had acceded to this assembly, chosen at this second higher echelon. I thought of several women whose Christian faith, culture, and experience would enrich this gathering. Some of them were "marginal," fighting and serving in different movements and institutions. Others, alas, had broken all connections with their church.

Being outside of the deliberative assembly, I had some difficulty in following the debates. I knew only a few deputies, either pastors or laymen, besides those of my region. Since I did not know the position of those who were speaking, a certain number of subtleties must have escaped me. I knew that the moderator[14] of this National Synod would be Pastor Pierre Gagnier, a colleague from our years of ministry in Lozère. (Besides, he had asked to read the text of my report to the regional synod at Quissac.) I was comforted to see him in the place of the presiding officer behind the table on the platform.

I took note of the decision that "in conformity with the provisions of chapter VI of the Discipline, these votes (having to do with the liturgy and the pastoral ministry of women) would be decided by an absolute majority of the members of the Synod and at least two thirds of the members present."[15] Chapter VI, here invoked, concerns "modifications to the Ecclesiastical Constitution." Thus, even if nothing else were changed, the ecclesiastical constitution itself would be modified by the single fact that the pastor might be of a different sex!

After the report presented by Pastor Eric Barde, the discussion seemed very confused. The motion which he proposed seemed to me full of wisdom. It recognized that the question of principle could not be decided now but did not wish to rule out any pastoral ordination which might be conferred on women. That motion was rejected. The moderator brought it to our attention that "Just when we see among future pastors a certain wavering about the meaning and the very reason for the ceremony of ordination" (these are the words of the report of the Commission on the Ministry) "here come women asking for ordination!"

I had the impression that a small group had prepared a very effective opposition. We were practicing democracy, as in the National Assembly. But for a Synod, one dimension was missing, that of the Holy Spirit. Some of the remarks appeared to me in the authentic tradition of the Reformation, those of Pastor Hébert Roux, those of Pastor E. Lauriol. The latter, who could not be suspected of being a militarist, exclaimed, "When a woman has stood her post in the forward lines, I stand at attention and let her pass!"

The discussions hinged on the interpretation of the scriptures. But none of these well-meaning delegates suspected that they were reading the scriptures through a screen, that of the society in which they were living. Furthermore, it was a society which dated from before the war. The delegates had not yet been able to profit from the studies in biblical theology which appeared during the following years.

When it was a question of tradition, it was never invoked in a normative fashion, as in the Roman Church. And finally, those who were most opposed to the pastoral ministry of women never referred to the affirmation of Roman theology, nourished by Thomas Aquinas, that the priest is the image of Christ, or, as the Orthodox would say, "the icon of Christ."

In his bass voice, with passion and authority, Pastor Cadier (by his forthright affirmation) may have stirred up the opposition of those who were perhaps hesitant. And to my great surprise, Pastor Boegner put the weight of his prestige and his authority as president behind the request for my ordination. His motion was rejected.

I left the temple, sliding noiselessly into the sacristy, where I let my tears pour out. I felt that between my church and myself there was a break. My sadness must have been a little like that of a child deceived by her mother. But it was not the image given by Christian theology which came to my mind (church=mother), but the quip which Suzanne de Dietrich had repeated to me several times: "I have only gone to one Synod. It made me think of the Sanhedrin." This old sin of clericalism smacks of the Sanhedrin. Christians are apparently unable to forget it. It makes the Christian church hypocritical and, we would say today, phallocratic.

Pastor Charles Westphal came to join me. He understood my suffering and knew how to bring the message I needed. "Elisabeth, you know that if one wishes to break the defenses of a fortress, the first attackers get themselves killed to make a breach by which their followers can pass. Perhaps you will never be ordained . . . but you will have made a breach and others will be ordained. Perhaps you will have to accept this sacrifice." But must Christians then suffer until the end of time from all the Sanhedrins of the churches, even the Reformed churches?

I did not know as I left the Synod that it had decided to take the question up again at its next session, "when fully informed."[16] In spite of my suffering I was not tempted to leave my church. Other women had done it in the past: Catherine Booth, who with her husband had founded the Salvation Army, and at Sète itself Mlle. Coraly Hinsch,[17] who in 1846, after much searching and many battles, started another Evangelical Church whose fruits are still visible, and so many others. We were women in different times; the circumstances of their period constrained these women to a rupture. At Quiévrechain Madame Bourquin had, in fact, been a pastor, even without pastoral delegation. I had that delegation, and a parish had been entrusted to me. I knew that God was asking me not to flinch.

The Different Reactions to This Refusal

An abundance of mail was waiting for me at Sète and continued to arrive on the following days. In reading all these letters, I seemed to find again the true face of the church, the aspect I had lost at the Grenoble meeting. Certain of these messages deserve to be quoted in their entirety, to comfort and encourage those who have been deeply wounded by a hierarchy, or by ecclesiastical regulations. There were letters freighted with affection, which expressed the grief of colleagues or lay friends, and their indignation on learning of the synodal vote of Grenoble.

One letter was particularly important to me, that of the moderator, Pastor P. Gagnier, writing me from Grenoble itself: "Many of us regret sadly—and for me it is a good deal more than a regret, because I reproach myself for not having known how to orient the Synod—many regret that we did not know how to assert God's freedom to call people imperiously. For after all, no Synod can deny the fact that God has called you to be a pastor by exactly the same right as all the rest of us. And no Synod can deny that, where he calls, his authority is fully at work in the ministry, whatever our human decisions may be." He concluded by saying, "Who knows if yesterday's decision, and the grief which many of us feel as a result, may not be the means which God will use with power, to lead the church some day on another course?"

It was striking to me to realize the unanimity with which colleagues, even those whom I did not know, were reassuring me that: "We don't consider you in any way a supernumerary member of the pastoral corps, but rather as a useful and necessary member, under the same accreditation as ourselves" (Pastor du Pasquier, the president of another region). The reactions of women were what you might guess. They denounced masculine pride, heightened by clericalism. My friend Marc Donadille, while exhorting me once more to patience, wrote, "What can you expect? I suppose the true reason for pastors to oppose the ministry of women is, on the part of many, their sense of inferiority, their fear of being surpassed. They are few and far between who have enough inner freedom to tell themselves that the presence of a woman on their pastoral team could be an enrichment."

Some friends were concerned about my reactions; I received from Pastor Roger Chapal a magnificent letter, the letter of a brother and a father confessor:

> Remember that this unhappy hour is the place of clear-cut testings and also, perhaps, that of secret graces. Watch out for what the apostle calls "the root of bitterness." If the body of the church has appeared to you distant and closed, the essential thing remains: this miserable but confident parish, and this community of pastors who, in Lozère, as here, have recognized you as being completely theirs.
>
> We would wish that you could experience today, as we feel it, the sense of communion which binds us to you. You know very well that none of us who are your "companions in royalty and service" feels less near to you. On the contrary! Doubtless that is the surest judgment of the church.
>
> You have known, since you entered the ministry, what it is to suffer with him whom men despise and wound through us. If you suffered at Grenoble, may that suffering be once more the occasion for knowing yourself bound to him.

Such letters were a great help to me. This unhappy Synod definitely strengthened me in my vocation. I had also discovered that through the question which I was putting to the church, others were raising different, related questions, questions which you could not at first separate out. They were all the problems concerning new forms of witness by the church and new forms of ministry in an evolving society.

Joys in My Continuing Ministry

Naturally the presbyterial council of Sète, in its meeting of July 7, decided to write a new letter to express its "grief and astonishment" that the Synod had not taken a decision concerning me. The lay delegate of the Sète church to the regional synod the following fall (at Montagnac November 29–30) brought a renewed request for my ordination, and the synod voted a resolution which backed up this request; in other words, the base and the region were opposed to the central power!

Nothing had changed in the carrying out of my ministry. During this period it was the young people who brought me the most joys. First of all, the Sunday school children, whose number I saw growing. Then the confirmands, a large proportion of whom did a third year of religious instruction voluntarily. The "retreats" preceding the first communion —a Catholic idea, according to some families—became a tradition which gave good results.

On June 17, 1948 I had received a letter from Monsieur Nègre, chairman of the committee of the Musée du Désert, asking me in the name of his committee to be one of the pastors who would distribute the elements of the Lord's Supper at the big annual Assembly of the Musée du Désert on the first Sunday of September 1948. He also invited me to the meal with the orators of the day.[18]

How could anyone fail to see in this request a gesture of protest against the vote of the Grenoble Synod and a way of affirming before this numerous gathering (around 10,000 people) that I was a pastor in the full sense of the term? I thanked the committee, telling them how touched I was by their letter and explaining to them why I believed I should respond in the negative. I wanted to avoid any possibility that my presence might seem like a kind of provocation.

Monsieur Nègre understood very well what he called "my pastoral discretion" in this matter.

At the end of September of this year 1948 I went to a series of theological studies on baptism. A small group of pastors were refusing to baptize infants, raising an old question for the church. Karl Barth, in person, was going to help us reflect on this question in advance of the Synods of 1950 and 1951, which were to put the question of baptism on their agendas. In the course of these days, which were held at Bièvres in the beautiful eighteenth-century house which had been given to the Fédé, I met Pastor Pierre Maury. He almost apologized to me for the way in which the Synod of Grenoble had debated. "I want to tell you one thing: My daughter wants to study theology and I am requiring her to do it in full, with Greek and Hebrew. It can't be on a bargain basis." Had his concern as a father led him to consider the problem from another point of view?

As for Monsieur M. Boegner, who could only come for one afternoon, he showed me his manner of a feudal lord: "Always write to me if you have something to tell me, even if you're 'giving me a piece of your mind.' I'll take anything from you!" Then he asked me two questions. The first reassured me: "Whom should I ask to prepare the next report on the pastoral ministry of women?" The second worried me: "Do you think the time has come for you to leave Sète and how do you picture doing it?" Was this because he thought the next National Synod would vote in the negative once again?

But there was one who did not disarm in his attitude of opposition to the pastoral ministry of women. That was Pastor Conord. He forbade several women, all of whom were following the theological questions of the time, from entering the room where the discussion of Karl Barth's study on baptism was to take place. Even Madeleine Barot, who had been a delegate to the ecumenical conference at Amsterdam, could not pass the door. Monsieur Conord said to me, "It's just because you have protectors in high places that

I let you pass." Was it possible that a general secretary of the French Reformed Church had come to this? Was it any use to answer? There is a masculine churlishness which women know well. It displeased me to meet it in a pastor.

In the spring of 1949 the triennial elections of presbyterial councils were to take place in all the parishes of the French Reformed Church. Except in certain cases, there were very few women on these councils. In the parish of Montpellier, Brueys, Madame Marie de Montbrison d'Adhémar, the wife of Amaury d'Adhémar, had often requested that women should sit in the presbyterial council. In the course of a skit which gently satirized several personalities (yes, Protestants are sprightly), this request was put into a quatrain. I suggested to the meeting of the presbyterial council of Sète on March 30 that they should nominate one or two women to the electors.[19] Since the councilors did not see the necessity for it, I did not counter them. I knew that I had to be patient. But at the session on May 9, I wrenched from the councilors their agreement to propose, among other names, that of a woman, Mlle. Jeanne Boissière, a retired teacher. I knew that she was well known by the children and their families, that she was respected for her devotion and her conciliatory spirit, and that a good number of the parishioners wanted to see her join the council. I could also tell them, "If you do not nominate her and she is elected (which is almost sure to happen), you will be a little bit embarrassed," and I added, "Sirs and brothers, spare me from recalling to you the famous words, 'by the will of the people.' "

Mlle. Boissière was elected on May 22 with a fine majority. Her presence on the council seemed quite natural. The councilors had already been in the habit of conversing with her. Once more, everything was simple in practice, but it had been necessary to blow up the theoretical bolts of opinions received and not revised. I noticed that in the course of the following months these men set great store by the advice of Mlle. Boissière and willingly unloaded on her several responsibilities which bored them.

7

Ordination and Continuing Ministry, 1949–58

THE NATIONAL SYNOD was to take place in Paris (parish of Saint-Esprit) June 11-13, 1949. I didn't go at all. I knew that the reporter on the pastoral ministry of women was to be Charles Westphal, but I did not allow myself to make any predictions. Could opinions have evolved in one year?

I shall never forget my emotion, on coming back from the church toward noon, when I found three telegrams in my letter box. On opening the first, I read, AM HAPPY TO ANNOUNCE TO YOU AUTHORIZATION GRANTED SIXTY-TWO VOTE MAJORITY. AFFECTION, BOEGNER.

What conditions were attached to this authorization? I was to learn about them in the following days. But I did understand that something must have happened in this Synod. Emotions often translate themselves into a sort of physical paralysis. I remained glued to my chair, without falling on my knees. I had never wanted to make of my ordination a personal question. All the problems and all the discussions of the past, all the memories of trials and graces throughout my life were whirling in my head, but one joy dominated all the others. A breach had been made in the fortress of clerical prejudice. I saw in this a sign of hope for the march and the witness of the church.

Finally I telephoned my family, the members of the presbyterial council, and some friends. And I heard the first reactions. Others were to follow, unforeseen, agreeable, or irritating.

Assailed by Journalists

In the middle of the afternoon, Monsieur R, an elder, and his wife came to visit me; they were followed by a man of forty whom I took to be their nephew, passing through Sète. It was a local correspondent of the agency France-Presse who slid in behind my visitors. He asked me to excuse him, telling me why he was in my study. "I was on the beach for the day when my mother had me called. I was to telephone Paris right away. I thought a car accident had happened to a cabinet minister in the vicinity of Sète. I didn't understand very well what was going on. I answered the questions of my agency: 'Yes, I know Mlle. Schmidt. She is a pastor here.'"

I refused to let this reporter take my picture. He did not insist but said to me, "You are a pastor in Sète and I want to keep on good terms with you, but tomorrow you will see journalists who have come from Paris who will not be as considerate."

The next morning an energetic ring of the doorbell resounded. A man, armed with a big camera, engulfed himself in the partly opened door. Sure of himself, blinding me by his flashes, he seemed to me completely ignorant of what a pastor could be, and a fortiori, a Synod. He had to take a "candid shot." I said to him awkwardly, "Why don't you go and photograph the movie stars and leave me in peace?" but my protest did not register at all with him.

Instead of trying to understand why the major papers were suddenly interested in the pastoral ministry of women, I first wondered anxiously what some of my colleagues would think, seeing my face in different newspapers. In the *Midi-Libre* under local news, it would not make a ripple, but elsewhere? At that time we were not accustomed to see the pack of journalists on television screens. Would those who opposed my ordination, perhaps (like me) unaware of the realities of the media, accuse me of having created propaganda?

A presbyterial councilor, and then parishioners, telephoned me that journalists had arrived in town and were waiting for the time when I would come out of my house. They had bribed some children to warn them when they saw me. My immediate neighbor came to tell me that reporters had encamped in her corridor, consuming sandwiches and beer from the café across the street. "I chased them out, but they installed themselves in the corridor of the house next door!" What to do? I couldn't stay home, barricading myself in my house as though it were a fortress. Another councilor, aware of the situation, advised me to go to the children's choir rehearsal, scheduled for five o'clock, without worrying about the journalists. "Anyhow, those folks seem to be determined. It's their trade and we mustn't make them lose their jobs."

Thus I came out of my house. At a sign from a youngster on the waterfront, a journalist emerged who, on his haunches, machine-gunned me with his camera. I did not stop. Still squatting, he jumped backward to keep ahead of me, while others followed me on bicycles along the embankment. The rehearsal was bad. The children, very much excited, wanted to get photographed with me, gratis.

After that for the whole week I had the most varied journalists coming to my house. A handwritten letter from Monsieur Boegner said to me, "I have been assailed by news agencies and journalists. I refused to give anyone your name. And lo and behold!, I do not know by what means, *France-Soir* has got it and printed it Wednesday in big type! Try to defend yourself." What made Monsieur Boegner imagine that in our close neighborhood here in the south of France, informers could not spot the first woman pastor to be ordained?

Foreign correspondents (*New York Herald-Tribune, New*

York Times, Constellation) asked me for interviews. Most of them seemed to know Protestantism; it seemed very interesting to them that the synodical decision had been taken in a country whose majority had more or less a Catholic training.

I was so anxious about this publicity that I asked advice from the pastor who seemed to me the most competent in these things, the editor of *Réforme*, Monsieur Albert Finet. His letter reassured me and brought me an answer to the real questions which I was asking myself during this agitated week:

> There is nothing to do. A public assembly has decided that you should receive a responsibility in full right. It is normal that the press should swing into action to photograph you, give your curriculum vitae, etc. As for me, I would accept without any second thought this involuntary publicity, which puts you on the map without, I think, shackling your action. Furthermore, I don't believe that those who tell you that God is using it are far off the mark. After all, you are under grace, enjoying the freedom of the children of God, and what the world says cannot hinder your witness.

Put differently, that was what several presbyterial councilors had said to me. The Protestants in Sète seemed happy that people were talking about their pastor. They certainly had the right to be happy, those who had accepted a woman as a pastor. But above all, Protestants always rejoice in anything which can even momentarily cure their minority complex!

I finally learned by letters from the delegates to the National Synod how the discussion had unfolded; more precisely, I became aware of the text which had been voted. The three first paragraphs of the proposal submitted by Pastor Charles Westphal had been rejected. The fourth, worked over, was retained:

> The Paris Synod considers that if the ministry of women in the French Reformed Church is not normally the pastorate in its present form, the Church, in exceptional cases which the

National Synod alone may take up, and of which it will be the sole judge, may entrust to a woman this ministry with the authority which ordination to the pastoral ministry confers, it being understood that this authorization will not be granted or continued except to an unmarried woman.

It was in an executive session (since it had to do with a question of personality) that the Synod took the decision to grant me pastoral ordination.[1]

These texts could not satisfy me fully. They betrayed a theological embarrassment. The Synod had been as though constrained by the discernment of the Holy Spirit to make an exception. But the decision was hedged with all kinds of precautions which revealed the sociological and psychological unreadiness in which it was taken.

At the time I had not dreamed that I had been placed in a difficult situation: that of being an "abnormal woman." A presbyterial councilor had an immediate reaction to this text: "It is not in the Reformed tradition that a church ruling should require celibacy. The practical questions are something else again." This man, an independent spirit, showed himself a good theologian. When the French Reformed Church was to take up again the question of the pastoral ministry of women at the Synods in 1964 and 1965, it would revoke this condition. But we were not there yet!

At this time the French Synods had far less sense of solidarity with the Reformed churches in other countries than the youth and student movements. The fact that there were women pastors in Germany, in the Anglo-Saxon countries, and in that part of France which is called Alsace-Lorraine, seemed hardly to have helped the synodical delegates in their reflection.

I received not only the journalists but a voluminous mail. The news, which was spread widely by the press, allowed me to discover the reactions of very different people, of Catholics, agnostics, and of course many Protestants, pastors or lay members of our churches. I shall analyze these reactions later, in conjunction with the even more voluminous mail that I received at the time of my ordination. Here I shall only pick out several lines, almost identical in several letters, affirming that this Synod lived up to its name, "The Synod of the Holy Spirit." The thirteen-year-old son of a pastor friend jumped with joy when his father told him the news. He asked, "So Taty will be crowned at Rheims, won't she?"[2]

Preparations for My Ordination

The place for my ordination posed no problem: pastors are ordained in the parish in which they serve. But I had to decide rather quickly who should preside in order to fix the date. Two personalities had more reasons than others for doing it, Pastors Marc Boegner and Charles Westphal. I knew what I owed to each one and what I owed to their interventions in the course of the last Synods.

It was Charles Westphal whom I asked. It was with him that I had always felt myself in a profound communion of faith and hope, in a peaceable atmosphere, without clashes, and without his affection ever being tinged with paternalism. To my request he responded by a letter characteristic of his spirituality: "Do you really insist that I should preside at your ordination? I will do it willingly, with as much affection as conviction, as you know. But for the church would it not be better for it to be done by a colleague less involved than I was in the struggle which we have just won?" I was able to convince him to accept.

Another letter was harder to write, the one I sent to Monsieur Marc Boegner to express my gratitude to him and at the same time tell him that I had asked Charles Westphal to preside at my ordination.

The date of Thursday, October 20, 1949 was selected to accommodate everyone's time schedule.

My ordination necessitated an unaccustomed amount of preparation. It was only natural that the presbyterial council should take this occasion to make some repairs and renovations in the parish buildings. But we had to safeguard the atmosphere of reverence befitting this service of worship. How could we put up barriers against the novelty seekers, the journalists, and fend off the noisy enthusiasm of the population in this extreme south of France? After much hesitation, the presbyterial council and the friends who shared this concern with me had decided on a careful watch at the gate of the church. Only those who had personally-addressed invitation cards would be admitted.

Thus I sent to all the Protestants in the parish and to my friends a card reading as follows:

Mlle. Elisabeth Schmidt invites you
To join in the intercession of the church
At the time of her ordination
To the pastoral ministry.

This ceremony will take place
On Thursday, October 20, 1949
At three P.M. in the church of Sète, 32 rue Neuve-du-Nord.

"While they were worshiping the Lord and fasting, the Holy Spirit said, 'Set apart for me Barnabas and Saul for the work to which I have called them.' Then after fasting and praying they laid their hands on them and sent them off [Acts 13:2-3, RSV]."

"I commend to you our sister Phoebe, who is minister of the church in Cenchrea, that you may receive her in the Lord as befits the saints. Take care to put yourselves at her disposal in any way that she might need you; for she has been a protectress of many, including myself." (Paraphrase of Romans 16:1-2 by Charles Westphal[3])

I had also wanted to limit the number of ordaining pastors, fearing that a little bit of curiosity might prompt pastors whom I hardly knew to decide to come. According to tradition I addressed an invitation, with a confession of my personal faith, first to my colleagues in the region, then to Pastor Barde, whose report at the Grenoble National Synod I by no means forgot. I also invited Pastor Pierre André, remembering his father, who had given me such a good welcome in 1935 in his capacity as president of the Cévennes region. In spite of his great age, Pastor Benoit-Bergis wanted to take part in the ceremony because he had been ordained in the church at Sète fifty years earlier. (Besides, there had not been any ordinations in this church since his own.) I invited friends whom it was precious to me to count among the ordaining pastors (Pastors M. Dona-dille, P. Gagnier, S. Jordan). Two pastors from Geneva were able to join them, Roger Campiche[4] and Madame Marcelle Bard. Madame Bard had been the first woman ordained by the church in Geneva in December 1929. Called as the titular chaplain at the Cantonal Hospital, she also had the pastoral charge of a district in Geneva but remained in title "auxiliary pastor."[5]

The Sète parish undertook the organization of this day: registration and hospitality for friends or pastors coming from a distance. The youth movements took the responsibility of welcome at the railroad station and transportation to the temple or to the homes of the hosts. They did it "in full dress" and with great joy and seriousness. A former scout-master said to me, "It's marvelous, the socks and the gloves are still white." They had not forgotten to provide a traffic policeman to ensure a smooth flow of traffic and quiet on the rue Neuve-du-Nord.

In *Le Lien Protestant* for October, I had explained the meaning of pastoral ordination for the most involved members of the community as well as the most marginal. On the previous Sunday I had made a point of gathering my former confirmands to tell them the degree to which this ceremony concerned the whole church. For me, more than for a man, the judgment of the church had been very important.[6] I was concerned that no one should miss the whole thrust of the teaching of the church and the generations of Protestant family tradition and see this ceremony only as a "clerical spectacular."

Finally, after all of us had done our best to remove ambiguities, equivocations, and misunderstandings, we could only entrust ourselves to the grace of the Savior for the living of this day.

The Ceremony of My Ordination

The ceremony was quite as we had wished. I made my way into the sanctuary where 700 to 800 of the faithful had gathered. No noise, no flashbulbs going off to disturb the general sense of reverence. To quote the article which Pastor Roger Chapal wrote for the paper *Le Christianisme au XXe Siècle* for November 1949:

> When, early in the afternoon of October 20, friends from a distance came into the neighborhood of the sanctuary at Sète, they realized at once with how much love and with what painstaking care the parish had prepared for this day. At Sète they had prayed that this day should be, for all the faithful, an occasion of grace. They also wanted the respect and the affection with which the pastor of Sète is surrounded to be truly expressed. A solemn expectancy, a restrained blitheness, could be read in the attitudes and were incarnated in imperceptible details. If anyone had allowed himself to be distracted from the main thing, the seriousness of the honorary guard of Sea Scouts would have been enough to bring him back to it.
>
> After having led in the worship, Pastor Charles Westphal delivered the sermon with a radiant clarity and simplicity. " 'And his gifts were that some should be apostles, some prophets, some evangelists [Eph. 4:11-12].' Here we are again placed before this act by which God, ever since he formed a people for himself, has set apart this one or that one for a given ministry. And now we are under the New Covenant, where each ministry is joined to the fundamental ministry which Jesus Christ exercises himself, the priestly

ministry. The pastoral ministry is not a priesthood. It is none the less a bearer of the Word and the Grace of Jesus Christ. In the people of the New Covenant all human distinctions are reduced to a secondary significance. There is no longer male or female, etc. And the Head of the church calls and qualifies whomever he wishes. This is why, although the French Reformed Church still judges it preferable to entrust the pastoral ministry to men, it does not wish to close itself against precise indications from its Lord. The church is there to discern humbly and in thanksgiving the wishes of its Master.

"Thus it is with great joy and full assurance that today the church ordains Mlle. Schmidt to the pastoral ministry. Separated from the world (belonging to Jesus Christ), the pastor is completely given to men (as Jesus Christ gave himself). In this total gift of self, which is not without the gnawing of suffering and solitude, the pastor is regally free and serenely happy. May the whole church, before this act of her Savior, glorify God and receive from him this ministry which the church is to live out with her who has given herself to it."

Now it was time for the kneeling and taking of vows, the laying on of hands, the prayer of the whole church through the voice of Pastor R. Chapal, then through that of the choir: "Divine Head of the Church, intercede for her" [*Louange et Prières*, No. 225]. After the installation by Pastor Berton, Mlle. Schmidt mounted the pulpit to bring the testimony which she owes to her Savior.

"Thou hast seized me, thou hast conquered me." In a firm voice she told how God had prevailed on the path which has brought her to this day. It was he who had filled with his presence the solitude of a godless adolescence. It was he who had strengthened her in the faith in the bosom of the community of students in the Fédé. It was he who had broken down all the resistances in her heart during the period while her call to the ministry was becoming clear. All this while it would have been so easy to hide behind the advice of friends and the rules of the church. It was he who at Sainte-Croix and then at Sète, and even more in the camp at

Gurs, had given her the vision of the church and the strength to serve in it. On this long path of combat and grace, the hardest thing had not been for a Synod to take the decision which it had taken, but for an obstinate heart to let itself be seized and conquered.

After the service, in the courtyard of the temple, I found parishioners from the Cévennes, thirty of them who had come by bus from Sainte-Croix, others by car, mingled with the parishioners of Sète and other friends. While I was speaking to one or another, the photographers had time to take me from all angles. I did not object, since they had been willing to wait until the end of the ceremony.

It was a long line. The parish had prepared a sumptuous collation in the parish house. Everybody did it so much justice that when I could get there, hardly a cup of coffee was left!

I still had the evening to spend with friends who were leaving by night trains, and I could begin to open the letters which were piling up impressively on my desk. I had already taken note of some thirty telegrams delivered throughout the day, from Pastors Boegner, Maury, Balfet, and other colleagues; telegrams from Geneva, from pastors or former professors; not to forget the one from Madeleine Barot!

A very dear friend quoted to me in her letter, which I read on the evening of this October 20, a verse which I had introduced her to some twenty years before: "I am too small for all the graces and the faithfulness which thou hast shown to thy servant [Gen. 32:10]."[7] Hadn't this word been sent just to express my prayer on that evening?

I still have in my possession most of the letters which I received at the time of my ordination. They all brought me messages of affection. Sometimes they came from friends who were far removed from any Christian faith, and I was surprised at the seriousness with which they all considered this ceremony. Most of these letters had been sent by Protestants. The sociologist and the historian would find in them a picture of the Protestantism of that year, an echo of its theology, and also the language in which it expressed itself. If the style is the person, it is also the milieu and the period. Today I would classify these letters in two groups:

First of all, letters from pastors or lay people who, in one way or another, congratulated me for my patience or for my obstinancy and saw in my ordination "a sign for the church," "a spiritual crisis which the church has surmounted," "a first step taken by the church," a "road marked out for other women," "a victory of the Spirit."

Pastor André Dumas wrote me from Pau: "We rejoice *with* you and *for* the French Reformed Church. At last, losing sight of its habits, the church has followed through to the end a spiritual and biblical conviction when it gave you the authorization to be ordained."

Pastor Henri Roser spoke his conviction that the decision which had been taken was a victory of the Holy Spirit: "I bless God for the fact that your patience and your fidelity has convinced our authorities that God had already consecrated you, without any possible doubt, to the point that the authorities fell in line in order to be obedient. Oh! how good God is, to give us this further sign that he is speaking to our church and that finally she has decided to answer him! So she is alive. One can serve him in her midst."

I shall also quote this passage from a letter from a friend: "I know that this abnormal situation was weighing on you. There is a time when one accepts living outside the rules and structures, and a time when that is no longer possible. It is hard to be a pioneer, and what you have done is health-giving for the church itself even more than for the feminine cause. You have brought it to rethinking a whole series of problems, of traditional attitudes, of ready-made judgments, of twisted quotations of scripture, drained of its life-giving substance and spirit in favor of preconceived human ideas."

This is what my former professor, Franz Leenhardt, wrote

me on the morrow of the National Synod: "To the joy which you have personally, you can add the satisfaction of having troubled the conscience of the church for its own good. To be sure, I do not know if the desirable decisions in principle have been taken, or not, but it is already something to envisage particular cases; that shows at least the church's willingness, even grudgingly, to let itself be taught."

On the other hand I received a series of letters, all from pastors or professors of theology, which could have substantiated the humor of a doctor who assured me of the sincerity and the seriousness of the good wishes which he and his wife felt toward my ministry: "How could this not produce in the spirit of many lay people a suspicious aversion for the over-wise cogitations of theologians past, present, and to come? God could not hold it against the laymen if they preferred the serene clarity of the Beatitudes, if only the first, to these sterile, Pharisaic rivalries!" A pastor who took part in my ordination, Prof. Georges Crespy, felt the need to explain to me in a long letter the meaning he gave to the laying on of hands: "With joy and without hesitation I will take part in the ordination of Elisabeth Schmidt, our sister, in the ministry to which God has called her in spite of the hesitancy of the church. But I would not feel at ease if I were only taking part in the ordination of the 'first woman pastor.'"

Finally, others insisted on explaining to me why they did *not* wish to participate in the ceremony. In the perspective of time, I am even more sensitive to their desire to express to me their confidence, "the consideration that they have for my ministry," or "their profound esteem" for this ministry and "their complete certainty that your future ministry will be fruitful for the work of God."

Dean Henri Leenhardt, brother of my former professor, took the trouble to write: "As you know, I have a notion of the pastoral ministry which does not jibe with 'exceptions' and 'reservations.' If, like some others, I could have seen in it the investiture of a qualified person to practice a ministry in the church, I would have taken part with pleasure in the laying on of hands that you are about to receive. I would dearly like to be among those who will surround you on this occasion and to bring you, by my presence, a fraternal witness to the esteem in which I hold you and the good wishes which I am forming for your ministry. But I do not think it would be appropriate for me to figure as one of those taking part, however pleasant it might be, and I am constrained to tell you my feelings by this message."

The conclusion of the letter from Professor J.C. Cadier seemed to me especially interesting: "Pastoral delegation has been established specifically to give exceptional cases the possibility of entering the pastoral ministry of the church. Your beautiful ministry, supported by the pastoral delegation of the church, had in my opinion no need for pastoral ordination in order to make clear its full effectiveness."

Its "full effectiveness," no doubt, but within a limited horizon. A woman pastor who might for her whole life keep on receiving "delegations" could not be elected to a regional council or, still less, serve as a delegate to the National Synod. Thus she would be excluded from the assemblies or councils of government and authority.

Men have exactly the same reactions in all the professions to which women accede for the first time: medicine, the judiciary, administration . . . or even in political parties. Women are accepted on the first rung of the ladder of responsibilities, but not beyond. The embarrassed tone of these letters, however well it might have been concealed, betrayed a searching thought, a curious mixture in which the separation between theological and sociological notions had not yet been made. Was my former professor, Franz Leenhardt, right when he wrote me that "I had troubled the conscience of the church for its own good"?

A cultured man who, because of his responsibilities, was closely in touch with young people, wrote to me that

Catholics and atheists were taking the synodal decision more seriously than Protestants! Why?

The Hinschist Community

Among the Protestants in Sète, one small group had indeed taken my ordination very seriously—those who were called "the Hinschists." When I arrived in 1942 I had first believed that we were dealing here with a small community growing out of the revivalism of the nineteenth century. In the course of conversations with people brought up in this "church," I quickly perceived that it showed some unique characteristics. The first of these was the fact that it had been created by a woman.

Mlle. Coraly Hinsch was born in 1801 in a milieu of businessmen of great piety. When she was quite young, she experienced a great need for prayer and a true hunger for the Word of God. Neither the somewhat dry rationalism of the period nor the conformity of the church brought her the spiritual nourishment she needed. All alone, and without any theological teaching, she began to plumb the depths of the scriptures, counting on the Holy Spirit to illumine and guide her. Her apostolate began modestly. Ernest Krüger[8] fixes the year 1833 as the date of the founding of the Hinschist Church. She gathered some children and then their relatives and friends for prayer meetings at her parents' house. Then, thanks to a subscription, she made bold to open two schools, one for boys and one for girls. She would always show her care for the instruction of women!

Having heard about her efforts, the pastor in Montpellier, Monsieur Lissignol, made contact with her. Subsequently, joining with the Wesleyan Society, she worked with the Methodists in the region. Their chapels were open to her, and there she exhorted and preached. She even made a trip to the island of Jersey, where she stayed for six months. She probably followed a course of studies while she was preaching in numerous churches, where she confronted five to six hundred people, as she specifies in her correspondence.

Disillusioned by the imperfections of these churches, even though they were churches of believers, she decided (1846) to split off from Methodism, "sadly breaking ties with well-loved pastors," as she writes. Her aim was to gather "righteous hearts in one single body." And she was able to write in 1861, "The church which he [God] has given me to found is and will be the pillar and the buttress of the truth, for there God is adored in spirit and in truth."[9] In her letters she often goes back to the comparison: "I rose up like Deborah to be a mother in Israel."[10]

The little community became the "Evangelical Church in Cette." She wanted to make it live like the first Christians, of whom the book of Acts tells us: "And all who believed were together and had all things in common; and they sold their possessions and goods and distributed them to all, as any had need [Acts 2:44-45]."

It is easy to imagine all the attacks of which Mlle. Hinsch, who had now become Madame Armengaud, must have been the victim. "I am insulted and threatened," she wrote on April 18, 1850.[11] She disturbed lukewarm Christians and aroused the indignation of families who saw their fortunes put into a common treasury.

At the same time that she was trying to direct an authentic church of Christ at Sète, she was awakening little groups to a life of prayer in the Cévennes; also in the Tarn, in the Haute-Vaunage, and even in several cities like Alès, Avignon, and Lyon. She wrote, either to individuals or to the churches whose "mother" she called herself. She wanted frequent news reports sent to her, even though she assigned someone—a man or a woman—to be specifically responsible for them.

All her letters, now published, show the care for souls, whom Mlle. Hinsch wanted to pluck from temptation, to lead to the experience of pardon granted by Christ, and to bring to sanctification. Their tone is at the same time full of authority and full of love. Her urgency might seem unbearable. These letters, made up of biblical quotations from Genesis to Paul's letters, linked together in a chain without transitions, are quite without reference to time. No allusion is made to the circumstances of the day, to revolutions, to the changes in regime, or to the wars she went through in the course of a long life. She died in 1890, leaving the direction of her church to her Krüger nephews.

When I came to Sète, the vast buildings which had sheltered the faithful, living in communities, were empty. They no longer welcomed modest families for a sea-bathing season in the summer. But the training received by the members of this "Evangelical Church in Cette" had borne fruit. I found Christians who had a good knowledge of the scriptures, even among those whose piety had grown cold. They kept a real generosity toward welfare institutions, a fraternal concern for one another, and the taste for a life without luxury. Each week a prayer meeting still brought the Hinschists together in their chapel.

In this chapel Madame Schlegel had celebrated the marriages of her grandchildren, one of whom had recently become the leader of the girl scouts in our parish. Since she did not find what she needed in the little Hinschist group, I had somewhat filled out her religious instruction. Madame Schlegel sent word that she wanted to make my acquaintance. I thought this meeting would be difficult. A hundred years later, the situation between the French Reformed Church and the Hinschist community had reversed itself. I found an old lady seated in her Corniche garden. The late-afternoon light outlined her thin face, which I saw back-lighted. Her big eyes fixed me as though illumined by some inner light. "I thank you for having done good to my granddaughter" was her greeting to me. I found a real nobility, that of the Spirit, in her expression and in her observations. We readily found ourselves in spiritual communion.

I was not especially interested in the dogmatic expression of the Hinschists. Furthermore, this system of dogma was only formulated little by little. All sects and revival movements underscore aspects of the Christian faith which the churches have veiled or forgotten. Mlle. Hinsch was, in her own way, a "charismatic." She was persuaded that the fullness of the Spirit had been given her in order that she might understand the scriptures, receive God's orders, and, like Abraham, pursue this venture of faith. When a pastor said to her that to understand the Bible we have to read it in the original texts, she answered, "Sir, I have a good translator—the Holy Spirit."[12] She affirmed that the scriptures give woman a place which the churches deny her, calling herself a new Priscilla, to teach people like Apollos (an allusion to Acts 18:26).

The fact that a woman was preaching in the church at Sète had pleased the members of this "chapel." Some of them joined our Sunday worship. Two of them, however, had not crossed the threshold of the church. They did so after my ordination. Their presence made a big impression on the tradition-minded Protestants. It did not surprise me at all. While I deplore the Hinschists' indifference to the history of their times and some dogmatic peculiarities, the Hinschists had at least raised the question, before the society and the church of their era, of the place of woman in their structures. And that is a rare virtue!

The Work of the Lazaretto

The day after my ordination I assumed another responsibility of my ministry at Sète. I chaired for the first time the board of directors of the Lazaretto. The Lazaretto Society had been founded in 1865 by the pastor of Sète, Lucien Benoît. At that time the sea air and sea bathing were credited with all sorts of benefits. Families with modest resources came for a stay by the sea in deplorable housing and sanitary conditions. Pastor Benoît, struck by the deaths of many little children during the hot months, induced his parishioners to create a "Sea Bathing Society" (following the Hinschist example).

A board drawn from the Reformed Church of Sète obtained from the Ministry of War the concession of a part of the buildings put up in 1855 for soldiers returning from the Crimean War: hence the strange name, "Lazaretto Society,"[13] by which it was known at the beginning, and which it has kept. The board, wishing to shield the work from the unexpected (the ministry had taken the buildings back several times), and realizing what a real need it was meeting, incorporated itself and bought a waterfront property. Some vines were pulled out. Monsieur Benoît had pines planted there and began the construction of the first building. The purchase of adjoining properties and villas over the years increased the project's ability to welcome summer residents. Pastor and Madame Camille Leenhardt, who came in 1922, developed the Lazaretto splendidly. With new pavilions, it then spread over seven and a half acres, and could accommodate 700 people at the same time.

Already requisitioned several times during World War I as an additional hospital, the Lazaretto had also been occupied several times during the last war. Buildings and equipment suffered havoc and pillage, but the pine groves, the jewels of the Lazaretto, had been respected. Monsieur Leenhardt reopened the Lazaretto in 1947, but fatigue and age forced him to abandon this heavy responsibility.

I had been invited to sit on the Board of Directors in my capacity as assistant pastor at Sète. I was not familiar with the way the project had functioned before the war. Monsieur Leenhardt, the president-director, held the reins with gentle and competent authority. Therefore, I kept my role down to a "walk-on" part. When Monsieur Leenhardt announced that he would be retiring soon, the board realized that it would not be easy to find a successor for him. It decided to dissociate the functions of the director from those of the president of the board. It was then that the members of the board asked me to seek, on my own, for a possible director.

During the time of this search I became better acquainted with Pastor Leenhardt. I had read his book on Oberlin.[14] He invited me to come see him at the Château de Fonfroide (Coldspring Castle) near Montpellier. (This family mansion had been built in 1872 in reinforced concrete, an innovation at the period. The painter Burnand was a guest in this home. He found the light of Galilee in this land of Languedoc, and painted at "Fonfroide" some of his illustrations of the parables of Christ.)

I mentioned, as a possibility for the director's job, a man who seemed to me to have all the necessary qualities, Pastor Jacques Demeret. Pastor Leenhardt said to me, and wrote later, "God has guided your hand." Before I left "Fonfroide" that day, Monsieur Leenhardt said to me, in almost a confidential tone, "You understand: we cannot have any of those men from Sète as president of the board." I found in him that nuance of superiority with which the Montpellier bourgeois look on their neighbors from Sète. My host added, "It must be a pastor who presides over this project. And you are eminently qualified for that!"

I protested, not out of politeness but from conviction, since I had had no experience with social work institutions. But my host continued, "I shall not give up the presidency of the board except to an ordained pastor. You are going to be the one!" At that time the National Synod's decision was known and the date of my ordination fixed. "So everything is in order," he concluded. Thus at the board meeting which I chaired on October 21, 1949, Pastor C. Leenhardt was named honorary president of the Lazaretto and Pastor J. Demeret, director.

From then on I gave a small part of my time to the Lazaretto. The board had to make many decisions for repair of the buildings. All social work institutions had to apply the new standards imposed on the different installations (electrical, sanitary, etc.). We had to adapt the work in some way to the social change brought about since the close of the war. The new director improved the comfort of the different buildings so that they could take boarders year round. The vocabulary we used was a reflection of these changes. We no longer spoke of welcoming "bathers" but of "vacationers," "pensioners," and "groups," as at the fellowship centers.[15] We added the word "campers," since the Lazaretto had bought a nearby property to set up a campground there. The guests of the Lazaretto came from all the provinces of France, whereas before the last war the project had been known only in the South.

How many papers I had to sign over the nearly nine years! I was a little frightened by the magnitude of the figures in our audits. As president of the board I received the laments of those who hankered after the past, when the project had a familiar and paternalistic character. They were indignant, for example, when they saw families coming to the Lazaretto by car. It was also to me that the townspeople of Sète complained when they were in conflict with the director. Then I had the impression that the waves were bringing in all the pollution of human nature, with its vanity, smallness, and stinginess—all of this washing up on my desk.

But as I crossed the threshold of the Lazaretto, I was delighted at the liveliness of all the different services, from the nursery to the library. I was pleased to follow from year to year the improvements made to the housing units for the comfort of the guests and for the working conditions of the staff. I admired in my colleague Demeret his organizational gifts, the promptness of his response to unforeseen circumstances, and his breadth of view, when he brought future plans to the board.

In summer, I preferred to go to the Lazaretto at the end of an afternoon, when the heat was less strong. It was the time when families were coming back from the beach in groups, in bathing suits, towels over their shoulders, with slow steps, as though drunk with sun and fresh air. The children, tireless with their pails and shovels, were still running. The splashes of lively colors in the dresses and bathing suits under the pine grove made an impressionist painting, while the blue sea sparkled at the end of the central avenue in the slanting rays of the sun. The day ended with an open-air service. Under the deep sky of Mediterranean evenings, those who wanted it, gathered in front of the main building, quite simply and naturally. After the reading of a scripture passage, the group sang hymns with zest. The hymn "Abide with Me" was one of the favorites. It fitted the form of piety which marked a period. But the psalms became more familiar to the guests in the years 1954-58, as I was leaving Sète.

A Regional Synod Chaired by a Woman!

In 1953, as I did every year, I left Sète for the regional synod with the lay delegate from the parish. This synod was held in Avèze, a little Cévenol village almost two miles from Le Vigan. Pastor Henri Bosc was the man whom the regional council had in mind as the moderator. Not expecting his refusal, the regional president nominated him for the vote of the synod, and he was elected by 45 votes out of 52. (Synods usually follow the recommendations of the regional council.) But Pastor Bosc would not let them force his hand. (Did he have other reasons which I do not know?) He refused again. Thus we had to have a second election. A delegate behind me whispered, "This time it will be you." "No danger!" I answered him. "Not a chance!"

The assembly, a bit surprised at this unexpected refusal by Monsieur Bosc, could not form discussion groups to propose one or two names. The counting of the ballots showed 16 scattered votes, 13 votes for Pastor Baud and 23 for Pastor E. Schmidt! Some people were astounded at this result. I saw the smile of the only two women lay delegates to the synod. I was in the most awkward situation to moderate a synod. First of all, I had not had time to get ready to do it. Again, I had a report to make there: the proposal for a new order of service for baptism. Nevertheless I did not refuse and took the moderator's chair. Women do not come into certain responsibilities except by unforeseen roads. I had already had this experience!

Although the regional council had not had the idea of asking me to preside over the synod in 1953, three years later they asked me to conduct the Sunday worship service at Le Vigan at the time of the regional synod which was to be held there November 17-18. The text of my sermon was "So Peter was kept in prison; but earnest prayer for him was made to God by the church [Acts 12:5]." Disregarding all the prohibitions, a photographer disturbed us during the service by a flash so as to sell us, later, souvenir photographs of a woman pastor in the pulpit.

The coffee hour, after the meal, allowed a moment of détente before resuming work. Pastor Jean Valette, with the brio and humor with which he has delighted so many Protestant assemblies, told us the latest "synod story." During the worship service he had sat down in the balcony. During the singing of the first psalm, he saw sliding in next to him a man from the country who seemed to be coming from the depths of the ages. When the hymn was over and he heard my voice, the man half stood in his pew and stretched out his head to see the pastor in the pulpit. Poking his neighbor vigorously with his elbow, he said in dialect, between his teeth, "It's monstrous![16] That's a woman!"

Responsibilities Away from the Parish

Beginning in 1951, I had been asked to serve on the editorial board of our regional paper, *Le Cep* (the Vine Stock). At that time the Sète parish made another gesture of solidarity: after having given up its financial independence, it also agreed (not without regret) to give up its own house organ and, like the other parishes, use *Le Cep*. This board did not require of me any more work than the late lamented *Lien Protestant de Sète*, but it obliged me to be away, outside the boundaries of my parish, for one day out of every month.

Another responsibility necessitated regular absences of several days at a time. I had been named to the National Commission on Feminine Ministries,[17] which met about two or three times a year, generally in Paris or, less often, in the provinces at the time of meetings with the parish assistants of several regions.

I had pretty well guessed that some members of the parish criticized these absences and that certain members of the presbyterial council agreed with them. During the council meeting of October 7, 1954, the board came to grips with the question. Some thought a pastor ought to give full time within the limits of the parish alone; for others, "The council cannot dissociate itself from the common ministries of the French Reformed Church. The parish itself has had the benefit of these services from the outside."

During my vacation I had met a friend of my sister's, a faithful and devout Catholic. She was coming back from the rectory and venting a certain anger: "Our abbé is still gone, another indispensable meeting! All the same, his place is here!" So you met the same problems everywhere—the problems which the evolution of society was bringing up, and which the majority of the faithful did not understand. I had asked myself whether I ought to give in to the hostile misunderstanding of some, but that struck me as cowardice, so I kept on going to the different meetings of the Commission on Feminine Ministries, ready to meet a conflict which might lead me to submit my resignation from the Sète parish.

What, then, was the meaning of these trips for which I was

being criticized? As I have already written, there have always been feminine ministries in the French Reformed Church. But a great diversity, not to say disorder, reigned. This was true as much in the matter of the responsibilities as in the remuneration of those who were called as "auxiliaries" or "aids," almost always dependent on a local pastor. The officers of the Reformed churches were aware of this disorder, without always seeing the intolerable aspects of it. In this or that big city, the parish assistant was the specialized worker of the church, but she did not even attend the presbyterial council of the parish. Elsewhere, the parish assistant had to obey the pastor's wife. Women submissive and sometimes exploited—weren't they called to practice Christian humility?

The National Synod meeting in Bordeaux (1939) created a Study Commission on the Question of Feminine Ministries. It was this Synod which renewed my pastoral delegation. Had my presence in a pastoral post needled them? Without waiting for the end of the war, the National Synod in Valence (1942), "in the presence of the urgent needs of the church and of the many feminine vocations which it is happy to note, decides that a program of preparation for these future church workers shall begin on a trial basis next October, following the guidelines laid down by the Commission."[18] During the war, Frenchwomen could no longer go to the Institute of Feminine Ministries in Geneva. Then the Deaconess House accommodated a "training school" directed by Denise Hourticq, but this school did not have a long life; the National Synod of 1949 recorded its closing. No more women candidates were entering than the leaders of the French Reformed Church had estimated. Pastor Lestrigant was right when he said in his report, "No one can flatter himself at having been a prophet."[19] Actually, the Synods, assemblies made up uniquely of men, continued to try to define the nature of woman in order to find the specificity of her ministry, referring sometimes to nineteenth-century authors like Michelet and Emerson.[20]

The Study Commission was replaced by a national Commission on Feminine Ministries, to which the Synod named two women. Later the commission was reconstituted, with the nomination of pastors M. Ferrier, S. Jordan, Dean Henri Leenhardt, and several women: Claire Jullien, Colette Roullet, Madeleine Barot, and myself. This commission undertook to transform the relationships between parish assistants and pastors and presbyterial councils.

I remember vividly a meeting at Lyon. Madeleine Barot had persuaded Sarah Chakko to take part in it (Ms. Chakko was then one of the presidents of the World Council of Churches). She was always draped in her Indian national costume, which made a great impression. Even before she had taken the floor, her presence brought a vision of Christians from another continent. To pastors as to assistants, she opened up a little the horizons of the universal church and showed the diversity of ministries exercised by women. Did we have to listen to a Christian personality from India in order that pastors and their assistants might be able to work together in another climate?[21]

Another concern of the commission had been to give to all the women serving the church a "status" and an official recognition of their ministry, taking into account the diversity of the tasks entrusted to them. In any case it was necessary to offer women church workers an adequate theological training. Dean Leenhardt suggested organizing a program of two years of study at the Montpellier Seminary, but the commission thought it wise to require that women who wanted to enter the seminary should have a professional skill for which they were trained (as a teacher, a nurse, etc.). That seemed to me an excellent requirement. I allowed myself to assert that it should also be imposed on men before their theological studies.[22]

The status which the commission worked out allowed in every instance for these women to be protected against exploitation or the unfortunate initiatives of local churches. It was clear that the parish assistants in the Geneva church were a good example in the matter of their training and the bonds which united them. Their ministry had been officially recognized for many long years.[23]

Unfortunately, the whole work of reflection and research on the part of the commission seemed to me to be stymied. Traditional concepts concerning woman continued to bear down. I could not discriminate between attitudes which came from prewar French society and attitudes which came from a Catholic theology which had partly influenced that society. Sometimes the closed horizon opened, and I hoped that we could look at tomorrow's church. And then, *crack!* —we were back in the same ruts, like an ox cart stuck in the mud. During this time society was transforming itself very quickly, and here we were, twenty years behind in bringing our witness! We had "institutionalized" the ministry of women at the very time when men were calling into question the whole pastoral ministry as it was organized. We ought to have worked together, studying the ministries of the church as such, instead of having two commissions working separately, one on the pastoral ministry and the other on feminine ministries.

Protests by the Young People

In 1955 the sufferings of the war seemed far away. Business was good. Money was spoiling those who were amassing it. At Sète, as elsewhere, a generation of young people was asserting itself as independent, disrespectful toward old traditions, sometimes leaving their parents in a quandary. The former confirmands whom I had taught, and whom I loved, brought their healthy dynamism into the life of the parish. I was glad to see the increase in the ranks of the "troops," "packs," and "flights" of scouting.[24] The presbyterial council noted the fact that there had never been so large a proportion of young people at worship and at the Lord's Supper. I thanked God that young people, in searching and in prayer, were taking the gospel seriously, for the world and for their own lives. It was they who had expressed the desire to have a time of meditation and intercession once a week in the morning before they went to the lycée. In rotation they led the prayer after the scripture reading. In winter we used to go into the church while it was still night and come out in daylight.

But on the day of the annual meeting of the Sète congregation, February 13, 1955, the young adults caused an explosion. After my general report on the activity of the church during the year and the presentation of the accounts by the treasurer of the Association for Public Worship[25] (i.e., the church as such), the leader of the girl scouts asked for the floor. Frightened, expressing herself with a certain confusion, she reproached the presbyterial council for not having paid enough attention to the youth movements. Leaning on the priesthood of all believers, she claimed that the older young people who had been given responsibilities should be treated like "adult Christians."

We had not yet lived through the student-worker protest of May 1968, and this interjection had the effect of a bomb which shook the whole assembly. Unfortunately, the discussion began with the brutal response of one of the elders: "Child, you are all wrong!" I suffered at seeing young people misunderstood—young people who, instead of slamming the door of the church, were showing their faith and their dynamism.

The presbyterial councilors handed me their resignations, with the exception of the treasurer and the secretary. I felt some hurt and sorrow as I tried to understand the reasons for this gesture. It is true that, in spite of the separation of church and state, the Napoleonic traditions still carried weight when it came to electing presbyterial councilors. They were truly "notables."[26] "Notables" do not accept the idea that young people, without experience and without prestige, should allow themselves to take the floor and challenge the habits established in the society and in the church. "Young people, like women, ought to keep their mouths shut and listen to their elders!" That the youth of a church should cause the resignation of the presbyterial council is scarcely an everyday occurrence. I had to notify the president of our region, aging and near the end of his term. Pastor Berton disapproved of the attitude of this group of young people. He saw all the risks this situation was creating. But once again he showed his faith in me.

We had to proceed to new elections two weeks later. The balloting on February 27 put an end to all parish-wide agitation. The retiring elders were reelected, with the exception of the one who, without the excuse of youth, had so rudely opposed the girl scout leader.

The young people, at first very much disconcerted by the resignations which they had brought about, redoubled their gusto in getting ready for their carnival at the end of March. Before Christmas the new president of our region, Pastor Valette, began his "episcopal visits" with our church. He dedicated the new youth rooms which the presbyterial council had arranged to build or refurbish.

The 1955 annual meeting had signaled, at the echelon of one local church, the tremors (we were later to call them the "protest movements") which shook the society, as it shook the churches across the entire world. Young people were demanding and difficult. They were turned toward the future and they marched fast, while their elders were looking at the road in the rearview mirror. I tried to understand each group and explain the one to the other. The love inspired by Christ is compassionate (in the strong sense of the word) with sufferings. But it refuses to share partisanship and prejudices.

During the last years of my ministry at Sète, I lived in the midst of these tensions. But these same years also brought me many causes for joy and thankfulness, with the confirmands, the adolescents, and the leaders of the youth groups.

The Sète Period Draws to an End

Even as late as the beginning of this century, pastors remained a long time in the same posts. Toward the middle of the century it was deemed preferable that pastors should not prolong their terms beyond ten or twelve years in the same parish. Putting in parentheses the war years until 1946 (because of the evacuation and the slow return to the city), in 1956 I was beginning my eleventh year of ministry at Sète. It would have made sense for me to leave in July 1956.

Because I was still the only woman pastor, I had thought best not to offer myself as a candidate for a vacant parish or one that was looking for a pastor. The general secretary of the French Reformed Church told me that he had suggested my name to a parish in a prefecture city,[27] so that its presbyterial council might consider calling me. But the council had just finished repairing an immense house which served as its manse and would not for a moment consider a single pastor! (How far the consequences of our property reach!)

In 1957 I was approached by the president of another region, in a cold part of France, concerning a vacant parish in his area. He stressed the comfort of its parsonage, which had a good heating system. I answered him that I did not see, in the comfort of which he spoke, any clear indication that the Holy Spirit was leading me to answer his appeal. He thanked me for my letter, even though it brought a refusal.

I had advised the presbyterial council that I would be leaving Sète in July of 1958, but it was only at my farewell service that I told the parish I would be leaving for Algeria. I had been feeling closer and closer to the problems and the sufferings in Algeria and now, without my volunteering to go there, the church in Blida-Medea had asked me to come and take the post of pastor in this parish in the Algerian region of the French Reformed Church.

8

Pastor in Algeria, 1958-1962

Using a flashback technique, Elisabeth Schmidt told the story of her ministry in Algeria[1] within the framework of her recollections and meditations during the long weekend from Saturday, June 30, to Tuesday, July 3, 1962, when Algeria was celebrating its independence. She calls that weekend "the turning of a page of history for my country and for this land of Algeria, where French soldiers had landed in 1830." It is worth noting that in another dramatic event—the freeing of American hostages by Iran in January 1981—independent Algeria played a significant role.

It was in 1958, the very year when General de Gaulle was recalled to power after his self-exile at his country retreat, that Elisabeth Schmidt was called to minister in Algeria. Here is her story in her own words.—A.H.

Saturday, June 30, 1962,
The Face of Blida on That Evening

THE HEAT HAD COME ON SUDDENLY those last days of June. I found it overwhelming as I made my way home, earlier than usual, on that late afternoon, on the eve of Algerian Independence Day. I had gone on foot to visit one of the few members of the parish still in Blida, an old and ailing woman who had stubbornly resisted all attempts to get her back to

France. I wanted to make sure that, with her two servants gone, she would be safe during the celebrations.

I was walking slowly, to see the face that was turned that evening by the city where I had spent four years as a pastor. I followed rue Lamy, the central artery of the European quarter. There was very little traffic. There were more shuttered houses. The rubble and the broken glass had been cleaned up in front of Arab stores bombed by the OAS (Secret Army Organization).[2] Big boards, hastily nailed up, closed the abandoned storefronts.

I threw a friendly glance toward the drugstore, closed for the weekend. (Only one druggist had closed up shop and left for France.) Across from the drugstore the big department store was as bustling as on the previous Saturdays.

I kept on climbing the rue Lamy. My grocery woman had also gone. As I passed the blind store window I remembered the few words we had exchanged when I was the only customer in her shop. "Now there is nothing to do except to leave, after what we French have done." Then, carefully dissociating herself from her compatriots among the wealthy colonials and in the higher echelons of the army, she added, "They have lost everything, with their OAS." Even so, she spoke calmly of her imminent departure and even smiled at the thought of seeing her grandchildren again in France.

What face did Blida show that evening? Not that of a bombed-out city (my memories of the last war remained clear), but of a ghost town. I thought of *The Plague* by Camus. A kind of dejection seemed to have struck the few Europeans I met. They were normally warm and authoritative. The visible signs of departure revealed a brooding sadness, made graver still by the beauty of the evening.

Now, as I went on, the street became more and more animated. The side streets, where the Arabs lived, rang with the shouts of children chasing each other. The grandfathers sipped their coffee, seated with dignity on their doorsteps. Nobody paid any attention to the only European who was going by, and I had not caught any hostile looks. What did this indifference conceal? What surprise did the morrow hold for us? Would the vicious circle of assassinations and crimes keep on, as those who had just left in panic predicted so loudly?

Finally I came to the top of the street, to drab Franchet-d'Esperey Square. From a distance you could see the Ricci fountains, but they were without water. There was a group of concrete vases, covered with blue and gold mosaics. Since "the incidents" they had been wrapped around with barbed wire, to prevent the planting of grenades.

The church, like the parsonage, stood on the right-hand side of the square. Their common garden was surrounded by a low wall, on top of which was a green iron fence. There was a grilled iron gate in front of the church and a doorway in front of the pastor's house. No Arabs were seated on the wall. Ordinarily, the old men used it as a bench, their hands clutching their staffs, watching their grandchildren playing in the square, while they chatted endlessly.

The facade of the church, with the four columns of its peristyle upholding a triangular pediment, was not without harmony or solemnity. But without the signboard attached to one of the columns, who could have guessed that this building could be a place of Christian worship? One of the soldiers we entertained at my house thought it was the employment office! The parish house, recently built, surrounded the sanctuary on three sides.

Arab Workmen at the Parsonage

When I got home, I had the feeling of coolness. The parsonage was a solid and undistinguished house from the beginning of the century, with narrow windows and high ceilings. A strong smell of flowers and bushes came from the garden at this hour, heightening the feeling that I was a long way from Paris, my native city. There was a little of everything here: a bougainvillea which filtered a pink light, two spindly palm trees, a lemon tree, and two cactuses which climbed along the facade like green snakes.

Back in my study, I picked up the telephone and noticed that it was still out of order. Ordinarily, it would be merely annoying, but the lack of a telephone was worrisome on this night of June 30, 1962. I tried to believe that the cutting of the wire was caused by a local tree trimmer hurrying to finish work before quitting time, and not a plan to cut Europeans off from communications during the Independence Day celebrations. To reassure myself, I remembered my contacts with different sets of Arab workmen.

The manse had been in need of major repairs for a long time, but the mayor's office had delayed undertaking this piece of work.[3] This was one aspect of life in Algeria which had surprised me, as the daughter of a deputy who had voted for the Law of Separation of Church and State! Upon my arrival I had called on the mayor, who sent for the city architect and got the work started the following Monday.

I had decided not to move out during the repairs, but when I left the house the foreman had to have a key. My parishioners said, "It's impossible, these are Arabs. You will be assassinated, or at least robbed." I decided that the only Christian attitude, in these circumstances, was to trust the Muslim workmen as I would have trusted Frenchmen. One day a mason asked me for a knife to cut a piece of string. I asked him naively, "You don't have a knife?" He answered, "No, Mademoiselle, we Arabs are not allowed to have knives." I decided that love of neighbor ought to banish fear. I insisted on informing my parishioners that I had without regret discarded their advice, I was safe and sound, and nothing had disappeared. I concluded on that June night that my telephone wire had not been cut on purpose.

My *Fatma*

Thus on the evening of June 30, 1962 I was completely isolated in my big, old house. My European and Jewish neighbors to the left had gone. So, too, the teachers across the square. The little street behind the house was lined with Arab dwellings. Some of them looked prosperous. All were blinding white in the sun. I felt cut off, not only because I was probably the only European in that quarter of Blida, but because I was the pastor of a church which would henceforth be foreign in this Muslim country. One thing was certain: There was no Arab or Kabyle Christian church in Algeria.[4]

I was at this point in my thinking when the key turned in the lock and Madame A opened the door. She had been my *fatma*, housekeeper, ever since a little after my arrival, when one of my parishioners helped me locate someone who spoke French.

"Do you have everything you need?" she asked. "Is there anything lacking?" This question surprised me. Madame A had come this morning and laid in food for several days. Of middle height, well-built, with a round, intelligent, and expressive face, she wore a little bonnet of thin cloth, always of bright colors, which partly hid her faded henna hair. She exuded goodness and energy. She gave the impression of being a fighter, rather than someone resigned to her fate. I had guessed right away that she and I would hit it off well. She seemed happy to come to me every day and had said as much to me in the kind of picture only the Orientals know how to find: "When I open the door of the garden, the sun comes into my heart."

Like all mothers, Madame A talked to me about her daughters, their characters, their futures. Fatirah, the youngest, who had just finished her last year in the girls' lycée, struck me as the most feisty. Dressed like a French schoolgirl (in very good taste), her pigtail down her back —and without the enfolding veil—she walked down the street with a determined step. How had she contrived to go without the veil, against her father's wishes? (Fathers and schoolmasters whip hard.)

Of the older ones, Madame A said, "We'll marry them off after the war. Not now! There are too many troubles. For the time being they are at home, but it is hard for Nadiah to ply her trade. She is a dressmaker, but she can't go to the French houses for fittings, nor can Frenchwomen come to our house. She can only work in the neighborhood, but our neighbors are poor and slow paying!"

I hate to waste time on fittings, but I had asked Nadiah to make me some dresses and tailored blouses. Since she was a good seamstress friends staying with me also gave her work. Coming on mornings when her mother was there, Nadiah slowly took off her veil. Then I saw a girl with regular and refined features. You did not read in her eyes the energy of her mother, but her gentle look suggested hidden sensitivity.

Once, when I had the time to stay with her in the kitchen, Madame A had told me some details of her past. She was stringing some beans which she had bought in the Arab market near my house. The Europeans did not go there any more after "the incidents," but traded at the "French market" in the city center.

"My parents were poor, very poor. You can't imagine how we lived. When I was a teenager, my father gave me to an old man—to be his wife." (Here I knew she was shading the truth to protect her father's reputation. In reality, she was sold, and the relationship could scarcely have been called a marriage.)

She spoke slowly, with long silences. I sat with my hands folded, beside her. I had noticed that my *fatma* interpreted any effort I made to help her with the housework as a distrust of her abilities.

"I don't remember it all, but a short time later I was in the hospital at Orléansville. There everyone was so kind to me! Then I went back home. I asked my father if I could stay. My father nodded his head 'yes,' without a word. I stayed."

A Frenchwoman who had called on her during her hospitalization asked her to come to work as a maid. From there she went to a doctor's house, where she learned more French and became a health purist—scolding me for not boiling water for ten minutes before I gargled! At the doctor's house she met a fellow servant who became a loving husband to her and the father of her girls.

A daily visitor at my house, Madame A extended a discreet invitation for a return visit in the Arab quarter, no doubt first clearing with the neighborhood representative of the FLN. There I met the girls again and Muhammad, a foundling two-year-old boy whom they had taken in and were beginning to spoil.

Now, on this thirtieth of June, the eve of the celebrations of Independence, my *fatma* repeated what she had said several times already: that she could not come, perhaps for several days, but would be back as soon as possible. Then, suddenly, she asked, "You won't go out any of these days, will you, my little mistress?" She spelled out her solicitude. "Here people know you, but there will be outsiders in town for the fête, people from the mountains who do not know you. So stay home all these days!" As she put on her veil, she added, "There won't be any St. Bartho—"

"There will be no St. Bartholomew's night!"[5] I wondered at this reference from a Muslim woman who had never been to school yet knew that St. Bartholomew meant a massacre. She said it a third time as she hid her face, all but one eye, and then set off quickly, with her loping gait, toward the Arab quarter.

Everything Seemed Calm

When night fell, I went up to my bedroom. My parishioners had made me promise not to work late in my study on the ground floor. They had installed a second telephone upstairs. Tonight it was no use and seemed to be eyeing me! I looked out toward the 4,500-foot range of mountains, which reminded me of the Cévennes. On the "Tell" some of my parishioners had chalets, which gave them cool nights in summer and a base for skiing in the winter. (Yes, there was an Alpine Club in Blida!) Since "the incidents," guerrilla bands of the FLN held the mountain, necessitating a military convoy for approaching it. Each Sunday and each Thursday I saw such a convoy, with civilian and military vehicles, winding up the steep road.

Nearer at hand I saw more people than usual in the square, talking with many gestures. Yet everything seemed calm as they took the cool of the evening. My thoughts kept whirling. "No, I ought not to let fear get the better of me. If an organized massacre on the order of St. Bartholomew's night was ruled out, there would probably be uncontrolled small killings. Are killings ever controlled? Stop your head from spinning around—around the fixed point of anxiety for tomorrow!"

Little by little the healing coolness of the night invaded my room. I put out my light and saw the depth of the summer night sky, with the stars shining, standing out in relief against the dark blue vault. Remembering that Jesus had advised his disciples to be "wise as serpents and innocent as doves [Matt. 10:16]," I decided to stay clothed that night.

A page of history was being turned for my country and for Algeria. I was there, at that hour, and at that point on the globe, experiencing intensely the fact that we are "strangers and exiles on the earth [Heb. 11:13]." I was there because I had been called as a pastor and "installed" (an incongruous word, given the recent dispersion of the parishioners). In the midst of the anxiety, fatigue, and tension of these last months, there remained nevertheless the peace of knowing that I was where I belonged. I found some reassurance in remembering how I had been led to Blida.

Algeria Seen from Sète

As a Mediterranean port, Sète had commercial relationships with Algeria. We saw Algerian ships, tied up or heading for the open sea. Besides, the picture left by school geography stayed with us: the three departments[6] (Alger, Oran, and Constantine) colored pink, just like France, in the school atlases.

Yet, paradoxically, the Protestant communities in France were closer to the black Africans than to the Arabs in Algeria. The Paris Evangelical Missionary Society had no mission station in Algeria. We celebrated in 1957 the "coming of age" of the Evangelical Church of the Cameroun, but of Algeria we knew only that there were some churches for Europeans. The Arabs were Muslims, and who cared about their faith or culture?

But Algeria came closer to us all in Sète with the increased anxiety of families as their soldier sons did their compulsory military (or alternative) service in North Africa. The family of Paul Dupuy, a teacher, was part of our parish. Monsieur Dupuy was kidnapped by terrorists, led on forced marches at night in the mountains, and harangued about the inquisition and torture carried on by the French army, which had requisitioned some rooms of his school. Finally released at night on the main road, he had been picked up by a patrol of our army which was looking for him. When he came to see me, he still walked with difficulty.

In February 1958 it was Lucien Valente, a medical student, who was killed in an ambush near Constantine; his body was brought back to Sète on March 24. While the military chaplain had charge of the committal at the cemetery, I conducted the funeral at the church, where I had married Lucien to one of my former confirmands and baptized their little Denise. The young widow chose the text for my sermon from Isaiah 40:6-8: "All flesh is grass . . . but the word of our God will stand for ever." Lucien, with great humility and good judgment, had wanted to care for the disinherited, to serve suffering humanity, and Laura shared this ideal. He had started by caring for the miseries of the Algerian populace, as was often the case with the army medical corps. The FLN had spared Paul Dupuy, the teacher, and killed Lucien Valente, the doctor. It all seemed incomprehensible.

It was in the course of that day, March 24, 1958, that I began to feel drawn toward service in Algeria. I was sure that if God wanted me on the other side of the Mediterranean, a door would be opened for me.

The Postscript and the Call

One day, when I was in Paris for a church commission meeting and saw the new secretary general, he said to me abruptly, "Do you have a driver's license?"

I answered, "Certainly, since 1940!"

"By any chance, would you be willing to take a post in Algeria?"

I had answered right off. "Why, yes, if you think I could be a useful pastor there in this period."

Pastor B wrote a few words about me as a postscript to a letter ready to be mailed to Pastor André Chatoney, the regional president for Algeria. Some days later I got a letter asking if I would take the post of pastor in Blida. Providence can also express itself in postscripts! Perhaps Pastor Chatoney was surprised by the speed with which I answered. "In the present circumstances, it is an honor to be called to Algeria!"

After Pastor Chatoney's letter I had one from the vice-president of the presbyterial council. "It's a splendid idea to have the pastoral charge entrusted to a woman. It will be a witness to the Muslims." I had not thought of this angle of the situation, and I found in it a new encouragement.

At a last meeting of our clergy group I was surprised at the violence of one man's opinions, a man born in Algeria with family still living there. He could not agree with our moderate resolutions. I also consulted a black African pastor on deputation before I flew to North Africa. I remember his sad face as he said, "We can put up with hunger, cold, pain—but not contempt!" I guarded this saying close to my heart.

As I got ready to say farewell to the parish which had

asked for my ordination and shared it with me, I tried to crystallize my working philosophy. The service of Christ always leads toward those who suffer, to share their grief and their hope. I would try to keep myself available, without letting myself be imprisoned by a party, always trying to seek the truth. My early university training was still alive in me. But it was the thinking of Calvin, Kierkegaard, and Karl Barth which would help me even more in traversing this period of crisis. I knew that it is easier to enlist God on our side than to serve God; that care for the neighbor requires us to be free from the prejudices of our milieu; that true love toward those who walk with us requires as much humility as discernment, one of the gifts of the Spirit being discernment, according to Paul.

Arrival and First Contacts

On this night of June 30, 1962, I recalled vividly my arrival, which seemed so long ago! Leaving Toulouse on the cool fall afternoon of October 2, 1958, I met a ground swell of heat as I came down the steps of the airplane at Algiers that night. The temperature seemed to me suffocating where we waited for our luggage.

The baggage handlers were all Arabs or Berbers. When I finally got hold of my bags I said, "Thank you, sir," to the man who handed them to me. He looked up at me with a kind of astonishment which I did not understand.

Standing next to Pastor André Chatoney, who was expecting me, I saw the former pastor of Pau, who had arranged for my hospitalization when I left Gurs with typhoid: Jean Nouvelon. He was now chief chaplain of the French army in Algeria. He greeted me with: "Knowing you, I'm not surprised to see you here! Did you see my wife on the plane?" (I had not, in the crowd.) Then Pastor Chatoney took me in hand, asking about my trip, telling me about the hot wind (the sirocco—no friend to my asthma). He had to give me necessary information and advice.

I learned that the parish which had been entrusted to me entailed various responsibilities and covered a vast area geographically. The larger number of Protestants were in Blida, where there was a church and manse. At Medea, on the High Plateau, more than twenty-four miles south, a small number of the faithful constituted a branch church with a worship room. Then there were some dispersed Protestants among the Europeans, fewer and fewer as you neared the oases of Laghouat and Ghardaïa, on the fringe of the Sahara desert.

The next morning Pastor Charles Bolay took me to my post in his little four-horsepower Renault. We had left the big city, Algiers, a replica of Marseille except for the veiled women. I saw my first Algerian road, lined with aloes and eucalyptus. At a turn of the road I saw the range of the Blidean Atlas on the far horizon and in the plain, a city. The smell of the earth and the trees seemed to me different from that of France. I had heard of Blida—that little city, the "city of roses," with its orange groves watered by the Oued-el-Kébir, which flows down from its gorges on a bed of pebbles. But I was taken to a European subprefecture town, built up little by little by the French since General Valée had captured the town in 1838.

On the following Sunday I went in to the church for the worship service. It was a bright, high-ceilinged building, without vaulting, lighted by six rounded windows on each side, cheerful in contrast to its austere facade. The walls were covered with pink artificial marble—surely the idea of an Italian mason nostalgic for the churches and the palaces of his native land. The plaintive tone of the organ made me a little homesick for the organs at Sète.

At first blush, the little Protestant community hardly differed from the communities in France, gathered at the same time. I noticed the same looks, a little curious, a little nervous, sizing up the newly arrived pastor. The congregation included a number of soldiers, in khaki or in blue. Their strong young voices fortified the singing of the hymns. To my surprise, an airman, introducing himself afterward, said, "The squadron is inviting you to lunch today."

The manse was still empty, but the airmen took me to lunch in my future home, using a few pots and pans they found and an old hot plate. They turned out to be excellent cooks! Thus I found myself with young Protestants, a few years older than those I had left at Sète. But these in Blida were in uniform. On this first contact they impressed me as happy, anxious to relax, and quite at home with me. The assistant chaplain, after his theological studies, was doing his military service at the air base. Each Sunday I invited him to lunch, with soldiers he had chosen because they could not afford restaurant meals or for some other reason. My housekeeper would make a big roast and food for a big family. From the pile of dishes awaiting her the next day, she would guess the number of my guests.

I often saw at the service soldiers from black Africa, but I rarely had any of them at my table. They always had a pretext for refusing the invitation relayed by their chaplain. I tried to find the reason and concluded that the parsonage was not for them, as it was for the Frenchmen, a house that recalled their own.

After the meal, at the coffee hour, one of the intellectuals would sit down happily in the easy chair in my study, taking down a book and fondling it, without having time to read it. The handymen hung pictures or assembled a cabinet left in pieces by movers in a hurry to get back to Algiers by nightfall. The soldiers took endless photographs from upstairs, looking toward the mountains, promising to send me the good ones. I only got one. Back in France, they wanted to forget Algeria, with its tragedies and its problems, and close the parenthesis on this period of their lives.

It was moving to hear the old Sunday school songs to which these men, in these circumstances, gave a new meaning. This group of young soldiers, "the troop," as they called themselves, was appreciated by the parishioners. Their presence brought us all a great deal, without their knowing it.

The Workroom for Muslim Girls

Another aspect of my post at Blida was directing the workroom, one of several created to help fill the gap left when the FLN had suddenly ordered girls to leave school. On Wednesdays and Fridays the parish house was filled not with Protestant soldiers but with seventy to eighty Muslim teenagers taught by a dozen women from our parish. Some of the teachers were officers' wives and one was a Kabyle Protestant. As the girls arrived, they folded their capacious veils (haiks), revealing threadbare garments, always spotlessly clean. We taught them needlework (few knew how to thread a needle), reading, and writing. Some were listless, possibly because of undernourishment. Others were eager and moved ahead at their own pace.

I wondered, naively, why Muslim families would entrust their daughters to an institution directed by a pastor, in the shadow of a Christian place of worship. One of the teachers who was born in Algeria told me. "The parents know their girls are safe, and they know that Christianity is not going to conquer Islam!"

From the first months, I had wondered if it was worthwhile to continue the workroom. My question would not have been understood in the fall of 1958. We did not know the real problems in the lives of these girls: perhaps poverty, perhaps worry about a brother fighting with the guerrillas or a father held in a French prison. Besides our inability to reach the depths of the girls' problems, there was a subtler danger. I was afraid that, in spite of the teachers' devotion, there might slip into their minds an unconscious desire to work through the girls for a French Algeria. There was a certain ambiguity which left me uneasy. However, I persuaded myself that in any case we were doing a useful work. We were giving a little practical instruction. Then again, teaching a woman to read was a small beginning toward her liberation!

"We Lived Well Together, 'Before' "

The mayor of Blida had told me that the city had a population of 100,000 to 105,000. (It was hard to get a census because of population shifts caused by "the incidents.") Of these, there were only 18,000 Europeans, and the Protestants were a minority within that minority. We had the usual spread of socioeconomic groups, with more people of modest means than I had expected. Only part of the Protestant community lived in the city itself. The rest were on large or small plantations in the environs.

On my first round of visits to the Protestant families, I had gone to see two almost-neighbors, two sisters who had joined their lonely lives—the one a widow, the other a single woman. They lived in two rooms on the ground floor on a narrow street. One was an embroiderer, the other a presser who spent long hot days pleating, starching, and ironing linen for the city's rich women. The sisters spoke of "the ladies" with a certain obsequiousness belonging to another period. Poorly housed, badly paid, they had a social conservatism which disconcerted me. If they bowed before their clients, they were in any case persuaded of their superiority over the Arab people.

In other early conversations I learned about "the good life," Blida style—skiing on the slopes of the Tell, mushroom picking in the woods, swimming parties at the Mediterranean shore. A little refrain, always the same, slipped in: "Then we lived well together." It went without saying that they had the Arabs in mind. One day, when a family was describing the beach parties, I asked, "And did the Arabs come lie on the beach too?" I understood from the tone of the answer how incongruous my question seemed. "Of course not!" I had to conclude that the Arabs were completely left out of this "good life" before "the incidents."

I found one middle-aged couple tense because they had received a death threat from the FLN in their mailbox. The husband's father died, and on the way to the cemetery the man slowed his car and showed me a large farm. "That was my grandfather's, and I spent all my Sundays and holidays there as a lad. Yes, grandfather always kept a rifle beside him, just in case."

I noticed how often the conversations turned on what France had done for Algeria. "Algeria is—or certainly ought to be—eternally grateful." This reflection, in turn, led to patriotic rhetoric in the style of World War I.

I thought it best to offer in return the story of my grandmother, who showed me every vacation time the monumental armoire in which she had hidden a French prisoner of war in 1870. My two grandfathers in Alsace-Lorraine had opted for France after the defeat of 1870. The Gestapo officer who came to arrest my sister in 1943 had found, in searching the house, a certificate showing that my grandfather, Edouard Schmidt, had chosen French citizenship. The German officer exclaimed, "They're right patriotic in this family!"

The Arab Who Read *Le Monde*

Several times I had gone into the variety store of Monsieur G to pick up little things I needed. He introduced me to Ahmed, his chief salesman, an Arab dressed fit to kill in European dress. The proprietor and his wife treated the elegant Arab almost as an adopted son. This did not prevent Monsieur G from passing on to me the conventional wisdom: "Look out! The Arabs are thieves, good-for-nothings. You can't trust them." Arab workmen had sometimes used these same words in self-derisive humor, saying of a mistake, "This is Arab work!" This was said with a malicious light in their eyes, a mocking smile on their lips.

Some weeks after my first visits, Monsieur G told me that

Ahmed had been arrested by the French authorities and released soon after, suspected of ties with the FLN. "I told him," he continued, " 'it's not surprising, Ahmed, that you should be arrested. You read *Le Monde* and you hobnob with intellectuals!' " No, I didn't understand at all. But I remembered the advice of my president, Pastor Chatoney. "As to your subscriptions to papers: *Le Monde*, yes, but not beyond that. You would be putting up a barrier between your parishioners and yourself." *Le Monde*, bought on the sly by Arabs who sent their young children to the newsstand and had the paper read aloud by the best educated member of the family, was a means of culture and reflection as well as information.

At another time I struck up a conversation with the Arab who read *Le Monde* and asked him over for coffee. Having heard repeatedly how the Europeans felt, I asked Ahmed how the Arabs felt. He told me, with as much passion and volubility as the Europeans, about the suffering of the "despised" Arabs, the injustices committed by the French, the refusal of the colonials to implement the reforms voted after the 1939-45 war. He probably thought this was all new to me. In any event, he needed to be heard out by a European whom he respected and could trust. In the end he spoke with gratitude of his boss and his boss's wife, but added, "They don't understand!"

Protestants of Kabyle Origin

The Protestant church in Blida included two families of Kabyle origin. A Methodist foreign mission had been the means of converting the parents to Christianity. The children and especially the grandchildren, brought up in the midst of Protestant youth, attending the French schools and lycées, were completely integrated into the European community. I was especially drawn to these families. They brought me proof, so necessary in Algeria, that race does not determine faith. One picture remained with me as a vision of peace and of hope. It was the first Christmas service I had celebrated at Blida. Suddenly two little children, escaping from their parents' arms, came toward the pulpit, where I was. Of the same age, about two and a half years old, the one was European, the other Kabyle, the grandson of the first Christian of the line. Hand in hand, they were about to climb into the pulpit with me when their parents recaptured them.

In these unhappy years, the Kabyle Christians were in an especially difficult position, misunderstood in certain respects by both communities, and often wounded by both sides. Who could understand the rending they must have experienced in leaving their national traditions to become Europeans? With the transplanting of populations and the fighting in the mountains, the craftsmen had abandoned their native art (typically pottery with classic geometric patterns). I still found Kabyle woven blankets which I gave as wedding presents.

It was almost impossible for the several Kabyle families to find what the large African churches had taken time to discover: a specific Christian expression bearing the imprint of their heritage. Their co-religionists wanted to Frenchify them—perhaps a sign of friendship?

I had to ask myself, If there had been native Arab or Kabyle churches, what part would they have played in the unfolding of events? They might have made the unseeing Europeans understand better the claims of their people. They might have been an especially valuable link between the two communities, a place of real dialogue. But I was dreaming. You cannot rewrite history.

Medea and the Chaplains

At the end of December 1958 I finally made contact with the little community in Medea and its region. As a crossroads community, 3,000 feet high, between the sea and the mountains, Medea had been a Roman stronghold and had a few aqueduct arches to prove it. Now it was a departmental capital with nearly 50,000 inhabitants, of whom less than 3,000 were European. Since it was in a war zone, the general was the prefect. In spite of its altitude, Medea had a high incidence of tuberculosis among the Arabs, and you heard coughing in the streets.

You would have missed the Protestant place of worship if you had not been told to look for a signboard on an apartment house near the square and to go up to the second floor. An accommodating chaplain took the service every other week, and in return he had a little apartment which he used when making the rounds of his scattered army units. High-ranking chaplains also called on me. It occurred to me that a grain of curiosity might have been mixed with this fraternal approach. But since I had rounded the corner of fifty, I smiled at it. I found it harder to establish spiritual communion with the chaplains who were superior officers than with the recent seminary graduates.

Though our worship center in Medea was adequate, once you found it, I persuaded Pastor Chatoney that in a prefecture city the Protestants ought to make a better showing, and that a modest church building would help to put us on the map. The soldiers contributed their labor, and a young artist soldier delayed his return to France to complete the wrought-iron lectern he had designed. But by the time we had finished the building in 1962 it was virtually useless; the people had gone back to France. When we decommissioned it, the CIMADE team members took the lectern as a memento of their sojourn in Algeria.

During the first services of the Lord's Supper in Blida, some aspects of the Algerian tragedy came home to me in a new light. I saw, gathered around the Lord's table, European families, a Malagasy family whose father was a noncommissioned officer posted at Blida, and soldiers of different races, including black Africans in French uniforms. These services could have been an anticipation of the kingdom of God. However, it was not their faith but the French army which had plucked these non-Europeans from their land and their culture and made them put on the same uniform.

But while the French army uniform quite unintentionally broadened the Christian fellowship around the communion table in a parish church, it had—once more inadvertently —an opposite effect among the Algerians of Muslim faith. Some Muslim Algerians became aides-de-camp to French officers and thereby became the enemies of their Muslim brothers who were guerrilla fighters striving for independence. In some instances they betrayed their French chiefs; in other cases, they disappeared and went over to the liberation army. Did anyone among the colonials feel guilty about forcing the Algerian Muslims to fight against their brothers in the faith? Had anyone raised such a question, would the prophetic voice have been heard in this heavy time of waning colonialism?

In my first three months of life in Blida, two realities seemed to dominate life. The first was the barriers, visible and invisible, which existed between the two communities. I had to accept a system of human relationships which was alien to me as a European. The second factor was insecurity. It accompanied each day's life, insidiously or brutally. Algeria had known for several years the dangers of FLN terrorism. Little by little the population had gotten used to a number of protective measures which were imposed upon them. Like everybody else, I became accustomed to searches at the doors of the big department stores (opening your bag, being frisked by women in white gloves who knew quickly how to find the places where grenades could be concealed under one's clothing). One day I forgot to lock the car trunk when I parked in the square and received a warning: A grenade could have been put there. All these measures formed a protective framework which allowed us, instead of recalling the dangers, to lead as normal a life as possible. But it was travel which dramatized the danger and the insecurity most vividly for me.

I preferred to go to Medea by car on Route 1. The train, christened "The Puff," was an "accommodation train" in the fullest sense of the word. Driving interfered with my crowded schedule, but I learned that there was real danger as well as inconvenience involved in train travel in Algeria. In front of every train a motorized handcar set out, with a French soldier in charge, to explode any mines which the FLN might have planted along the track. The detonating devices were cleverly set to explode under the first-class carriages. (Not that I had any idea of traveling first class!)

The national road follows all the curves of the Chiffa gorges. A military post at the valley entrance checked the car's registration, and another, near Medea, either asked nothing or made a new check. (It was wise to make sure that all the cars which took the gorge route came through it!) All along the way there were doorless concrete blockhouses. I had a grateful thought for those who were watching. One hairpin curve, where we had to slow down, had been named "the curve of the missing" because of the people who had mysteriously disappeared there at the hands of the guerrillas.

At Medea, Pastor Chatoney took me to meet the general. He welcomed us in his huge office, whose walls were covered with maps and flags, just as I had imagined it. The general took Pastor Chatoney for a bishop. He was deferential to us but quickly led the conversation to his own familiar territory—the latest military successes. "In twenty years, we will have stamped out every trace of rebellion." I broke the silence I had kept until that moment. "Twenty years? Do you think the civil population will put up with twenty years of this kind of war?"

Pastor Chatoney and his wife also took me south beyond Medea toward the oasis of Laghouat on the ruler-straight road which stretches toward the shimmering blue haze on the horizon. Green is abolished; only earth and sun remain. I was delighted to see a dark nomad tent, and dromedaries en route to who knows where? It brought back Abraham and Lot. Suddenly two Arabs appeared, signaling us to halt. Pastor Chatoney, with his usual politeness, said, "Good morning, sirs. What would you like of us? I am Pastor Chatoney, and this is my wife, Madame Chatoney, and my fellow pastor, Mlle. Schmidt." The two men did not introduce themselves. One, in guttural French which I did not understand very well, said, "Go along," signaling us ahead. Pastor Chatoney kept them in the rearview mirror while he quickly picked up speed. I broke the silence by asking, "Who on earth were they?" Pastor Chatoney answered only, "They must have been looking for someone else." He did not want to deter me from my next trips.

During our free time in Laghouat, Pastor Chatoney went to the monastery of the White Fathers (a missionary order working primarily in Africa), hoping to find a monk with whom he had shared a jeep during World War II. Meanwhile Madame Chatoney took me for a walk in the monastery gardens, pointing out the three-layered cultivation which the oasis requires—palm trees on top, then fruit trees, and vegetables below. I followed her without anxiety, knowing that she was impervious to fear. Pastor Chatoney was relieved to find us again, relaying what one of the monks had told him: "Two women together were probably safe enough, but it was well that Pastor Chatoney had not gone into the garden himself."

When it was time to go on south to Ghardaïa, ninety miles farther toward the Sahara, Pastor Chatoney wanted to use every quarter hour when it was possible to drive. There was an all-night curfew, ending at dawn, and we were at the barrier when it was lifted. We were given instructions: Stay at least a quarter mile behind military vehicles. They roared past us—a kind of small tank and a weapons carrier with machine guns. They had the same function as the motor-driven handcar on the railroad: to "open the way"—what a euphemism!—in other words, to explode any mines the FLN might have planted during the night. Yes, this was war . . . which I had almost forgotten while I was looking at the palm grove at dawn and the sand dunes catching the first rays of the sun.

Coping

My pastoral calls on the big planters and their families offered them the chance to tell the beads of their past dangers and of the present fears which insulated them from every other influence from outside. Some showed me their underground fortresses. One could reproach them for many things, but they certainly had courage! Many paid monthly "dues" to the FLN as a kind of preemptive ransom, an insurance of survival. But they drew a veil of silence over these payments to the enemy.

Insecurity and strangeness combined to weigh on the teachers from metropolitan France who were sent to country schools. On one of my rounds of visits, I spent the night with two such teachers in a fortified village south of Medea. They did not know the Arab customs or religious habits. They were not welcomed by the Europeans round about. They were up against the teaching problems of beginners, with children whose mother tongue was Arabic. The school building, including their apartment, was at the junction of two small ravines. Almost every night they heard bullets whistling over their roof, as if each valley were firing on the other. I did not sleep very well that night, thinking of the life of these young women. I had known teachers who complained of the loneliness of their first jobs in the Lozère. What would they have done here?

One night, back in Blida, the loudspeaker blared, in French and Arabic: "Curfew from noon until six o'clock."

The next day my *fatma*, Madame A, told me how the Arab families had had to pass buckets of water from roof to roof, since they had no running water in the Arab quarter. But Fatirah, who had her mother's intelligence and a schoolgirl's assurance, got two French soldiers who were passing the door to go with her to the fountain and back. When she arrived with two pails of water, nobody thought of scolding her for her rashness!

A Cup of Cold Water

One July morning, just before I left on vacation, I saw an especially large number of soldiers in my neighborhood, in combat uniform. Toward noon, when my housekeeper had gone her way into the Arab city, I realized that a big military van had stopped across from the gate of the church. Soldiers were pushing into it several Muslims, clearly under arrest —"suspects" who were to join others in overcrowded detention camps. The arrested men were standing in the sun, which was burning hot at that hour. What had they done? Probably they would keep silence under torture.

I came out of my garden, looking for an officer. I had to find him by intuition because the stripes were hidden by the combat uniforms. "Excuse me, sir!" and I introduced myself.

"Ah, Madame the pastor! I have not yet had time to come to greet you, nor come to service. Lieutenant V."

"These arrested men," I said, "know that this building is a place of Christian worship. I cannot accept the fact that the picture of the church and the cross above it should be linked with their arrest. You will let me bring them something to drink, as Christ asks us to do? It is only a small gesture. But it can be a sign to them, in their unhappiness, of all the spiritual realities in which we believe."

The lieutenant could not refuse. In a basket, I quickly fetched from my house cold milk, hot coffee, glasses, and sugar. The detainees looked at me, a little surprised. A man about thirty, in a white shirt, handed me back the basket with all my china piled up neatly. I shall never forget the tone in which another said, looking at me squarely with his big, lively black eyes, "Merci, Madame, merci!"

Should I Continue?

In the French Reformed Church a pastor is not imposed on a parish against its will, nor the reverse. It had been clearly understood at the outset that my first year was a trial year. The presbyterial council of Blida unanimously asked me to continue. I noted on the negative side that the little communities had not been as accepting as I had been promised. I wondered if the unity which did exist might be rooted in the isolation of a minority. I felt that our unity was already fissured by the unfolding of the present conflict. Yet the geographical spread of the parish, the unforeseeable events, and the new undertakings actually gave me more scope for initiative and more freedom than a typical parish in metropolitan France. I gave an affirmative answer to the request of the presbyterial council and the friendly persuasions of Pastor Chatoney.

Too Much Prudence

It had struck me at once that in Blida, this subprefecture of Algeria, the signs of intellectual life were almost nonexistent. While I observed among the Arabs a real thirst for knowledge, I saw the Europeans losing all curiosity about anything except their own future and that of Algeria. I had proposed to the presbyterial council that, in the tradition of the Calvinist church, we might present lectures on various subjects in a neutral setting. We took advantage of distinguished visitors and offered "Christianity and Marxism," "An Expedition in the Himalayas," "The Reformation and

Christian Unity"—to steadily diminishing audiences, dwindling as their own ideological and political conflicts became more obsessive.

Our regional church paper, *L'Algérie Protestante*, received instructions from the regional synod "to be circumspect about articles which might affront or divide its readers." Thus we lived out the tragedies of Algeria closed in upon ourselves. We carried pastoral prudence to the point of cowardice. I sometimes had the impression that we were living among sick people whom we had to treat in gingerly fashion. Looking back, I was sadly aware of a lack of the prophetic spirit among the Protestant churches during our time of torment.

An Extraordinary Pastoral Visit— the Relocation Camps

But during my long sleepless night on the eve of Independence Day, I remembered signs of the solidarity of the Church Universal. Early in January 1960 we had been helped by the visit of three outstanding leaders of our churches: Pastor Marc Boegner, who had followed my career from the beginning, gauging the temperature of the National Synod in relation to women in the pastorate; Pastor Charles Westphal, who had preached my ordination sermon; and, from Alsace-Lorraine, Pastor Étienne Jung, leader of the Lutheran Church of the Augsburg Confession.

For the Europeans, harried by their anxiety for the future, Pastor Jung brought the assurance of the concern of his constituents. Pastor Westphal, speaking quietly as though imparting a secret, dwelt on the things he believed most essential in a time like this: "To offer ourselves humbly to that which inspires us." But the principal purpose of the visit was to make contacts on behalf of CIMADE. Seasoned by its experiences in World War II, CIMADE was continuing its compassionate ministry to "refugees," even when they were still in their own countries. Thus Algeria's relocation camps drew the sympathy and interest of CIMADE, and these three leaders of the French churches came to establish contact with civilian and military leaders, including the Army Medical Corps.

These camps, not to be confused with detention centers for political prisoners, were designed to offer protective custody to "fellahin," or peasants, whose normal ways had been disrupted by FLN raids. The guerrillas, often natives of a given village, would come back to recruit "volunteers" and to spread propaganda among the villagers, confiscating money and food. To resist them was to sign one's death warrant. Over a million Muslims, or 12.5 percent of the non-European population of Algeria, had taken refuge in such relocation camps. Beginning in May, Pastor Boegner, as usual in concert with his Catholic counterpart, had launched a joint appeal, so that the distress of these evacuated populations might be known and relieved.

Once the delegation of three arrived on the spot in Algeria, Pastor Boegner asked me to guide them. We went first to the camp at Sidi-Nahman, near my second post, Medea. The distinguished visitors had been invited to lunch at the officers' mess, normally off limits to women. The general had given a special dispensation for me; at Pastor Boegner's request, an officer's wife was also included. Afterward this young woman thanked me for letting her see her husband's place of work. She had not known about woman pastors and "thought it was a nice idea."

The officers, still shaken by their captain's recent "death in action," responded to Pastor Boegner's fatherly friendliness. When, at the close of the meal, he rose to speak, I believe that Christ's message was heard. The camp officers, themselves isolated in the sorry loneliness of this Algerian plateau, were guarding and protecting other uprooted people.

The fellahin, snatched from the little plots of land where

they and their animals had cultivated the soil with tools three centuries out of date, were now crowded, 3,000 to 3,500 strong, into the relocation camp. Their tents and cheap block houses were clustered around the fortified headquarters like a medieval village at the foot of its castle. These were the little people, always the victims of wars and revolutions, those who cannot read or write and need others to tell of their distress. There were few young men or women in evidence, but many old men with ashen faces and plenty of children of all ages, running or looking at us with quizzical expressions.

We went to a school, just recently opened in a huge green military tent, Pastor Boegner stooping his tall frame to get under the door lintel. All the children stood up. "Sit down, my children," said the pastor, shaking hands with the teacher, who had a rifle leaning against the shaky table which served as a desk. "What were you in civilian life?" the visitor asked. "I installed central heating," was the reply. (What a picture, in this setting: comfortable houses with radiators!) Pastor Boegner encouraged the soldier with a few words on the importance of education and then spoke simply to the children.

Pastor Boegner wanted to meet Commandant G of the Army Medical Corps, a specialist in respiratory diseases. He worshiped at our branch church in Medea, and his presence, with his great height and attentive look, spread a beneficent force. It was said that he would go all alone into the villages and the poorest Arab houses, to heal. No other French doctor had gone where he went.

After their conversation, Pastor Boegner wanted to visit one of Dr. G's patients. He went down a slippery ramp to a sort of cellar. God alone knows what passed between the Muslim patient and the Christian pastor. The dying sometimes have remarkable intuitions. I hoped that the presence of the "great Christian holy man" might have been for the Arab a sign bringing God's love, peace, and hope.

The CIMADE "Presence"

With his intimate knowledge of the health needs of the villagers, particularly the children, who were prime targets for tuberculosis, Dr. G proposed that CIMADE establish a fresh air station for preventive care. In the spring of 1960 a one-story building of concrete and wood was finished near Medea, with some help from young work campers. Dr. G decided on the admissions. The normal quota, soon exceeded by emergency cases, was fifty children. They had two months of this healthy community life. Then their turn was up and others took their places. They would come at eight thirty, join in play groups on the lawn—later enriched by some literacy training—have a nourishing meal and a nap, and go home before curfew. Soon the mothers wanted to stay in the friendly ambiance of the center, and the resourceful director, Mireille Derez, introduced a program for them. Older brothers and sisters were corraled in adolescent groups, so that it became a multipurpose center. On my frequent visits I felt that European-Algerian hostility was mercifully absent between the Arab kitchen workers and myself. No doubt their friendliness was enhanced by the increasing responsibility which Mireille and the other CIMADE team members were giving to their carefully selected co-workers.

CIMADE maintained another "presence" in a large middle- to lower-income apartment house. In this concrete building, the Arab families were forced into a life-style quite alien to their native villages. This was a community of women and children, living in suspense because their men were in the guerrilla armies. The CIMADE team, Marcelle and Claire, bought wool in the form of fleece and trained the Arab women in spinning, dyeing, and weaving on home looms. Hereditary skills came out of hiding and inborn creativity was released. In all the coming and going, women poured out their griefs, got help in filling out papers, and found comradeship with other Arabs and with the team workers. Their artistic products were sold in Algeria as far as possible, to avoid shipping costs, but also in France, giving the women cash, a scarce item.

As a former CIMADE worker and as a Frenchwoman still feeling myself "in a strange land," I tried to offer the team members hospitality, comradeship in Christ, and practical help—such as a small kerosene stove for a worker in a trailer. Their visits always brought me a great deal. In particular, they gave me other perspectives on the Arab world, in the midst of which they were living more closely than I could.

I went to spend Christmas Eve with Claire and Marcelle in their workshop apartment on the top floor of the concrete apartment house. We had a quiet evening as Europeans, separated by thin partitions—and by our different faiths —from our Arab neighbors. We were guests, possible hostages, coming to them in the name of Christ and yet cut off from them. In the morning service at Blida, in the bright sanctuary, and in the evening shadows at Medea, I had reread Luke 2:10: "Behold, I bring you good news of a great joy which will come to all the people." But I could not make this news known to the Arabs and share with them my joy and my hope. In the present circumstances, only gestures and acts could bring this message. Was this the silent time for the church in Algeria?

9

The Deepening Rift

As THE POLITICAL PRESSURES MOUNTED, I was intent on keeping the freedom of the pulpit. My first Armistice Day celebration in Algeria, on November 11, 1958, brought together a large congregation, mostly of soldiers, some assigned, others coming of their own free will. I had chosen for my text Isaiah 32:17: "And the effect of righteousness will be peace, and the result of righteousness, quietness and trust for ever." The expressions of their faces and the quality of the silence gave me the impression that my preaching was not rejected.

We had quite a contrary experience at a meeting of our consistorial church (a subdivision of the region, grouping the churches in Algiers with the two communities which I served). We arranged a gathering for May 1959 at which Monsieur R. Pujol, the newly arrived secretary general for the prefecture of Medea, would give the keynote address, which was to be followed by discussion. (It turned out that he had been a boy scout leader in the Cévennes and remembered happily our meeting there.) He qualified himself as "a Christian engaged in public action." His carefully prepared message was that if, among Protestants living in Algeria, we lack the courage to speak truth to each other in a spirit of mutual understanding, we are admitting that there is no church and, a fortiori, that there is no chance of agreement among French men and women of good will. But no dialogue was possible. We dispersed without having experienced a communion of faith transcending our differences. When the secretary general left, stating that the Chiffa road would soon be closed, it seemed to me that I could guess a movement of sympathy toward him on the part of some of the delegates. They must have said to themselves that this man, in order to show the unity of the church, had been willing to go through the Chiffa gorges, which we all knew were dangerous. The light of a May afternoon revealed the whole plain as far as the Saharan Atlas mountains. But the splendor of the creation could not dispel my sadness, that which we experience after a defeat.

At the Time of the Putsch (April 22, 1961)

I had tried to understand the state of mind of the members of our Protestant communities. I had tried to explain to myself their blindness, attributing it to the weight of habit, the lack of information, and the absence of spiritual links with Protestants in France and in the rest of the world. Since the last quarter of 1960 I had felt an added element, an unconcealed hatred for the government and more specifically for the person of General de Gaulle, the chief of state, and for his representatives. I saw this hatred grow like a tide, until it lapped at the very souls of those who considered themselves Christians in the face of Islam. This hatred slipped out unconsciously: "If only I could find some way of killing General de Gaulle!" Since he was following his Algerian policy, looking toward self-determination,[1] these people felt that eliminating him would be justified as a measure of public safety.

Live in the midst of dangers—yes, I could do that; but live in the midst of hate, no. That was not possible for me. I thought particularly of the young people for whose religious education I was responsible. What defense could we offer them against the climate of hate? Boys were asking for paratroop uniforms as Christmas presents and were fascinated by noisy fighting. Scouting, weekend camps, which had given so many of us a training that stamped and oriented much of our lives—these were impossible under the circumstances.

With the consent of the parents, I did manage an overnight retreat at the parsonage for those who were finishing their two-year confirmation training. This kind of encounter was something new to these young people. Coming in from the garden on Saturday evening, they set the table for the lunch they were giving the next day, after their first communion, for their parents. Many would be coming from a distance. Was I wrong in thinking that the joy of this service was a victory over hate, and that the young people had helped their parents? Children bother older people; that we know full well. There was even a small child who upset the whole world by being born in Bethlehem and whom we are still talking about! Had the soldiers, the chiefs, the leaders who wanted to keep Algeria French felt the eyes of the children upon them? Had they felt the serious looks of these young people who would someday contest their ideology and accuse the Algerian Christians of failing to ask the true questions?

It was a rude shock to hear over Radio Algiers on Saturday, April 22, 1961, the sound of martial music, then General Challe's proclamation: "I am in Algiers with Generals Zeller and Jouhaud to fulfill our oath, the army's oath to keep Algeria French!"

Algiers, the principal city, was invested by troops commanded by generals who were opposed to the legitimate government in Paris. They began to install prefects and subprefects who were sympathetic, hoping to carry out their coup and land firmly in the saddle. While there were many Protestants who sympathized with the purposes of the coup, many of the prefects and subprefects designated for dismissal were among the thirteen Protestant administrators whom General de Gaulle had chosen. The president had learned that the so-called "Protestant rigidity" had no room for compromises and ambiguities and led to courageous stands in perilous times. Of the thirteen, two in particular were friends and parishioners: Monsieur Pujol, already mentioned, and Monsieur Bosc, subprefect of Blida.

On the day of the putsch, Monsieur Pujol of Medea was visiting the Boscs, and I joined them for a quiet and refreshing hour. Madame Bosc had a plan for taking shelter with a friend but suggested that I guard their treasured family album. I answered that since my ideas were opposed to those of the putschists, the parsonage might be the object of a house search. Monsieur Pujol heartened us by saying that our coming together thus, in full trust, reminded him of the resistance movement in France twenty years before.

There was a reverent spirit at worship the following day, except that the young people slipped out before the sermon. "You can't understand," they told me. "We had to join the others"—presumably those excited by the putsch. "We could not listen!" My sermon was on the text in Matthew 10:28: "Do not fear those who kill the body but cannot kill the soul; rather fear him who can destroy both soul and body."

I saw that after church everyone was talking excitedly in the courtyard. There was a news blackout, and we had to rely on the old word-of-mouth method. A great deal hinged on the air squadron posted at Blida. I had heard contradictory things about it on Saturday.

After church on that Sunday several members of the presbyterial council came to dinner at my house, including a noncommissioned officer and his commander. At other times the lower officer had been quite ill at ease in the presence of his superior, though they were equals on the council. But on this occasion he was completely self-assured. He told us that the air base would have no part in a politico-military operation in metropolitan France, as it had been rumored.[2]

Simply, but not without pride, the subaltern detailed a second point: When the colonel in charge of the air base hesitated too long in choosing sides, the noncommissioned officers had put him under obligation to remain faithful to the legitimate government in France. Given the importance of the Blida air base, it was reassuring to know that our paratroops were *not* going to leave to invest Paris! Was there a fascist coup d'état brewing in France? We did not know. But around my table we had broken the bread of friendship and shared the certainty that "God is the solid rock" when the powers of this world are tottering.

During Sunday dinner our thoughts often turned to Monsieur Bosc, our subprefect. On Saturday he had tried to make contact with the lieutenant colonel in command of the "Red Berets," the principal unit involved in the putsch, in order to determine his status. On Monday he renewed his approach to the military officer, who came to call at the subprefecture. The Red Beret officer, somewhat embarrassed, tried to pass it off as a courtesy call on the occasion of his taking over the sector, aimed at keeping good relations between the military and civilian authorities. The subprefect took the occasion to make it clear that he represented the legal government and could not countenance or lend a hand to an insurrectional situation imposed by force. He then closed the prefecture until further notice, except in cases of emergency.

At the end of that same Monday morning Monsieur Bosc went home, only to see his garden overrun by Red Berets, machine guns in hand, under the command of a captain who seemed ill at ease. Monsieur Bosc gave himself up and was spirited to the air base at Zéralda, which had served as the launching pad of the putsch. His fellow prisoners were a score of private soldiers who had refused to follow the generals in their takeover and remained loyal to the de Gaulle government. The guards were members of the Foreign Legion, which was composed, in large part, of men who were happy to have police records expunged in return for their enlistments. I learned later from Monsieur Bosc himself that the Legionnaires remained glued to their transistors and appeared to be wavering in their support of the putschists. Some, realizing Monsieur Bosc's rank and quality, offered to help him escape, an offer he brushed aside. The officers who commanded the guards became aware of this rift within their movement and transferred the prisoners to another air base. Monsieur Bosc, long schooled in dealing with the public, perceived the hostility of the Europeans who watched his convoy from village sidewalks. Clearly, the putschists had the sympathy of a great many of the colonists! Among them, not to my great surprise, were friends and parishioners.

On the Monday following the putsch, I was in Medea as the guest of a couple who said, "This is the most beautiful day of our lives!"

After lunch I asked "What do you expect of the putsch?"

The husband and wife answered in chorus: "Why, that Algeria should remain French!"

I had then added, "I don't believe this is the best way."

I think my hosts and I must, each in turn, have been looking for some explanation of what we thought of as the blindness of the other. I believe that we were able to maintain our mutual affection and our communion in essential things. Because I was a pastor, I was constrained to be neither sectarian nor partisan. My Christian faith led me to meet all people lovingly and with understanding. I was obligated to be on guard against making a political party or a strategy into an idol or an absolute. I was under the necessity of discerning the mistakes and the lacks and of recognizing what good there might be in those whom I judged to be in error. That was, for me, the only way to hang on to a certain idea of humankind, with its grandeur and its misery, the humanity whose face Christ has discovered to us.

Back in Blida, I learned that the putschists had found and

installed a complaisant junior civil servant, Monsieur J, in place of the legitimate subprefect. Monsieur J was also a Protestant, but inactive. On Tuesday when I went to the subprefecture to ask for a pass to visit Monsieur Bosc, I found a strange situation. (I knew my chaplain's pass for the civilian prison would not be honored at the putschist air base.) The door was wide open. The staff, usually at work behind their desks, stood with their arms folded. When I asked to see Monsieur J, an employee said, in a hostile voice, "He's not in." When I asked whether I might see him later in the day, I was told, "He won't be in the rest of the day!" As I turned on my heel to go out, the chauffeur caught up with me to give me news of Monsieur Bosc, and a secretary whispered, "I was in the Resistance during the war—here is my card! I'm a Gaullist, the only one here; it's frightful!" The chauffeur then added, "The puppet subprefect has been taken away also." I asked the chauffeur and the secretary to come to the manse for coffee after the office closed, so that we could talk quietly.

Then the story unfolded: One or two military vehicles had stopped in front of the subprefecture, and a handful of air corps soldiers had sprung out. They shouldered aside the policeman at the entrance and forced their way into Monsieur J's office, whisking him away before anyone realized what was happening. He was taken into custody at the Blida air force base. I tried to comfort the two functionaries. The chauffeur had nothing to lose and could hope for the return of the true subprefect. The secretary was so upset that I offered to take her the next morning to a regional headquarters for better information.

In point of fact, on that Tuesday evening we had no civilian administration in the district of Algiers. Soldiers made the law, but which soldiers? I would ordinarily have gazed into the depth of the night sky on that spring evening. The beauty of creation had so often helped me to find once more the true dimensions of things. But I had my eyes fixed on the dial of my transistor, going from the stations in metropolitan France to those in Algiers.

I learned that the situation was evolving more swiftly than I had dared to hope. On Radio Algiers I heard still one last appeal, pronounced in a young voice, vibrant with passion: "Get to the Forum at once!" Then, after one of those scratchy records, so often played over the last four days, another voice picked up: "This is France Five . . . we are resuming our broadcasts." We had found France again! I could sink into sleep, lost during the putsch.

The recapture of the radio station by the Gaullists signaled the end of the putsch and, at certain levels, a rapid return to normal. At the air base where Monsieur Bosc and his fellow prisoners had been sent for safekeeping, a captain woke the prisoners at three on Wednesday morning, announcing, "The war is over! You won! We'll take you back to Algiers." As they went along the coastal route before dawn on this superb spring night, they met units of the First Foreign Parachutists, their revolution quashed, returning to their base. Monsieur Bosc found his wife and daughter and resumed his duties. But I had to think of the other detainees who had become such as a result of the overturn. The one Protestant I could readily identify was Monsieur J, subprefect for a day.

"I Was in Prison"

The subprefecture, functioning normally again, quickly gave me permission to visit the military camp where Monsieur J was detained. But the colonel in charge of the internment camp, himself just back from imprisonment at the hands of the putschists, asked many questions before he finally gave me the necessary permission. An unknown voice over the telephone asked for my car's license number. A sentry, reading the number, raised the barrier and told me where to park. A soldier led me down the central alley between military barracks occupied by Arab prisoners, who looked at me in astonishment. I thought I was at Gurs again, except that the distant mountains were the Atlas range, not the Pyrénées. The soldier snapped me out of my reflections, saying, "This is a sad state of affairs—arresting good Frenchmen as you would Arabs!"

I told him a bit dryly that I was surprised to hear him talk like that and went on to explain that I was not a relative of the detainee but came to visit him in the name of Jesus Christ and of his church. I quoted Jesus' words in the parable of the last judgment: "I was hungry and you gave me food . . . I was in prison and you came to me [Matt. 25:35-36]."

Monsieur J, the prisoner, was surprised and glad to see me. He drew up two gray metal taborets in a corner of the barracks and put his blanket on mine as a cushion. No sooner had we begun to talk than he excused himself and rushed out to talk with another prisoner, an Arab much older than himself. I saw the two men embrace and begin to talk in Arabic, with many gestures. At one point, both lifted their arms above their heads. The Arab, who had been in the camp first (probably for FLN activity), shared with the putschist a common love of the land, though they were defending their country by opposite means. Now they were behind the same barbed wire!

When "my" prisoner had come back and we had resumed our conversation, I asked, "If I am not indiscreet, what were you and your Arab friend saying to each other?"

"God is great!" he answered.

What an extraordinary confession of faith, common to a Christian and a Muslim, in this barren and distressing place! Here were material discomfort, promiscuous detention, and the smell of human misery—yet under God's sky. Leaving Monsieur J, I said, "Yes, God is great, but the most remarkable thing is that—as Christ has taught us—this great God loves us!"

The Time of Despair

The abortive putsch did not put an end to our troubles. On the contrary: The Europeans in Algeria, normally grateful to the army for protection against terrorists, now showed resentment against the soldiers who had remained loyal to de Gaulle—resentment evidenced in various ways. A fine-looking airman from Alsace told me that the daughters of colonials would not dance with him. I told him to forget it and turn to Alsatian girls, who had good sense and knew how to tease and laugh!

The July 14 parade usually drew great crowds, but in the summer after the putsch—1961, the last under French rule—the soldiers marched past empty sidewalks under the darting sun. This "sit-down strike" by the population was a minor token of last-ditch resistance against the Gaullist policy. The intransigence of Europeans in Algeria was a hindrance but not a fatal impediment to the negotiations in Évian, which were to conclude in the spring of 1962.

While I was in France on vacation in August of 1961, the Secret Army Organization (OAS) blacked out the regular television station in Algiers, announcing, "French Radio Algeria has decided today to interrupt the Gaullist broadcasts." The unknown voice continued, "In spite of the defeat of the putsch, the fight goes on!"

A certain number of Europeans had not returned from their vacations. They had left quietly. I learned that those who returned to Algeria were urged, by letter or by personal contact, to make donations to the OAS. Backed up by threats, the quotas were stiff (especially in comparison with voluntary contributions to the church). I saw a woman like an old-style charity collector leaving the house of a poor parishioner. The latter told me, "I'm sick and I'm not rich. I could only give her five francs. We have to do something for a French Algeria!" Somehow the OAS never asked me to give anything. Why?

Thanks to some friends, I had come to know a Kabyle family, Muslim in faith, the T's. The father had enough education to enable him to work in an office job. The mother, still veiled, was intelligent. Wanting her girls to have the independence which education can bring, she sent them to school in the city. Their apartment was furnished mostly in European style, but with woven wool hangings to recall the native Kabyle art.

The pride of the family was their twelve-year-old boy. Riding his bicycle around the block, he had fallen and broken his arm. I went to see him in the hospital and found him sitting up in bed, reading a travel story. His mother, at his bedside, told me that the fracture was not severe and that he would be home the next day with a cast on his arm.

The next day I had a phone call from the father. "Mlle. Schmidt, my son is dead. A nurse gave him an injection, and then he acted strangely and afterward he died! Go see my wife, you will do her good. The funeral is at four o'clock." I went to see Monsieur and Madame T before the time of the Muslim service. When I went in to their apartment I found many relatives, whom I recognized. They stepped aside to leave me alone for a time with the mother. Her silent and majestic despair was more moving to me than all the cries and gestures with which I have seen Arab women express their grief.

The father, in another room, seemed to me less resigned. In his look I read the desire to keep control of himself. He was also eager to show confidence and friendship toward me, the only European present. On a previous occasion, after I had said the grace at a dinner where we were guests of a common friend, Monsieur T had broken the long silence by saying, "Brotherhood is beautiful!" Had he perhaps discovered that we must go through God to recognize each other as true brothers in spite of all barriers? Among the friends and relatives, as well as the parents of the twelve-year-old whom we mourned, there was an acceptance of their grief which seemed to me quite different from Muslim fatalism as we Westerners imagine it. I would have liked to read them the Lamentations of Jeremiah or the words Job addressed to God, for in this sadness the greatness of God was present.

After the service and the boy's burial in the Muslim cemetery, with its simple tombstones, the inevitable questions arose. Who killed that boy, so full of life? In normal times, the parents would have ordered an inquest, but in such a climate it was impossible. No one would ever know who had ordered that injection. While my *fatma* attempted to restore me by her sovereign remedy—a cup of coffee—I remembered a conversation with a nurse, the daughter of one of the large plantation owners, at their pleasant country house. I had said to her, "In the midst of all the distresses of this hour, nothing has changed for you! You are still taking care of the sick and the wounded and comforting them." She surprised me by answering, "Not all the sick people! I don't like to take care of Muslims. They deserve death! They have done us so much harm!"

I had been saddened and surprised to hear such words from the lips of a young woman brought up in a cultured family, which had given her a Protestant training. I reminded her of the principles of the Red Cross as well as the teachings of the gospel, but I was up against a stone wall; I left with the sadness of the defeated. The propaganda of hatred had prevailed in the mind of this young person, and of how many others? What could reawaken in this young generation that which makes the true nobility of humankind?

Beyond their terrorist attacks on individuals, the OAS bombed buildings. The graffiti blared out on the walls: "The OAS strikes *where* it will, *when* it will, and *whom* it will!" It was civil war, Frenchmen against Frenchmen, for there were still some liberals who were loyal to the constituted authorities.

The FLN, meanwhile, held the natural desire for reprisals under a tight rein. This countered the OAS strategy, which was to provoke the Algerians to commit atrocities which would stall the delicate negotiations in progress at Évian. Undeterred, both before and even after the Évian agreements were signed on March 19, 1962, the OAS played on the conservatism of the big property holders, using their conscious or unconscious racism and their fear reflexes to nourish an insane hope. Discussion became, for all intents and purposes, impossible. It was pitiful and tragic to see men and women who had been intelligent, able to take initiative, close themselves into intransigent positions.

When Preaching Is "Unacceptable"

At Christmastime in 1961 I sent a written message to all the Protestants in the parish and to several other friends. I reminded them of the worship services rebroadcast by Radio Algeria. It seemed to me that the Christmas congregations, visibly diminished by departures, were looking for the light of Christ in the midst of their sufferings and their uncertainties. I urged them to "discover the abasement of Christ from the crèche to the cross."

The spring of 1962 brought new disruptions even as the delicate negotiations at Évian were drawing to a conclusion. General Salan ordered "total mobilization" (even though the army was in place). Mail was censored by OAS sympathizers. Travel to France was cut off—not a boat sailed, not a loading crane operated, much less an airplane.

I was not the only pastor who wondered how and what to preach under these circumstances. Several of us addressed a letter to our newly arrived regional president, Pastor Max-Alain Chevallier.[3] We felt that he was bearing with us, and even more than we were, the tragedy of "sad Algeria." We asked simply, "What should we be preaching in these days and when the cease-fire is proclaimed?"

His response was, "All human exhortation, even if it is only repeating the Word of God, is inadequate, ambiguous, and unacceptable. We are now at the time for the confession of faith and at the time of prayer!" I could understand how Christian preaching might be unacceptable to non-Christians who saw Christians committing violence to defend a so-called "Christian civilization." But that church members should find the call to repentance unacceptable? The preaching of the cross unacceptable? Trust in God on unknown ways, unacceptable? Where in the world were we?

I knew that beginning in April 1956 the Reformed Church in Algeria, ahead of most other parties, movements, or journals, had protested against the practice of torture. In 1957 the Synod of the French Reformed Church in Algeria had called on its member churches and church members "to recognize their share of responsibility for the present war, and, remembering that the future belongs to Jesus Christ, to consider it their Christian vocation to work for reconciliation between Muslims and Europeans."

In 1959 the French Reformed Church in France had called for an end to the war in Algeria. But the French Reformed Church in Algeria did not see reality from the same angle and refused to put the same question to itself. This may explain in part the disarray lived through by the people of our churches during the spring of 1962.

Little by little I guessed that my advice and my preaching were being rejected because I had been accused of "agreeing with those who are selling Algeria down the river." I knew that—alas—it was the same in the Catholic communities. They had the advantage or disadvantage, depending on your viewpoint, of having a majority of priests who had been born in Algeria. At the time of a funeral service I had talked with a Catholic woman who wanted to tell me about her experience the previous Sunday. The parish priest had read a pastoral letter from Monsignor Duval, archbishop of Algiers. With an evangelical concern for peace between the two communities, he had recalled the dignity of every man and woman and the duty of justice. The Europeans had nicknamed him "Muhammad Duval." When the letter was read, many in the congregation had begun to cough, blow their noses loudly, and scrape their chairs. My informant "was completely upset by it all!" I had wished that she could see the gospel message in Monsignor Duval's, but I was willing to settle for endorsing her resolve to obey her ecclesiastical superior.

After the Évian Agreements

Who would have dreamed of a cease-fire in Algeria? I had imagined that it would bring a great sense of relief, that we could on that day go about in complete security, meet each other without fear, without suspicion. I had dreamed that trust between the two communities could be built on new bases. Alas, March 19 did not allow us either to dream or really to rejoice. The OAS immediately called a twenty-four hour general strike, ordering that "doors, windows, and shutters should remain closed, and that no one should be in the streets." I was completely unwilling to keep this quarantine. My shutters stayed open all day, and I went out to see what I could see, walking down the middle of rue Lamy to the post office—though I knew that no letters would go out. My footsteps echoed from the buildings. Soldiers with submachine guns were posted every sixty feet to protect French or Arabs from attacks by the OAS. Only one car was on the streets. It was driven by Madame Boulle, directress of the lycée. We greeted each other in the dead city much as we greet our fellow countrymen in a foreign land.

Some days before the Easter vacation there had been demonstrations at the boys' lycée in Blida; the students, following several ringleaders, wanted in their turn to protest the Évian agreements. Next, it was the girls' turn. I heard singing from early morning on, girls' voices singing the "Marseillaise" at the top of their lungs. Depending on the wind or the street noises, the sound came to me in successive waves.

"That comes from the girls' school," my *fatma* told me. "Fatirah did not go today." She said nothing more. I closed the windows and tried not to hear.

At noon I saw Mlle. H, the literature teacher, arriving. She looked pale, her clothing a bit rumpled. As soon as she came into my study she sank into an armchair saying, "That was frightful! I was more scared than at Ravensbrück, the women's concentration camp in Germany!"

Mlle. H had been arrested by the Gestapo in Paris when she was twenty. Since her arrival in Blida she had been a frequent guest at my house. Her experience as a deportee had drawn my sympathy and special care. Remembering her own experience as a prisoner, she had asked for and received permission to give courses to Algerians who were held in Paris. She then volunteered for a teaching post in Algeria. Did her pupils in the lycée know her previous activities?

Wiping her face with an angry gesture and straightening her hair, she explained to me the reason for her state. The boarders at the lycée had begun their rebellion at breakfast, shouting the "Marseillaise." Madame Boule, the headmistress, confronted them. "You don't need to teach *me* the 'Marseillaise'! I come from Strasbourg, where it was first sung." The day students, joining the boarders, had refused to go to their classrooms. All the European girls, sticking together, had stayed in the big courtyard while the Arab and Kabyle girls, just a handful, gathered in another corner of the courtyard. The teachers, arriving for their courses, joined the European girls—except Mlle. H, who went to the group of Arab and Kabyle students. The headmistress had telephoned the parents to ask them to fetch their girls. Most of the parents said, "It does them good. It lets them unwind!"—an expression often used to explain and excuse excesses.

Mlle. H continued her explanation: "Yes, of course the police were there, but they didn't come in, since the headmistress had not called them. Some leading citizens had looked in at the door and then moved on, unable to help. Some Arab parents had also arrived, hiding knives under their blouses."

"Was there a fight, and was anyone hurt?" I asked.

"No," she answered, "but there was danger of it. The day students had Molotov cocktails in their briefcases—or so they boasted—made by their brothers and their friends." After this long morning the European girls, far from "unwound" but working themselves up into hysterical excitement, had mobbed Mlle. H and spat on her. The police had wanted to protect her, but she waved them off. There were no Molotov cocktails thrown.

I persuaded Mlle. H to stay with me for two nights, fearing that she might not be safe on the street. When she returned to her apartment, Arabs in native and European dress gave her a military salute, with great respect. Was this because the story of her courage recalled to them the statues of Joan of Arc as a warrior?

A few days later, at the Good Friday services, when I read "they spat upon him . . . [Matt. 27:30]," I thought I saw her shudder. After the same service a parishioner came to me saying, "This is truly a Good Friday! General Salan has been arrested."

Reassured about Mlle. H, I still wondered about the way in which the Arab and Kabyle girls had been protected. I learned the answer directly from Madame Boulle, whom I had invited to tea to meet Suzanne de Dietrich, my former leader in the World's Student Christian Federation group in Paris. I surmised that Madame Boulle might be the only other person in Blida who had read Mlle. de Dietrich's books. As she knows so well how to do, Mlle. de Dietrich listened to the story of the demonstration and showed particular interest in the safety of the Arab and Kabyle girls.

The director of the social service department of the FLN rang the doorbell of the headmistress' house, offering his services to take the boarding girls from Arab and Kabyle families back to their homes. He had a number of buses ready to leave at once. Madame Boulle accepted the offer on the spot, knowing that the student demonstration might lead to something worse at any moment. She laid down one condition: that the parents should telegraph her as soon as their girls were safely home. The promise was faithfully kept, and every girl's parents, without exception, wired the headmistress as the buses delivered the girls.

Madame Boule had not been gone fifteen minutes when a terrible explosion shook my windowpanes. The telephone rang and the anguished voice of the headmistress told me that the treasury building had been plastic-bombed and she was afraid that the fire might spread to part of her school nearby.

Suzanne de Dietrich said, "But that's crazy, to call us instead of the fire department!"

I explained to her that everybody who was supposed to respond would have heard the explosion. "They will let it burn until the records are destroyed. The OAS have accomplices everywhere, and once more the culprits will not be found."

After a long silence, Suzanne de Dietrich said, slowly and gravely, "I had thought of the physical dangers of grenades and machine guns. But I had not imagined that you were living in such moral tension here."

"Yes," I said, "Here we're descending into hell."

As soon as it was possible, I went to survey the damage. Mingling with the little group in front of the treasury, held back by the police, I saw that one whole floor had been wiped out by the force of the explosion—the floor where income tax declarations had been stored. The roof and the rest of the building had settled on what was left of the bombed portion. Everybody was giving his or her commentary, with never a word of regret or condemnation. As I was leaving I heard a European, properly dressed, saying in a loud voice, "That's neat work, that!"

What happened in Blida was repeated elsewhere. In

Algiers, French people, supposedly the guardians of civilization and culture, set fire to the public library, destroying priceless manuscripts. More and more of the planters left for France, their workmen now unemployed. Many people were like the fragments from a shipwreck thrown up on the beach.

In the last days before independence, the OAS leaders manipulated the dreams and fears of the credulous, including such average people as Monsieur and Madame R, who kept a store in the rue Abdallah. As I turned a corner while running an errand nearby, I saw that the glass of their storefront had been broken. Before I could express my regrets and ask if anyone had been hurt, they said, "No problem, look!" Across from their store an Arab boutique had been completely devastated by an explosion. "That's neat work, that!" they said contentedly. The expression must have been the ritual formula for self-congratulation on plastic bombings.

The husband left us to go about his work, but I detained the wife to ask about their seventeen-year-old daughter. "She is to be married and return to France, but we shall stay on until the victory."

"What victory?" I asked, but she ignored my question and ran on.

"We are very strong, you know, we have a cruiser" ("we" meaning the OAS).

I was so taken aback that I asked, "A cruiser, where?"

"Oh, it's dismantled now. We have only to put it together!"

It struck me as useless to carry on the conversation any further, and I said "Good-bye."

The woman pressed my hand and whispered to me as a secret, "Then, too, we have stolen an atomic bomb."

I was so troubled that I hurried home, forgetting my errand. For some church members there seemed to be a clear dilemma: choose the OAS or the church. They were constrained to choose by the fact that the Reformed Church in Algeria never recognized the OAS as a legitimate power, even in the cities where, for a time, it had all the instruments of power (as at Oran). Even with a meager theological training, they were aware of the opposition between the most traditional piety and the undisguised ideology of the activist commandos.

Some chose the OAS. I cannot bring their faces to mind without sadness: mature men, prisoners of a political passion, prisoners also of fear. (To quit the OAS was to become a "traitor" and draw on oneself the swift justice of those who handled guns so easily.) I am also picturing the faces of some young people—especially that of a parishioner whose confidences I had received. He had given up all participation in worship. He was on the run. But I had noticed the expression of hardness in his eyes and on his face. He must have thought of himself as virile and strong. They had fallen prey to false shepherds, those whom Christ describes as abandoning the sheep and fleeing when there is danger (John 10:12-13). What would be the future of these young people? Would the memories of this terrible period remain repressed until death or a psychoanalytical cure brought them to the surface again?

These were some of the images and reflections which kept running through my head as I lay, fully clothed, on my bed. But in the end I sank into sleep.

The light was dazzling when I woke up on the day which was to mark the nadir of the French colonial spirit in Algeria—a state no less bitter for the fact that it was the result of mistakes by my country and my church. This day was for others a zenith, as Algeria became an independent country, throwing off a mantle of fear and anxiety.

The Joy of Independence Day, Sunday, July 1, 1962

A dull roar came to my ears. Against this monotonous ground note I heard loud exclamations and calls which I could not understand. At the window I saw that the boulevard and the square were swarming with people, the men embracing each other. There were more Arab than European costumes. But it was not only the European dress that was scarce. The Europeans themselves were conspicuous by their absence. The celebration was beginning. The air was light. The day gave promise of being hot. Lighter than air was the mood of this joyous crowd.

I picked out unusual colors, like the points of an impressionist painting, in the clothing of boys and girls—red, white, and green. The children did not play among themselves. They did not run. They carried themselves with gravity, aware that they were wearing the national colors: green skirts or trousers, white blouses or shirts, red foulards or caps. There were alternative combinations, but always the red, white, and green. I forgot the words of my *fatma*, intended to reassure me that there would be no "St. Bartholomew," and concentrated on the sight before me. The idea of these children's costumes was ingenious. I thought of the preparation required to produce this kind of demonstration: giving out the cloth to poor families, and the mothers seeing to it that the costumes were made on time! I thought how much it meant to some to have their first brand-new clothes—clothes for which nobody had to say "thank you."

The idea of wearing the colors of the flag is not new. I remembered an elderly cousin of mine in Alsace who made my childhood vacations happy. She told me that during the 1914-18 war she and two friends would walk around a French prisoner-of-war camp. She would wear a white dress and the others would dress in blue and red. I remember myself choosing a dress with red, white, and blue to wear on July 14, 1941 in occupied Paris.

July 1, 1962 was a Sunday. Church time came and went and no one had come to the church. The parishioners thought of themselves as soldiers "confined to their barracks." I thought I heard a distant noise, then clapping. The children began to wave flags and seemed more excited. The roar clarified. I heard distinctly the sound of motors and horns. A motorcade, coming from the rue Lamy, went around the square and turned toward the beltway. These cars were almost all convertibles, with young people—boys and girls—standing up, banging the sides of the cars, and yelling *"Algérie yahia!"* ("Long live Algeria!") in the same rhythm, three short beats and two long. The cries of the children and the applause of the spectators added to this deafening noise.

I did not know what to think as more and more cars came on, faster and faster. Were they going round and round, as on a carousel, or were there more and more cars? No way of telling. There were cars of all makes, all colors. Where did they all come from? I remembered that Pastor Chevallier had had his car stolen a few days before. Many Europeans had fled, leaving their cars. Some had, no doubt, been commandeered.

The midday sun struck hard, 104 degrees in the shade in my garden. Would they stop for lunch or a siesta? No. The race continued with the same frenzy. Intoxicated with speed, with joy, the young people kept going by, bareheaded in the sun. Hammered by the noise and the untiring rhythm—three short, two long—I could not read theology or history or even a novel. I kept thinking, Where will it empty out, this flood of emotion? In a St. Bartholomew? Clearly not!

I preferred to think about why the organizers of this day had chosen this form of celebration. In a Muslim country it was out of the question to arrange dances as we do in our French villages for the national holiday. All adolescents in all countries dream of driving a car. They love speed. Hands on the wheel, they affirm their personal freedom. What a symbol today for the Arab young people who had watched the Europeans drive by in their cars for so long!

I thought of the education of Muslim girls and of what

their mothers must have been going through, as they watched their daughters riding by, unveiled, hair streaming in the wind. Then I concluded that the idea was rather ingenious. These young people—in little groups under the conduct of a responsible person, the chauffeur—were, so to speak, supervised and guarded by the people who were watching them. The heat did not seem to bother this crowd, which remained thick in the square and on the sidewalks.

I tried to decide whether I should go out to show the Arabs that I shared their joy. (There was no order preventing us from going out.) But I decided not to, except for some valid reason. The Arabs had no need of us Europeans for these days of celebration. (It was just the reverse of the decision I had made when the OAS ordered everyone to stay home.) I went down to answer the doorbell. It was a boy of perhaps five who had climbed up on the little wall. Before I could say a few words to him, his mother had grabbed him, without even glancing at the house or at the person who was coming. I stayed and looked at this crowd, only two or three yards away from me. Nobody was looking in my direction or at any of the other European houses. The Arabs wanted to forget. To be happy, they wanted to live in a world without Europeans.

The rhythmic shouts and the banging on the cars continued until two in the morning and resumed at dawn, when we had barely had a few hours of rest. The celebration continued all of Monday and Tuesday. As a housekeeper, I wondered how the children's red, white, and green costumes could look so fresh each day, despite the crowds, the dust, and the heat.

It seemed to me that my garden was being pounded by the waves of an immense joy, a happiness whose depths we could not fathom. I remembered July 14, 1919. I had stood on a balcony on the Champs-Élysées near the Arc de Triomphe and watched the allied troops come up the broad avenue. When the French *poilus*,[4] in their horizon blue, arrived, a spontaneous "Marseillaise" arose from the crowd, which was dense on the sidewalk and clinging to tree branches and chimneys. I was so moved that not a sound came from my throat, which was tied in knots. In spite of the differences in time, setting, and circumstance, I found in Blida in 1962 many of the same elements as in my childhood memories of July 14, 1919—a people finding once more the joy of living after the harsh trials of a long war.

On Tuesday morning, while the celebration continued, my *fatma* came in quickly to find out how I was. Without taking off her veil, standing in the doorway, she said, "Oh! but my girls are hoarse from yelling so much. Could you hear it?"

Could I!

Sensing that I had been a bit surprised at the girls, hair flowing in the breeze, speeding by in the cars, she said, "It was very well managed. They weren't in any danger." Going toward the door, she added, "I'll be back as soon as the celebration is over. This afternoon my husband and I are going to X, baths and a holy man." Madame A melted into the crowd before I could ask her questions: pilgrimage, purification, offering, prayer? These may have been part of the religious life which she and her husband were looking for. The Muslim soul is a mystery.

On Wednesday afternoon, suddenly, an unbearable silence! Over the radio we heard President Ben Khedda order everyone back to work. The power of this joy seemed to me rich in hope, whatever difficulties might follow on the morrow of independence.

I remained at Blida after the proclamation of independence. Most of the Europeans being gone, there was no longer any parish activity. While I provided all along for the Sunday worship services, I answered the request of the principal of the Algerian lycée for boys and became a teacher there during the school year 1962-63. It was an interesting experience in this first year of the Algerian Republic. But I did not want to prolong it, and I felt that I should leave Algeria in July 1963. My colleagues, who were going back to France at the same time, knew what posts would be given them, but I myself remained in uncertainty until May 31. Finally, on that day, I received a letter from the general secretary of the French Reformed Church, proposing that I go for an interim year as part of a team ministry in Nancy. He did not conceal from me the difficulties which I would find in that parish. I read between the lines that several had refused the call of the Nancy church. To be sure, the letter ended with compliments to show me that "I was certainly the one who . . ."etc. Grateful that a door was opening, I could only answer "yes" to this call.

By Way of Conclusion

The war years in Algeria forced us all—civilian and military people—to call into question the directions of our lives and the values we had been aiming for. With so much violence unleashed around us, I, too, had to reexamine my Christian assurances to answer the problems of each day in all loyalty. French culture has taught us that truth must be sought after, however painful the search. But we always had to ask, "What is true?"

What is true: Whatever "works," the lies of people, of the princes who govern, or of a press enslaved to special interests?

What is true: The pride which uses the subtle play of human vanities and trusts in force or ultimatums?

What is true: A charity without imagination or self-criticism, which accepts the established order in which the little people are exploited and despised?

What is true: The haughty assurance of those who refuse to recognize their personal errors?

How many have given in to the temptation of repeating the words of the skeptical and arriviste Roman functionary Pilate to Jesus of Nazareth: "What is truth?" How many others, knowing that the spirit of truth can lead us into all truth, have stopped along the way, frightened, then ashamed and bitter? Finally, how many, who know the Beatitudes and the One who lived them even to Golgotha, have not been able to accept the sacrifices and the deprivation which a true encounter with another would have required?

Augustine already shared with his contemporaries in the fifth century a love of life. He sang of the light and the beauty of the horizons of his native Numidia. But this great doctor of the church recalled the power of evil in the depths of the human heart and helped us find the necessary path to repentance. The church could write its story of the tragic war years in Algeria by adopting the famous title: *Confessions*. And we would all find our places there.

10

Ministry in Nancy, 1963-72

IN ALGERIA, NOBODY PAID ANY ATTENTION to the discussions about the pastoral ministry of women which had disturbed the Synods nine or ten years before in France, and which were then shaking the churches in other countries. Instead, terrorism and the growing uncertainty about the future filled people's minds. Even I myself forgot all the questions left dangling concerning the accession of women to the pastoral ministry in my church. I forgot that I remained the sole "exception" which the French Reformed Church had allowed.

Arrival and First Contacts

After the grueling years of ministry in Algeria, I took three months' rest and went to the university city of Nancy at the end of September 1963. I entered the sanctuary for the first time in my pastor's gown to take part in the ordination of Monsieur A, who, after his probationary year at Nancy, was leaving for Africa.

This church building was a former Catholic church, built by the architect Richard Mique, closed during the revolution, and given to the Protestants by Napoleon. Its classic facade, its two elegant bulbous towers, and its high vaulting —all these factors combined to make of this historic monument a place ill suited to Protestant worship. I found it a nuisance to preach under the pulpit sounding board, which was topped by a funerary urn in pure eighteenth-century style. But after a while I paid no attention to it. Happily, the presbyterial council had conceived the idea of setting up a big plain cross behind the marble altar, and the open Bible on the altar proclaimed the Reformed theology. This church possessed the most beautiful organ in the city at that time. With a third manual, they had altogether thirty-three stops.

The three pastors then at Nancy welcomed me very fraternally. It was a new experience for me to be part of a team ministry in a large parish. Pastor Franck Hervé, who was president of the presbyterial council,[1] taught me right away how the work was divided. Each pastor was responsible for a sector of the city and its environs in connection with the regular forms of ministry (calling, baptisms, funeral services, marriages, and one year of confirmation instruction). Then the pastors divided among themselves the responsibility for the different groups and chaplaincies, according to their personal gifts or the necessities of the moment.

One question had to be settled right away—that of my lodging. I understood, immediately upon my arrival, that the presbyterial council at Nancy, like the one twenty-eight years before at Sainte-Croix, did not want to sign a lease with a landlord, since I was there as an interim; in other words, on trial. The suggestion of a cousin of mine, who lived in Nancy, to house me in a new apartment in a complex she had just had built, freed the council from any immediate concern. I was very happy in this small, comfortable apartment. And the "temporary" lasted until I left for retirement.

After having seen a parish disappear, it was marvelous to come into a live community. The great spread of its members determined a diversity of interests. The descendants of the Alsatians and Lorrainers who had come in 1870 preserved from their Lutheran training the love of liturgy and music. I was surprised to find so few activists among the "little people." (Is the cold in Lorraine a factor in social conformity?) Both small tradesmen and big businessmen seemed to have a patriotic fervor which reminded me somewhat of the world of my early childhood. As for the government workers of all echelons, the students, and others of the university community, they all brought the richness of their different types of training and of their backgrounds. In the fluid situation of modern times, my responsibility was not so much to fit in to the Nancy parish as to join in the common effort of being "the Church of God in Nancy," to use Paul's expression. I had been happily surprised to find in my new parish a great variety of circles and study groups. The meetings usually took place in the evening, and the coldest nights did not stop anybody. After having spent almost thirty years in the south, I was astonished at their hardihood.

Contrary to the traditions of our church, the president of the eastern region, Pastor F, had not been in contact with me, by letter or by telephone, on my arrival. This perplexed me, and I sought an explanation for this abnormal silence. Had the general secretary of the national church perhaps prepared the way for my coming to Nancy by dealing directly with the parish, without consulting the regional president? I had to conclude that I never came into parishes by the usual way! I did not ask myself, during my first six months in Nancy, whether I was going to stay there. My previous experiences allowed me to be somewhat easy in mind on this score. By the month of March, several people had said to me something to the effect that "Lorrainers don't show their feelings very much, but you have brought us a great deal. You must stay." For my part, I saw no reason for leaving the ministry at Nancy in which I was involved, or for breaking up a collaboration with my colleagues which seemed to me friendly and enriching. The decision, however, belonged to the presbyterial council. Deliberating in my absence on March 26, 1964, the council decided unanimously to call me as a regular pastor in the Nancy parish.

One year after my arrival, at the Sunday service on October 18, 1964, I was installed as an incumbent pastor at Nancy by the president of the region. I was very much moved by the beauty of the organ and the singing of the choir. The cold of Lorraine seemed for a moment abolished at the luncheon which the presbyterial council gave on this occasion in the vast, clean, and inviting room of the renovated quarters of the Croix Bleue.[2] In a narrow street where misery could be read on every house front, where music and smells came out of the little cafés frequented by North Africans, the Blue Cross had opened a "café without alcohol." I had already seen in the north of France, as I would see in Nancy, the results obtained by this rehabilitation service for drinkers. I had heard men, snatched from slavery to alcohol, giving testimony to the Christ who had freed them and transformed their lives. I was happy that on this day the two aspects of the Christian life had been linked together: *prayer* at the worship service and *service* in the midst of human misery.

Elected to the Eastern Regional Council and a Delegate to the National Synod

The synods of the French Reformed Church were to study the pastoral ministry of women at the regional meetings in the fall of 1964 and the National Synod in the spring of 1965. Fifteen years after the decisions of the National Synod in Paris, Saint-Esprit, why did the National Council decide to take this problem up again?

There were multiple reasons, which I shall summarize briefly. Certainly there was evidence of a change of mind in French society concerning the place of women. In other countries the question of the accession of women to the pastoral ministry had stirred up the churches, which had taken different positions on this question: some for, others against. Various publications, like the study documents of the World Council of Churches,[3] had no doubt led concerned Protestants to think afresh on the question. A certain number of these Protestants concluded from this rethinking process that the decisions of the National Synod of 1949 could only have been transitory. (The decisions were rather contradictory and ambiguous.) I had actually been not only the first woman but the *only one* to whom the National Synod of the French Reformed Church had granted ordination, and that as an exceptional case. Since 1949, several women had asked for ordination, but no Synod had studied their requests and they were still waiting.

Our regional synod was held at Bar-le-Duc, November 6–8, 1964. Under the gray sky, the countryside and the city seemed to be still in mourning for the dead of the 1914-18 war. We were meeting in the City Hall in a décor of the Third Republic. [4]

I admit that I did not bring a passionate interest to the discussions concerning the access of women to the pastoral ministry. I was a bit tired of hearing the same arguments, varied only by a few nuances, repeated for more than thirty years. However, the long set of resolutions which were finally voted contained some interesting ideas. After having stated that the decision of the Synod of Paris in 1949 should be put on a more solid footing, both "for the beneficiaries of this exceptional case and for the general notice of the church," the synod specified in paragraph 4:

> The pastoral ministry of women, if it is brought about in full community of conviction with the presbyterial council and the parish community, may present to the world of today a creative and life-giving innovation—the common ministry of the church being shared, at all levels, between men and women.

It concluded in paragraph 5 by proposing

> that women, whether single or married, should have full access to the pastoral ministry in the French Reformed Church. But at the same time the Synod proposes that a serious study of the pastoral ministry in the French Reformed Church should be undertaken. [Voted 36 in favor, 2 opposed.]

That year the synod was due to renew its regional council (six pastors and six lay persons). The retiring councilors were reelected, with the exception of one of the pastors who was beginning his retirement. On the first ballot, the vote to choose his replacement was inconclusive. On the second ballot, to my great astonishment, my name received the largest number of votes (15!). Three years later another woman was elected to the regional council. I myself was reelected twice (each time on the first ballot). I was to stay on the council until I left Nancy.

After this vote, while the synod went on with its work in the big hall under the eyes of Marianne,[5] the new regional councilors retired to a small, badly lighted room to constitute their executive committee. It was quickly done: Pastor F was reelected as president. We still had to nominate delegates to the National Synod. The president of the region is normally part of the delegation. Therefore there was only one pastor to be nominated, since the eastern region only had the right to four delegates, two of whom must be lay persons. Pastor Hervé had previously been the other delegate, with the president, Pastor F.

Monsieur Hervé took the floor at once to ask not to be nominated again. He added, "But there is someone who seems to me clearly indicated; namely, Mlle. Schmidt. Her culture, her experience, and her authority will allow her to represent our region very well. Besides, for the main question before the Synod, she has to be there anyway!" Nobody protested except me; Monsieur Hervé had authority. Impressed by the words of my colleague, and perhaps also caught short by his withdrawal, the councilors did not propose any other name. I had only been in the region thirteen months! Thus I accepted being a delegate to the National Synod. But just the idea of returning to a National Synod gave me the feeling which comes in an airplane going through storms and tempests. Into how many "air pockets" would I still have to drop before I reached the end of my journey?

The National Synod of 1965

The National Synod of 1965 was held at Nantes, April 30-May 3. As I expected, it was a male assembly. At the roll call of delegates, I had a presentiment that some were not rejoicing at my presence. Therefore, remembering Pastor Boegner's advice in 1948, I decided not to take part in the corridor discussions, even though I was an ordained pastor and duly chosen as a delegate from my region.

The societies and agencies[6] sent delegates to the National Synod. I spied two women among this group, seated together in an alcove. These representatives had the right to express themselves but not to take part in voting. They were "consultants," not "legislators." (This was an administrative and judicial question under study.)

At the press table I noticed a number of representatives of the big daily papers and of the Protestant journals. Friends told me that these journalists were following the discussions with a great deal of interest and quietly making predictions and bets about the votes. Being the only woman ordained in the French Reformed Church, I had to accept several invitations during the Synod to give interviews over radio stations, once to France-Inter and twice to Radio-Television Luxembourg. I also held a press conference for the reporters who were there. *Informations Catholiques Internationales*[7] gave more space to my statements than did other periodicals.

That year the National Synod was to choose a new National Council (i.e., Executive Committee). The retiring Council had proposed certain names for the vote of the Synod. (Evidently mine was not among them.) But I had been nominated, as is possible at the request of at least five members of the Synod. The absolute majority being 45, I received 31 votes. Wasn't that a kind of "demonstration," which might exasperate the opponents of the pastoral ministry of women?

Pastor Pierre André, the son of my regional president in the Cévennes, had been chosen by the National Council to bring in the report on "The Accession of Women to the Pastoral Ministry." (The expression used was pejorative.) His report, like all the others, had been sent to the delegates long enough in advance so that they could study it. The report seemed to me excellent. It pointed up the question and gave the responses of the regional synods. It quoted the end of Pastor Charles Westphal's report to the National Synod at Paris, Saint-Esprit, in 1949 and concluded, "The question is whether we can and whether we ought to go still farther today and open the door wide."[8]

When the discussion began on the early afternoon of May 1, I felt that we were coming into a turbulent zone. It was very clear that one part of the assembly did not want to go farther. However, the assembly gave me the impression of being much less the institutional church ghetto than in 1948. The discussion was long, reflecting a great human diversity in culture, in psychology, and in practical experience. At the same time it reflected a diversity in readings of the scripture. Some went back to the literal interpretation of the several passages in Paul which are always quoted (1 Corinthians 14:34), leaving other texts in the shadow. Others recalled how deeply the churches, including our own, were involved in a search, both speculative and practical, concerning all aspects of the ministry. Pastor Paul Keller[9] said, "The question raised today has its center of gravity not in relation to women but in relation to the pastoral ministry. We have to have women come in to the pastoral ministry in order to help us explode it." A good number of delegates preferred to use padded ecclesiastical diplomacy, offering weakening amendments and stating that the time was not yet ripe to settle the issue. To which one delegate, who was an arboriculturist, replied, "In the case of fruit, maturity is close to decay. Fruit is therefore picked and shipped before it is completely ripe!"[10]

The question of our ecumenical relationships had been raised, and in particular the difficulties which could arise between ourselves and the Roman Catholic Church if we recognized the pastoral ministry of women. On this point Pastor André identified himself with the opinion expressed in the report of Region II: "There is no real respect for the unity of the church except to the degree that each confession is loyally and firmly *itself*" (clearly with a recognition of the duty to give an accounting to the other confessions for the deep reasons behind its choices).[11] Pastor Hébert Roux, the Reformed Church's representative in interfaith matters, judged this remark pertinent, recalling that the Catholic Church's contention bears on the fact it considers the ministry a matter of order and a sacrament.[12]

Finally, Roger Mehl, a theologian who joined with a wide culture the gift of clear language, found words to say, among other constructive things, "The question which arises is to extirpate from our consciences certain nontheological factors which are weighing very heavily in the debate, but which often belong more to the field of psychoanalysis!"[13]

Some of the delegates deplored the absence of women in this assembly and wished that they might be able to express themselves. In spite of this veiled invitation for me to take the floor, I kept silent. Although I was ordained and a delegate, I did not want to turn the spotlight on myself again.

At the dinner recess, repulsed by the idea of sitting down at table with the members of the Synod, I left with Madame

D, who represented the movement of "young women" and whom I had known since our years at the Sorbonne, to tramp the streets of the city. It was a Saturday, the first of May. The sky was gray above a city that seemed dead. Everything was closed. Finally we found a little café which was still open, where a woman consented to serve us coffee and sandwiches. I continued to think that it would be better if a laywoman delegate should take the floor, rather than I. I encouraged Madame D to do it. At the resumption of the session, in the evening, she entered the debate and drew warm applause.

By the terms of the Synod vote in 1949, the decision to confer ordination on a woman is taken by an assembly of eighty delegates, whereas for men it is within the competence and left to the discretion of a commission of the French Reformed Church chosen for this purpose: the Commission on the Pastoral Ministry (some ten or twelve persons, with one permanent staff member and two consultants). This difference was stunning, and the decision taken in my case in 1949 had been the final result of a sequence of events strung out over fourteen years, which could not be gone through again. The steps were:

1935: Beginning ministry at Sainte-Croix in the Cévennes
1936: Decision by the National Synod to grant me a pastoral delegation
1945: Request for my ordination by a presbyterial council addressed, without my knowledge, to the National Synod through Pastor Boegner
1947: Similar request transmitted by a regional synod
1949: National Synod authorization, followed by my ordination at Sète

We were now meeting at Nantes in 1965!

The vote of the Nantes Synod was taken at long last by secret ballot, with a separate vote on each paragraph of the report submitted by the chairman of the committee, after it had been worked over again and again to harmonize it with two alternative proposals. At a quarter past twelve midnight, the National Synod had adopted a text allowing women, like men, to be pastors! There were two important things to notice. As with men, the ordination of women was to be decided on by the Commission on the Pastoral Ministry. Furthermore, a restriction in the text of the National Synod of 1949 was deleted, the clause at the end of the second paragraph that had said (in respect to women candidates alone), "This authorization will not be granted or continued except to an unmarried woman."[14]

There were no long discussions on this matter. Everyone seemed to be agreed that we ought not to make celibacy a compulsory regulation. As the chairman of the committee remarked, "No regional synod has dared to bring back that requirement, and this unanimity is symptomatic."[15]

A Special National Synod Has to Reopen the Question

Even so, I did not come back from Nantes very well satisfied. The decision concerning the pastoral ministry of women had not been taken with a very large majority. Soon after, a rumor reached me—and friends spoke to me —about a "cabal" and even of "enemies plotting together." Very much taken up with my ministry in Nancy, at first I did not attach very much importance to these noises.

On November 16, 1965 the presbyterial council of Nancy elected me as its president. My new responsibilities put me in touch with representatives of the government, the judiciary, and the university. The habits of French society were evolving. Nobody seemed surprised to see a woman pastor making these contacts.

On the day following the National Synod at Nantes, the National Council had received a written protest against the "result attained by a simple majority: a result explained by a tendentious and therefore inadequate preparation, a regret-

table haste, and a failure to apply the two-thirds rule."
(Fearing that my ordination might have been retroactively
called into question, I remembered that the 1949 decision
had been taken by far more than a two-thirds majority, so
that vote was unassailable.)

The National Council queried the juridical commission:
"Was there a procedural error which could vitiate this
decision of the Synod of Nantes?" The commission having
recessed, the National Council decided to call an extraordinary meeting of the National Synod, which would be
convened one day before the regular meeting in the year
1966. For the second time within a year, a National Synod
would review a decision concerning the pastoral ministry of
women. Who could tell whether good results would follow
from a second reopening of the problem?

We were to meet at the church in Clermont-Ferrand, in a
building which had just been finished. From the moment of
my arrival for the special session of the 58th National Synod,
in the late afternoon of April 29, 1966, I noticed that the
"headquarters staff" of the French Reformed Church
seemed very troubled. The National Council had decided
that this would be a closed session (which an article in the
bylaws allows). The press was barred, but a vote had been
taken to give the consultative delegates and the legal counsel
the right to be present.

The declaration of President Pierre Bourguet was listened
to with gravity. From the juridical commission's study, we
learned first: "It does not clearly appear that, by its nature
and its import, the question of the pastoral ministry of
women necessarily pertains to the Discipline of the church."
The jurists were confirming the opinion I had formed in
Grenoble in 1948! But one mistake had been made in
preparing for the Synod at Nantes. The Grenoble decision
had been overlooked. It required in this case an absolute
majority of the members of the Synod and at least a
two-thirds majority of the members present at the time of

the voting. Thus a new vote had to be substituted for the vote of the Synod of Nantes.

The debate was opened and the vote was to be taken on one single agenda item. A certain change seemed to have taken place in the atmosphere of the assembly since the preceding year. I felt freer in mind about taking the floor (as some of my friends had advised me to do). Addressing myself to the minority, I tried to tell them, in the form of a personal testimony, what had been my own hesitancies and my own searching questions. The printed minutes of this session could obviously publish only the conclusion of my remarks:

> The National Synod, stamped as it is by its masculine and parliamentary character, even when it acknowledges the complementary nature of manhood and womanhood, cannot help but be at a loss to describe the ministry of women. Can the Synod delimit in advance what women, coming into the pastoral ministry, can do? Ought we not rather let the liberty of the Holy Spirit have free play, to make itself manifest in this realm?[16]

The text finally put to the vote of the assembly had been prepared by Prof. Jean Bosc, accepted by Pastor André as reporter, and slightly modified in discussion. After a time of meditation, this text was adopted, voted on by secret ballot, paragraph by paragraph. It differed very little from the text accepted at the National Synod of Nantes. But this time the negative votes never exceeded the figure of seven, while the affirmatives were from seventy-four to seventy-seven![17]

When we came to the end of this special session at twelve forty, I think we were all relieved. As for me, I had the feeling that now my task was accomplished. I was in the eventide of the great battle, and I wanted to take some rest. But I was enmeshed in the gears. I had to sit in the regular National Synod which began several hours later. And, once back in Lorraine, I would shoulder again the responsibilities I had accepted and go on with my ministry in Nancy.

Evolution and Tensions in the Local Church:
May 1968

I spent nine years in Nancy (from 1963 to 1972) in the midst of a team of four pastors, in a parish which could be called "traditional," and during a period when France was not at war. But this period was troubled by challenges to the society itself and to the church, with us as in the rest of the world. In spite of the tensions between different mind-sets and the opposition of the generations, it seemed to me that the church was on the march. The lay people showed themselves mature and responsible, and the young people wanted to take part in the life and governance of the church.

Beginning in the month of March 1968, "student demonstrations" began in Nancy. My colleagues and I consented to having a representative of the Protestant students explain, at the Sunday worship service, the significance which their group attached to these demonstrations. The congregation was surprised to be told of a great movement bearing hope, of claims which the gospel had inspired. Many did not understand. Lorrainers love order!

Nancy was not Paris, but Nancy also knew violence. A group of students "occupied" Poirel Hall, a civic auditorium where concerts and plays were given. The municipality decided to have it evacuated. Without any recourse to violence and without any confrontation, the students left the premises. But where to go? A Protestant student suggested going to the church, quite near Poirel Hall. The communists would only agree to this proposition if the pastor gave authorization for it.

I saw arriving at my house a delegation of three or four students, of whom two were Protestants and pastors' sons. I reminded them that a pastor is not a bishop, and that important decisions are taken by the presbyterial council. Explaining to them that the church was an old building, cold and without any facilities, I suggested the alternative of the parish house, whose renovation had been started in 1967 and which had washrooms and toilets. We were just before the eve of Pentecost, when the students went back to their families until the following Tuesday, so they did not need an immediate answer.

I convened an emergency meeting of the executive committee of the presbyterial council for the Tuesday after Pentecost in the late afternoon. At the time of our meeting of the lay leaders, the students were already occupying our big hall. We were facing a fait accompli! No one of us envisaged having the premises cleared, and we did not waste time wondering how the students had got in without breaking any locks. The councilor who headed the buildings and grounds committee and controlled its budget expressed his uneasiness about possible vandalism in the newly refurbished rooms. My young colleague sent for two leaders from the student group. The young man and the young woman knew how to inspire confidence. They promised to leave the place in perfect condition and to pay for the electricity they used. Could you ask for more at that time?

The hall could be reached from Maginot Square. An alley between one of the side walls of the sanctuary and the neighboring apartment house led to a courtyard, on which opened the doors and windows of the parish hall. At the entrance of this dead end, the students had stretched a white calico cloth on which, in bold black letters, was printed OPEN FORUM. The most widely different people came to talk with the students all day long, at mealtimes or in the evening. Workers of all professions were on strike, or prevented from working. They had the time to talk and they did it as, perhaps, they had never done it before.

Each morning, I saw the students cleaning the rooms they were occupying, with an ardor they would probably not have had at home. The open forum sometimes took the shape of a meeting called for a specific time, where the participants, in a circle, spoke to one another. I followed some of these meetings. (They smoked a lot, and often an asthma attack suffocated me and prevented me from waiting until the end.) There remains with me an indelible memory. Everyone spoke to everyone else, with a new kind of freedom. All barriers seemed to be abolished. A workman asked a professor why the students were still studying Racine and Corneille. A Marxist asked Christians how they understood the prophets. No one was afraid of looking silly if he or she did not know how to put something. Time seemed to stand still while they talked on and on. Was it the outpouring of those who had never expressed themselves? But people listened, too! In this effort to be true to oneself and to others, perhaps there was for a moment the miracle of communication between people? In spite of all the inexcusable violences and the excesses of which we heard, this great surge of indignation had a deep meaning. Some saw only the foam left on the shore, instead of feeling the wind which filled the sails.

Then, as the fire goes out on the hearth in the evening of the day, the fervor of May died out. Economic and political decisions are not enough to explain the return to "life before May." The banner was taken down at the entrance to the alley. One morning I realized that silence had come back to our quarters. The hall was empty. Why did I feel such a sadness? Some months later we spoke of "the May incidents" much as we spoke of the "Algerian incidents" in 1959 and 1960—with the same fear and shame.

The shock waves of 1968 certainly accentuated the evolution within the churches. I realized it again when, in 1969, I was elected moderator of the eastern regional synod. My nomination and election went off in the same way as with a man, not raising any problem. We had come a long way since the Synod of Avèze.[18]

Evolution in Ecumenical Relations

At the same time another evolution was taking place: that which was evidenced in our ecumenical relationships. Pastor Hervé had asked me to serve as the Protestant representative in the local ecumenical group, a responsibility hitherto held by a colleague who was leaving Nancy. At the time of my installation on October 20, 1964 I had received a letter from this group. One phrase had encouraged me, more than the too many compliments: "We have liked the firmness, the simplicity, and the fervor with which you have brought us the message." One question bothered me: Wasn't it a little off the beaten path to send a woman pastor to dialogue with the bishop and the priests? I had not erased the painful memory of my encounter with the Bishop of Montpellier at the time of the funeral for the victims of the American bombardment in 1944. But I was quickly reassured. The welcome of the clergy in Nancy was simpler and more natural than I had imagined.

The third session of the Second Vatican Council had adjourned in November 1964. The Superior of the Great Seminary in Nancy inquired whether I would be willing to give a lecture to the seminarians on the polity of the French Reformed Church. I was to spell out in fifty-five minutes what I had explained in fifteen at a priest-pastor meeting in the office of Father F, the bishop's representative in ecumenical relationships. The Superior was waiting for me on the staircase of this immense building. He greeted me, saying, "Madame, you are the first Protestant pastor to cross this threshold. This is a red-letter day!" He led me through interminable frigid corridors, first to his office, where a portrait of Father Foucauld[19] got our conversation off to a quick start.

Could a professor dream of a more attentive audience than the one I had in the small amphitheater where all the seminarians and their professors had gathered? I caught glints of malice in some eyes when I explained that in the wheels of our church no mandate is given for life. I cited the example of Pastor Chatoney, president of the Reformed Church in Algeria. After many years in that office, he returned to the ranks and simply and humbly became the pastor of a small parish.[20] Inviting me to dinner, the Superior asked if I would be willing to answer questions later for three quarters of an hour. Why not? On February 2, 1965 I went to the seminary again to answer for an hour the questions which the students had sent me through one of the professors.

The Second Vatican Council closed in the beginning of December 1965. We were happy to see our contacts with Catholics, in every relationship of life, developing more understanding and freedom. The Protestants in the city were becoming a little less suspicious, their minority complex less painful. Everything was easier for the younger generation.

January 24, 1969 marked a date in the ecumenical relationships in Lorraine. Abandoning the neutral ground of Poirel Hall, we were able to have a vigil of prayer in the Reformed Church. Christians of the two confessions were squeezed together in the pews of the church, sometimes standing in the aisles and in the balconies. The big wooden cross, lighted by a spotlight, dominated the assembly, in which you could see only one pastor's black gown—mine —and the white gown of a Dominican. It was he who had been asked to preach the sermon. The text for that week of prayer for unity was "For freedom Christ has set us free [Gal. 5:1]." At the end the bishop conducted the prayer of intercession. He seemed to be very much moved. As we went out, Father F said to me, "Yes, it's an event! Now Monsignor's presence has removed an embarrassment for us. It felt good to be together!" These ecumenical meetings, as they multiplied, took differing forms: a group of ecumenical couples, colloquia, Bible study groups. But all the happy recollections of this march forward cannot submerge the permanent suffering caused by the division between the churches, a suffering always sharper at the time of the eucharistic celebration.

My Last Year at Nancy

I had announced in October 1971 that I would be leaving Nancy in July 1972. I would no longer have to await, anxiously, the call to another church. I would join the category which I had hardly ever thought about, that of retired pastors. During this last year several groups for which I was not directly responsible asked me to lead a study session or to give a meditation. After 1970 I had given up the presidency of the presbyterial council and therefore had more time to respond to these invitations. I had a little feeling of saying good-bye all year long! The weariness of a ministry with its many responsibilities in a university city muted somewhat the pain of departure and the suffering of separations. I made my farewells to the delegates from our region at the last regional synod at Lunéville, under the eighteenth-century vaults of the decommissioned chapel in the château built by Stanislaus Leszczynski, a smaller replica of Versailles.

The last National Synod in which I took part was held April 29-May 1 at Pont-à-Mousson, on the Moselle River. The Premonstrant Order had had an impressive monastic complex built there. Bombardments and fires of the two last wars had ravaged it. A restoration was undertaken and carried through with good taste. The old abbey became a conference center. It was in this setting, which united the elegance of the eighteenth century with the comfort of the twentieth, that the Synod met. At the suggestion of Pastor Jacques Maury, President of the National Council, I was elected vice-moderator. At the end of a short session at which I had presided, an old friend came to me to say, "You got out of that very well!" He thought he was making me happy. I did not quite dare ask him, "Would you have come to say that to a male pastor?"

At the last session of the Synod, Pastor Jacques Maury expressed to me the affection and the gratitude of the French Reformed Church. Then, gathering up all the Synod's best wishes for my retirement, he said to me in Greek, "May grace and peace go with you, Elisabeth!" At the farewell dinner in the refectory, I saw a bouquet of magnificent red roses being brought to me. Its thorns were very sharp, but the flowers had a dazzling beauty to the sight, and the petals had the softness of velvet. What a symbol, those synodal flowers!

I bade farewell to the Nancy parish in a very traditional way at the worship service on June 18, 1972. I had chosen among the texts suggested for that day the exhortation of Paul to Timothy, "Do not be ashamed then of testifying to our Lord [2 Tim. 1:8]." The parish choir sang a chorale of Buxtehude, giving me a translation of the text, with the signatures of all the singers. At the little gathering which followed the service, an album was given me. They told me (in view of my request not to have a present), "This has no monetary value—only the cost of a few pieces of paper." Put together by a small group of parishioners, this album, with beautiful photographs and humorous collages, brings back several stages of my life. It also shows the various activities of the Nancy church through the twelve months of the year. It is "one of a kind," and I only show it to those who can understand its value.

Envoi—God Gives the Church to Discern

THAT'S THE END OF THE EVOCATION of several stages of my life. Through a certain number of circumstances which seem fortuitous, surprising, or contradictory, I can discern today the line which was bound to end in the recognition of the pastoral ministry of women by the French Reformed Church.

For the sake of truth, I have to ask, "Did I deceive myself? Have I been duped? If it were possible, would I redo my life in a different way?" In all honesty, I answer, "No!" My only sad regret is that of my inadequacies and of my spiritual lacks. That is a suffering which all Christians live through. Our common grief is that we are not the saints whom God needs in this world.

When I had to make decisive choices, I scarcely realized how fully my home training had kept me from the constraints of masculine clericalism. I was never fully aware that I was the exception, the "test case," in the French Reformed Church's college of pastors. In the evening of my life I recognize, still more surprisingly, that it has been given me to carry out my ministry in varied places and in diverse types of parishes. I got to each new stage by unforeseen paths where chance (it seemed) had set a door ajar. I was a pastor in a Cévenol mountain village, in a middle-sized town, in a university city. Lastly, I was a pastor in unusual times and circumstances—at the Gurs internment camp and in Algeria during the last years of the war. Nevertheless, this richness of experience through which God has led me does not, objectively speaking, entitle me to offer general conclusions on the pastoral ministry of women, even though this will disappoint several of my friends.

In the past, the ministry of a woman pastor was more readily accepted where the weight of traditions bore down less heavily, that is to say, in unusual circumstances. But these exceptional situations require a psychic equilibrium, a personal authority, and a spirit of initiative which, at that time, no one thought women could muster.

Over the thirty-seven years of my ministry, I have seen a certain number of objections disappear—objections brought against "the accession of women to the pastoral ministry," to use the Synod's terminology. These objections, offered by some as though they were affirmations of the Christian faith, have been swept away by the evolution of society. The same people who brandished them have forgotten that they did it, like the Pétainists who in 1945 suddenly thought of themselves as having been resistants. I have also been on hand for the unforeseeable and rich development of the idea of ministry, to which the experiments made by the church through women have not been alien.

More than most, I believe that women ought to take part in the church's organs of governance and reflection. Their absence was an "interdict," in the biblical sense. Let us hope that today, now that they are free to apply for any pastoral post, they will avoid errors of judgment concerning their personal gifts and capacities. Let us also hope that they will not, in turn, fall into a clerical immobility!

New theologies will arise on the horizon and will then go into history, thus finding their relative value. For no system can lock up or express the fullness which is in Christ. Thus I refuse to make fictitious theology out of the accession of women into the pastoral ministry. But I would like, in closing, to come back to the fifteenth chapter of the Acts of the Apostles.

There we are told of an important difference among the early Christians. Paul, Barnabas, and some others "went up to Jerusalem" to look into the affair with the elders and the apostles. Some people from Judea wanted to impose, on the "pagans" who had become Christians, observance of the Jewish requirements, particularly the rite of circumcision. There was a very lively discussion. But a decision was taken and it became the object of a letter addressed to the "pagans" who had become Christians. On that day Peter declared that "god who knows the heart bore witness to them, giving them the Holy Spirit just as he did to us; and he made no distinction between us and them [Acts 15:8-9]." Such a statement was so upsetting that the author of Acts does not forget to note that "all the assembly kept silence [15:12]."

It was not the apostles, the elder statesmen in Jerusalem, who decided that Christians coming out of the "pagan" nations were Christians without any difference from the Christians who came out of the Jewish nation. They discerned God's will at work in the fait accompli (which upset all their habits of thought and belief). These Christians, who had come over from paganism, made it manifest that they were living in the fullness of the Christian faith. Then the little group of leaders "legalized" this fact. It was expressed, orally and in writing, as a decision growing out of the church's faith. Thus the practice outran the theory and illumined the reading of the scripture.

You see the same movement all through the history of the church. A clerical pride, clinging to tradition, opposes the novelties which the Spirit gives to the people of God on the march. Later on, the leaders of the church, or its governing bodies, give official recognition to what the church is already living out by the grace of God and put the now-accepted novelties into the discipline or the dogma of the church.

The life of the people of God is a march full of dangers and unforeseen hazards. We know it by the scripture and by history. In that march women will have new responsibilities. Thus it is all together that we look toward the future, with a listening ear for "what the Spirit says to the churches [Rev. 2:29]."

Notes

1: Some Landmarks—Childhood and Adolescence

1. A member of the Chamber of Deputies, the lower house in France's bicameral legislature. The deputy is an important person in France. At the time when Henri Schmidt was elected there were 548, one for each *arrondissement*, or roughly one for each 100,000 electors, chosen by direct vote by universal suffrage (then male only). The Chamber of Deputies and the Senate together form a National Assembly to choose the President—A.H.

2. Jules Ferry (1832-93) was a famous statesman who brought about the reform of public instruction, making it secular, free, and compulsory. The law carries his name. In 1880 he extended secondary public education to girls.—A.H.

3. In the French Reformed Church communion is not served in the pews or at the altar rail, but in groups of twelve to twenty around the communion table. The elders summon the groups, but the elements are passed from óne worshiper to another, as Elisabeth Schmidt indicates.—A.H.

4. This is roughly equivalent to the M.A. in the United States.

2: University Studies and Call

1. "The generation of church leaders who had the ecumenical vision were shaped by these movements [Young Men's and Young

Women's Christian Associations, the first student groups]. The World's Student Christian Federation stated explicitly by its by-laws that Christians of all confessions were admitted to the Federation." Madeleine Barot, *Le Mouvement Oecuménique* (Paris: Presses Universitaires de France), pp. 31-32.

2. This book, Karl Barth's first published work, consisted of a series of addresses given between 1916 and 1923. It appeared in Munich in 1925 under the title *Das Wort Gottes und die Theologie*. In the United States, The Pilgrim Press had the distinction of publishing Barth's work for the first time, with Douglas Horton's translation of the same series of articles, issued in 1928 under the title *The Word of God and the Word of Man*. Young student movement leaders were soon aware, in every country, of Karl Barth's pivotal thinking, which effectively punctured the balloon of liberal progressivism with its optimistic assumptions and reoriented theology around the priority of God and God's Word. —A.H.

3. Pastor Marc Boegner had begun his career as assistant to his maternal uncle, Tommy Fallot, served as head of training for the Paris Evangelical Missionary Society, and was, when Elisabeth Schmidt wrote him, the president or chief executive of the Église Reformée de France. Subsequently he was head of CIMADE and a "founding father" of the World Council of Churches—A.H.

4. Author of *Devoir de l'Imprévoyance* ("The Duty of Improvidence," which might mean what one author has called "The Higher Carelessness"), Isabelle Rivière's husband was also an author.—A.H.

5. "Probationary periods" in preparation for the pastoral ministry may be described as "field work," "internship," and "residency," corresponding roughly to preparation for general medical practice. The French words are simply *stage* (for the first two) and *proposanat*, which I translate as "probationary period."—A.H.

6. Calvin's expression is *dresser une église*. It can also be translated "establish" or "constitute" a church.—A.H.

7. This status corresponds roughly to licensure in some churches or to the status of a deacon in the Anglican Church.—A.H.

8. After the fall of the Second Empire and the disastrous Franco-Prussian War, the republican government was dominated by anticlerical leaders, who finally separated church and state in 1905, as Elisabeth Schmidt indicated in chapter 1. This freedom allowed divergence between the two camps in the Protestant Church. One group insisted on a creed to be adhered to word for word. The other was content with acceptance "in principle." Their reunion in 1938 created the present Église Reformée de France, in which Elisabeth Schmidt found herself theologically sustained. —A.H.

9. The National Synod had the responsibility of governing the French Reformed Church, of formulating its confession of faith and its constitutional texts, and of representing it. Members of the National Synod with voting rights are the representatives of the regional synods, elected and chosen from among their number. The number of pastors cannot be more than half its delegates. (Article 33 of the *Discipline*.)

3: The Decisive Years—Ministry in the Cévennes

1. President of the regional council in the French Reformed Church is what some American Protestants would call "area minister" or "district superintendent."—A.H.

2. I looked in vain in my dictionaries for the word *gardon*, only to learn from Elisabeth Schmidt that it refers to a tributary of the Gard, the river made famous by the Roman aqueduct the Pont du Gard, which spans it.—A.H.

3. The presbyterial council is composed of the incumbent pastor or pastors and at least six representatives of the local church. It is elected by the general assembly by secret ballot. The local church is governed through the presbyterial council in the general framework of the discipline, laws, and regulations of the French Reformed Church. (Article 3 of the *Discipline*.)

4. The Cévenol Club, founded in 1894, has a quarterly review, *Causses et Cévennes*.

5. It was only in 1975 (thirty-four years later) that the application, which had been renewed, finally got a favorable response.

6. This gave rise to the delightful *Travels with a Donkey in the Cévennes*. Observing the centennial of the original trip, the Club Cévenol, mentioned earlier in connection with Elisabeth Schmidt's first service, has published, in French, an illustrated paperback volume including original drawings by Stevenson and facsimile pages from his notebooks: *Robert Louis Stevenson, Journal de Route en Cévennes*, Première Edition Intégrale à Partir du Manuscrit de R.L. Stevenson (Toulouse: Club Cévenol et Edouard Privat, editeurs, 1978).—A.H.

7. The French is *Remettez-vous*—literally, "Put yourself together."—A.H.

8. Again, as in the passage about the words of greeting she received after the first service, Elisabeth Schmidt uses the word *languir*—to languish. In translating it "get discouraged," I am considering the fact that pastors characteristically take leave of each other with the words *"Bon courage!"*—a sign that they need to uphold one another in their lonely and *dis*couraging work. —A.H.

9. "Regional synods are composed of delegates from the presbyterial councils, named by them and chosen from their number in the proportion of one pastor and one elder for each incumbent pastor. The regional synod has the duty and the responsibility of expressing itself on doctrinal and disciplinary questions concerning the French Reformed Church, the final decision belonging to the National Synod." (Article 23 of the *Discipline*.)

10. *Oeuvres et mouvements* is the inclusive term which describes what we would call home mission activities, social action, Christian education, and social welfare. The yearbook of the French Protestant Federation devotes as much space to these organizations as it does to the lists of parishes.—A.H.

11. These are small groups of clergy generally of one denomination and frequently covering a metropolitan area or, in sparser regions, a county. They may well include parish ministers and pastors in specialized ministries such as army chaplaincies and youth work. They usually meet at regular and frequent intervals

for prayer and Bible study, discussion of common problems, and the sharing of responsibilities. They naturally vary in the dynamics of their relationships, but where they are strong they are crucial in maintaining the morale of the pastors.—A.H.

12. *Acts of the National Synod of the Reformed Churches, 1936,* p. 36.

13. *Acts of the National Synod of the Reformed Churches, Castres, 1937,* p. 78.

14. Nicholas de Bâville (1648-1724) was Intendant of the Généralité (i.e., district) of Languedoc in the time of Louis XIV. He enlarged his power as financial chief to become an autocrat. Persecuting the Protestants ferociously, particularly in the thirty-three years after the Revocation of the Edict of Nantes (between 1685 and 1718), he earned the title of "tyrant of Languedoc." —A.H.

15. Decision XXII, *Acts of the National Synod in Bordeaux, 1939.*

16. The Camisard war (1702-5) took its name from the white shirts (*camisos,* in patois) which the partisans wore to help them recognize one another at night. It was localized in the Cévennes mountains and in the Vivarais and never involved more than a few thousand Protestants, but the guerrillas were able to discredit famous commanders in Louis XIV's army. The rebels identified themselves with the Old Testament warriors who conquered stronger foes by the help of the Lord of Hosts. Psalm 68 was their battle hymn: "Let God arise, let his enemies be scattered." They had the added advantages of mobility, knowledge of the rugged terrain, and the support of the population. The shepherd on the hillside could spy on the movements of the uniformed troops and might at the drop of a hat join the rebels himself. Finally, the king's armies, by their superiority of numbers, the burning of villages, and human error forced the Camisards to capitulate.

From the time of the Revocation of the Edict of Nantes (1685) and well into the seventeenth century, the vacuum of trained leadership was at least partially filled by spontaneous inspiration, largely among young people of both sexes. The prophets and prophetesses preached both repentance and resistance. The Holy

Spirit was said to have prompted the partisans to free several prisoners by burning the Roman Catholic rectory and assassinating the priest at Pont-de-Montvert near Florac. This was after four hundred worshipers had been slain in a Protestant church. It touched off the Camisard war, in which the Huguenots continued to claim inspiration.

The prophets and prophetesses condemned immorality and the greed of the clergy. Their popular religious movement gave back joy and confidence to the "little people" among the Huguenots. *Histoire des Protestants de France* (Toulouse: Privat, 1977), pp. 202-11.—A.H.

17. In the time when there was no institution helping the severely handicapped, either with motor disability or mental illness, Pastor John Bost gathered some young people who had been excluded from other facilities. Beginning in 1848 he built the first shelter. Today the John Bost Foundation welcomes 1,040 residents in eighteen buildings spread over three quarters of a square mile of green lawns. In a setting of superior medical and technical facilities, the most handicapped patients are cared for with a Christian love which overwhelms all those who visit them.—A.H.

18. His watchword was, "It is not tolerance that I demand, it is liberty!" The motion before the Estates (introduced by a Catholic), stated, "No one should be disturbed for his religious opinions, nor molested in the exercise of his religion." Despite Rabaut's eloquent plea, the assembly passed a motion giving the freedom grudgingly: "No one should be disturbed for his opinions, even religious ones, provided that their manifestation does not disturb the public order established by law." Two years later, in 1791, the constitution declared, "Every citizen is free to practice the religious worship of the cult to which he belongs." Rabaut was guillotined during the Terror (1793), when the Montagnards defeated the Girondins.—A.H.

19. Or, "preterit . . . a verb tense that indicates action in the past without reference to duration, continuance, or repetition." *Webster's New Collegiate Dictionary* Springfield, Mass: (G. and C. Merriam, 1971).—A.H.

20. The Camisard chief was Pierre LaPorte, a sheep gelder, who took Chevalier Roland as his *nom de guerre*. He was the most famous and most popular of the guerrilla leaders who taunted the royal dragoons. The small rebel force kept eluding the king's troops until they were betrayed and the cave where they had established their hospital and stockpiles of food and weapons was captured. Pierre LaPorte was born in 1680 and died in 1704. Samuel Mours and Daniel Robert, *Le Protestantisme en France du XVIII Siècle à Nos Jours* (Paris: Librairie Protestante, 1972), pp. 82-90.

The Roland who sounded his horn at Roncevaux died in 708, almost a millennium earlier. This Roland is the hero of the "Chanson de Roland," the most famous of the *chansons de geste*.—A.H.

21. Emile Combes, prime minister 1902-5, expelled the Catholic orders and presided over the preparation and passage of the law separating church and state in France.—A.H.

22. The acronym CIMADE means Comité Inter-Mouvements Auprès des Évacués—"Intermovement Committee on Behalf of Refugees." Rooted in its wartime service of inspired improvisation by a band of dedicated women combining holy indignation with incredible tenacity, CIMADE today continues its work with refugees but focuses largely on migrant workers. It also serves the purpose for which the churches in the United States have agencies for Christian social action. The story of CIMADE's service in the internment camps and the underground railroad to Switzerland is spelled out in *God's Underground (Les Clandestins de Dieu,* 1968) collected by Jeanne Merle d'Aubigné and Violette Mouchon, translated by William and Patricia Nottingham (St. Louis: The Bethany Press, 1970).—A.H.

4: The Camp at Gurs, 1941

1. This is the way the non-occupied zone was referred to.

2. This worked out to one for every twelve and a half prisoners. —A.H.

3. Verlaine was a decadent nineteenth-century (1844-96) poet. He became an ardent Catholic.—A.H.

4. I went back to Gurs in 1964. No vestige of the camp remains. I could not orient myself in the midst of fields, trees, and small houses. Everything has disappeared from what was one of the shames of this period. Beginning in 1945 the Federation of Jewish Societies in the Basses-Pyrénées had a monument erected in the abandoned cemetery so that the suffering of these thousands of human beings who were victims of Nazism might not be shrouded in forgetfulness. Then the cemetery was restored, thanks to the initiative of the Jewish Consistory of Baden and the gifts of various societies in that region. In 1962, 1,187 tombs recalled the names of those whose bodies remained in this corner of Navarre.

5. This letter is reproduced in Pastor Marc Boegner's introduction to *Les Clandestins de Dieu* (see chapter 3, note 22). It is available in a fluent English translation, from which I have excerpted the key passage:

"Our church, which knew in the past all the sufferings of persecution, feels an ardent sympathy for your communities whose liberty of worship has already been jeopardized in certain places and whose members have been so abruptly thrown into misfortune. It has already undertaken and will not cease from pursuing steps aimed at the indispensable rewriting of the law." (*God's Underground*, translated by William and Patricia Nottingham from *Les Clandestins de Dieu* [Paris: Fayard, 1968]. *God's Underground* was published by Bethany Press, St. Louis, in 1970. The Boegner letter is on p. 14.)—A.H.

6. *Les Clandestins de Dieu*, p. 188; *God's Underground*, p. 194.

7. See chapter 2, p. 20.

8. A more detailed story of "The Flowery Hillside" is available in English in two places. In *God's Underground*, Marc Donadille conveys the anxiety of these times (pp. 113-16). There is another book in English, and now in French, which gives the same account from a slightly different angle (the cooperation of the whole village of Le-Chambon-sur-Lignon and the leadership of Pastor André Trocmé and his wife are in the forefront). It is *Lest Innocent Blood*

Be Shed by Philip Hallie, professor at Wesleyan University in Connecticut (New York: Harper & Row, 1979). The French version is called *Le Sang Innocent.*—A.H.

9. During a trip to Germany I saw Bertha Lenel again in a retirement home at Freiburg-im-Breisgau.

5: Interlude in Florac

1. The French word is *mail*. Elisabeth Schmidt explains: "*Mail* is an ancient outdoor game played with a mallet (Latin *malleus*) and wooden balls. Then the word was applied to the promenade, a broad avenue shaded by trees. Almost every city in the south of France has its *mail*."—A.H.

2. In the French Reformed Church the president of the presbyterial council is ordinarily the pastor, and the chief lay officer is the vice-president.—A.H.

6: Ministry in Sète

1. This was the law promulgated under Napoleon, which officially reestablished the churches after the French Revolution. It gave them, however, an elitist stamp because church officers had to be "notables."—A.H.

2. The spelling of Sète changed a number of times.

3. Pastor Boegner made frequent trips to Vichy as a spokesman for the Protestants, often with the Archbishop of Lyon. His letter of fraternal concern to the Chief Rabbi of France is a high-water mark of interfaith communion. See chapter 4, note 5.—A.H.

4. *Au pair* means "on an equality." A young person offers her services as a mother's helper in return for the privilege of learning the spoken language more fluently. Generally no money passes, but board and room are provided.—A.H.

5. "Jean-Foutre" is "John Doe," with a derisive twist. It means "this heel" or some similar word, as the tone of the elder's comment indicates.—A.H.

6. He had been imprisoned at Fort Montluc in Lyon for his part in the resistance.

7. The original French has a play on words: *On ne peut que servir ou desservir son prochain.*—A.H.

8. Elisabeth Schmidt explained in a letter what this reference indicates: "*Témoignage Chrétien* (Christian witness), founded in 1941 by Father Chaillet of Lyon, as a ten-page "notebook," opened up the problems raised for the Christian conscience by the German occupation—anti-Semitism, forced labor, the anti-Bolshevik crusade, etc. It went from a few thousand to 100,000 circulation, necessarily underground until the liberation. Protestants shared in the editing and distribution—my sister, Simone, had a depot in her house in Montauban, which the Gestapo did not find when they arrested her. At the victory celebration in Montauban Square, after one of the two resistant Catholic bishops had spoken, my sister announced that *Témoignage Chrétien* was now available and signed up new subscribers."—A.H.

9. The National Council is the executive committee which, between meetings of the National Synod, governs the French Reformed Church. It wields great influence. Its decisions, while they are ultimately subject to the Synod, are for all practical purposes, binding.—A.H.

10. The term "interior France" points to the many sharp differences—historical, psychological, and of course geographical —between the once-separated provinces of Alsace-Lorraine and the rest of the country.—A.H.

11. Elisabeth Schmidt told me in a letter that she had in mind the important probationary year (the *proposanat*), which was required for male pastors before ordination. This would be even more necessary for women pastors at the outset.—A.H.

12. Historian, Doctor of Letters.

13. The regional synod of the VIIIth Region of the French Reformed Church, meeting at Quissac November 10–12, 1947:
1. Believing that the Word of God makes no formal objection to the pastoral ministry of women, recognizes its legitimacy. (Adopted by 30 votes for, 14 against.)

2. Requests that the modalities of the ordination which should be given to those women whom God calls to this ministry, should be studied. (Adopted by 24 votes for, 6 against, 2 abstentions.)

3. Requests that pastoral ordination should be given to those women when, with all necessary prudence, their authentic vocation has been recognized. (Adopted unanimously, 2 abstentions. The abstentions were those of an aged pastor who had just come to the region and that of a young pastor who had recently come from Lausanne.)

14. Moderator: a sixteenth-century word which has been kept and which means president.

15. "The National Synod, deeming it indispensable that the votes to be taken on the proposal on liturgy and that on the pastoral ministry of women should have the greatest possible authority in the church, decides that, in conformity with the stipulations of chapter VI of the Discipline, these votes will be taken by an absolute majority of the members of the Synod, and by at least two thirds of those members present." (Decision IX, *Acts of the National Synod in Grenoble, 1948,* page 12.)

16. "The National Synod of the French Reformed Church, Grenoble 1948, called to pronounce itself on the possibility of granting to women the same ordination to the pastoral ministry which is given to men, does not feel itself ready as of today to cut to the bottom of the question raised, and charges the National Council to take all necessary steps so that the next National Synod, when fully informed, may be able to consider it effectively." (Decision X, ibid., page 13.)

17. See chapter 7, note 8.

18. This gathering, the "Assemblée du Désert," is the high-water-mark of French Protestantism each year, a holy and joyous "gathering of the clan." Each year families and congregations make the pilgrimage, in vans, buses, by bicycle and on foot, to touch their Protestant roots. Some come from Switzerland, some even from South Africa. There are two solemn services, plus communion and baptisms. There are historical addresses and a bountiful picnic lunch shared from table to table and family to family. The open-air setting, on a low hillside in the foothills of the

Cévennes (within striking distance of Nîmes and Montpellier), brings back to mind the services in the "wilderness," when the Protestants were persecuted by the dragoons of Louis XIV but willing to face the galleys or imprisonment rather than to renounce their faith. The little village of Mas Soubeyran, with its red-tiled roofs, where the annual service is held, is a site actually connected with the wilderness history and has the chief Protestant museum in France.—A.H.

19. "Electors" are members of the congregation who attend the Lord's Supper and contribute financially. The presbyterial council keeps the register of voting members.—A.H.

7: Ordination and Continuing Ministry, 1949-58

1. "The National Synod, responding to the request of the regional synod of the VIIIth region to authorize the ordination of Mlle. Elisabeth Schmidt, Bachelor of Theology, who is serving the church in Sète by virtue of a pastoral delegation regularly renewed in conformity with a decision of the Synod of Bordeaux:

"*Whereas*, by a previous vote, the Synod has granted the possibility . . . of granting to a woman the full exercise of the pastoral ministry, . . .

"*Whereas*, the long years of Mlle. Schmidt's ministry and the testimonials which have been given her allow us to discern in her an authentic pastoral vocation,

"The Synod is happy to grant to Mlle. Schmidt the authorization for ordination requested on her behalf and invokes on her ministry the blessing of God." (Decision XXI, *Acts of the National Synod in Saint-Esprit, Paris,* 1949, p.22.)

2. The child probably heard "sacrée" (crowned) for "consacrée" (ordained). The cathedral at Rheims is the French Westminster Abbey. It has particular associations with Joan of Arc.—A.H.

3. Without ignoring the discussions aroused by the translation of Romans 16:1-2, I had opted for this one. Charles Westphal explains it in his report to the 1949 Synod of Saint-Esprit, Paris:

" 'I commend to you our sister Phoebe'; our translations say: 'deaconess.' In Romans 12:7 the same versions say 'ministry' for *diakonia*. Why not translate *diakonon* here by 'minister'? It would surely be more accurate. 'Deaconess' has taken on a narrow sense which it did not have in the primitive church. . . . To understand the text well, we must, in all intellectual honesty, read: 'Phoebe, minister of the church at Cenchrea, put yourselves at her disposal! . . . she has been a protectress of many, including myself.' " (From the *Acts of the National Synod in Saint-Esprit, Paris, 1949*, page 93.)

[I make bold to add that the same verb *diakonesai* is translated "to minister" in the *King James Version* of Mark 10:45.—A.H.]

4. See beginning of chapter 3.

5. It was only in 1968 that the Consistory of Geneva allowed a woman to be the incumbent in a parish on the same basis as a man.

6. John Calvin emphasizes the necessity of a secret call to the candidate and a ratification of the call by the church, which examines and judges the candidate's gifts and capacities for ministry. See *Institutes*, Book IV, chapter 3, 15 (John Calvin, *Institutes of the Christian Religion*, tr. John Allen [Philadelphia: Presbyterian Board of Christian Education, 1928], Vol. ii, 270-71). Elisabeth Schmidt's Envoi deals more fully with "the discernment of the church."—A.H.

7. In the KJ and RS versions the sentence begins, "I am not worthy." It seems better to translate literally the French text which Elisabeth Schmidt gives as follows: *Je suis trop petit pour toutes les grâces et pour toute la fidélité dont Tu as usé envers Ton serviteur.* —A.H.

8. Ernest Krüger, *Doctrine de l'Église Évangélique Hinschiste* (Nîmes, 1919), p. 5.

9. Madame Armengaud née Hinsch, *Recueil de Lettres Pastorales, précédé d'une notice biographique*, ed. Edouard Krüger (Nîmes: Imprimerie de A. Baldy, 1862), p. 27.

10. Ibid, p. 265.

11. Ibid., p. 327.

12. Ibid., p. 677.

13. The name, referring to the Lazarus of the parable in Luke 16:19-31, generally applies to a quarantine station or a leprosarium.—A.H.

14. Camille Leenhardt, *Vie de J.F. Oberlin (1740-1826) de E. Stoeber refondé sur un plan nouveau, complétée de nombreux documents inédits* (Paris-Nancy: Berger-Levrault, 1911). [Yes, this is the man for whom the Ohio college is named. Though Oberlin never came to the United States, within seven years of his death his name was chosen for the new college and community by two New England home missionaries. They wanted to identify their new venture with the spirit which guided Oberlin, his wife, and their helpers in a fifty-nine-year ministry to the minds, bodies, and spirits of the people in four yoked parishes in a remote valley in the Vosges mountains near Strasbourg.—A.H.]

15. Here, Elisabeth Schmidt is referring to more than a score of Search/Encounter Centers which sprang up after World War II in France. This term, used by a young American staff member in the center at Pau, translates the French: "Centre de Rencontre et de Recherche." Though they are *sui generis* and each one has its own identity and mystique, these centers have much in common, and their directors meet from time to time to compare notes. They correspond roughly to conference centers in the United States and to the German Evangelical Academies. The *1979 Year Book of the French Churches* carries the following listing: "Family Center 'The Lazaretto,' La Corniche, Sète. Center for study and meetings. Small groups and conferences welcomed. Permanent staff leadership for cultural and worship activities."—A.H.

16. *"Monstre, c'est une femme!"*—evidently a strong and salty expletive for which I find no ready equivalent.—A.H.

17. This was a national commission, chosen by the National Synod.

18. *Acts of the National Synod in Valence, 1942*, pp. 13-14.

19. *Acts of the National Synod in Saint-Esprit, Paris, 1949*, p. 64.

20. A popular biography of Emerson includes this passage: "Emerson did not care to see the old courtly and romantic ideals

of womanhood abandoned for a dubious modern substitute. . . . He wrote Paulina Davis, one of the Worcester convention leaders: 'If women feel wronged, then they are wronged. But the mode of obtaining a redress, namely a public convention called by women, is not very agreeable to me. . . . Perhaps I am superstitious and traditional, but whilst I should vote for every franchise for women—vote that they should hold property and vote, yes and be eligible to all offices as men—whilst I should vote thus, if women asked, or if men denied . . . these things, I should not wish women to wish political functions nor, if granted, assume them.' " Ralph L. Rusk, *The Life of Ralph Waldo Emerson* (New York: Charles Scribners Sons, 1949), p. 370.—A.H.

21. The "oral tradition" from the first assembly of the World Council of Churches at Amsterdam in 1948 preserves this anecdote: Karl Barth was saying that only men should administer the Lord's Supper, since the celebrant represented Jesus (a man) who presided at the original Lord's Supper. Ms. Chakko replied that in India it is the woman who presides at festival meals!—A.H.

22. Elisabeth Schmidt, whose mother had insisted that she be qualified as a teacher, was anticipating by some twenty years the decision of the Synod of 1972, at which she was assistant moderator. That Synod endorsed and implemented the report of the Commission on the Reform of Theological Studies, chaired by Prof. Jacques Ellul of Bordeaux. From then on, every French pastor under the auspices of the French Reformed Church must have training and experience in an alternative but not incompatible field. This can be taken either before or during his or her theological education. Two national leaders of the pioneering Evangelical People's Mission (Mission Populaire Évangélique de France) are, the one a cabinetmaker, the other a bus driver!—A.H.

23. Cf. chapter 2, pp. 17-18.

24. In France the scouting movement, for both boys and girls, is closely tied in with the Protestant Church. The word for "scout" is *éclaireur (euse) unioniste,* stressing both the idea of reconnoitering and the idea of banding together.—A.H.

25. The French is "Association Cultelle." The English translation I have used is that of Albert Guérard in *France, a Modern History,* revised edition (Ann Arbor: University of Michigan Press, 1969), pp. 363f. On the local level as well as regional and national levels, the cultural, welfare, social-action, and missionary activities of the church had to be organized in legally discrete organizations, the societies and institutions. (See chapter 3, note 10.) Thus the service and social-action phases of parish life were under separate organizations of the same people. The old New England custom of separating the "church" from the "society" is somewhat analogous.—A.H.

26. We have seen (chapter 6, note 1) that the Code of 1802 required church officers to be chosen from among the "notables" (i.e., prominent men). The assumption was that their wealth and position was an index of qualities of spiritual leadership. We cannot blame Napoleon for originating this idea, but we must note that he got it embedded in bylaws and regulations for a century. (It is no longer required, de jure, but de facto?)—A.H.

27. At the time of the French Revolution the country was divided into ninety-five *départements*, such as Ain and Yonne, instead of the old provinces, such as Burgundy and Normandy. Each *département* is governed by a prefect, and the seat of government is the prefecture. Thus a "prefecture city" would correspond to something between a state capital and a county seat in the United States, and a church in such a situation would have corresponding prestige.—A.H.

8: Pastor in Algeria, 1958-62

1. When I received permission to include a condensation of Elisabeth Schmidt's first book (*Dans ces Temps de Malheur (1958-1962) J'Étais Pasteur en Algérie* (Paris: Les Éditions du Cerf, 1976) as an integral part of her autobiography, I felt the need for more background on Algeria. I found two books especially helpful: C.L. Sulzberger, *The Test—de Gaulle and Algeria* (New York: Harcourt Brace and World, 1962). The second was the general history, Albert Guérard, *France: A Modern History*, New

Edition Revised and Enlarged by Paul A. Gagnon (Ann Arbor: The University of Michigan Press, 1959, 1969). The quotations below are used by permission of The University of Michigan Press:

Algeria is a country of 12,500,000 inhabitants, more than twice the size of France, stretching from the Mediterranean deep into the Sahara and wedged between Morocco and Libya. In 1830, at the beginning of Louis Philippe's reign, his advisers perceived the need for something glamorous to offset his bourgeois, pedestrian style. The foreign adventure which offered was the conquest of Algeria, which required the full period of Louis Philippe's reign —1830-48. "When Bourmont landed near Algiers in 1830, he promised the natives that their religion, their institutions, their customs would be respected. . . . But the French, in defiance of the plain facts, declared Algeria to be an extension of France under the ministry of the interior." (p. 482)

From that time on there was opposition to French rule, sometimes in the form of guerrilla fighting in the mountains, and at sea the famous Barbary pirates preyed on commercial shipping. Nevertheless, there was enough stability in Algeria to lure enterprising French colonizers, who developed vast plantations using Algerian labor. In the cities the French colonizers duplicated the amenities of provincial cities in metropolitan France, including Catholic and Protestant churches which had virtually no relationship with the Algerians or the Berbers. Teeming ports like Oran and Algiers loaded ships with fruit, a cheap, sharp wine, and (much later) oil.

General Charles de Gaulle, who in 1940 had broadcast from London, "A battle is lost, but not the war," went to Algeria in 1943 as head of the "Fighting French." Coordinating his efforts with General Dwight Eisenhower's strategy and the gallant resistance movement in France itself, de Gaulle had the satisfaction of seeing French troops reach the Rhine before General Patton's tanks rolled in. But Algeria was to tax de Gaulle's skill as a diplomat and his staying power as a leader.

Swept into power on the tide of victory, General de Gaulle restored the French nation's lost pride, presided over an orderly purge of the wartime collaborationists, and won recognition for France as one of the "big five," with a permanent seat on the

Security Council of the United Nations. He succeeded in setting a number of former colonies on their own feet. He moved with caution and conviction, with astuteness and grace. Algeria was his most taxing and his most remarkable achievement. Aloof and proud, de Gaulle nevertheless believed in self-determination for third world peoples. He saw that "it must not be the partnership of the horse and the driver . . . that fraternity between nations, as well as between men, cannot exist except on terms of freedom and equality." (p. 486) "General de Gaulle's curiously subtle diplomacy and inflexible will brought into the conflict . . . prestige, courage and generosity. . . . (p. 484) Civil war was averted, without yielding an inch to the proto-fascist groups in Algiers." (p. 506) "He silenced the colonists by agreeing with them better than they agreed with themselves, and giving a deeper meaning to their slogan, *integration*. Integration? By all means? But this implies that every citizen in Algeria, without distinction of race or religion, must have exactly the same rights and opportunities. . . . Political equality would be immediate. Economic equality was to be achieved within five years. . . . The newly discovered oil wealth of the Sahara came as a *deus ex machina* . . . .It will not turn Algeria into another Saudi Arabia [but] it will make a vast industrial development possible. . . . What de Gaulle offered Algeria was not mere wealth, but 'the end of contempt.' " (pp. 514-15) Looking at de Gaulle's finesse not only in Algeria but in dealing with all of France's colonies, Professor Gagnon concludes: "The miracle he [General de Gaulle] achieved was to climb down grandly, in an apotheosis. He gave up every thought of holding France's dominance through sheer force: such is not his conception of *grandeur*. Instead of yielding sullenly to native and foreign pressure, he assumed the initiative. He was realistic enough to believe that, in the long run, generosity is the safest policy. So he turned over the whole problem to the native populations themselves." (p. 512)—A.H.

2. This was the organization that attempted to oust General de Gaulle. The FLN (National Liberation Front) was the Algerian secret organization. There was terrorism on both sides.—A.H.

3. With curious inconsistency, Algeria and Alsace-Lorraine revert to the Napoleonic pattern in which the state maintains

church property and pays clergy salaries, despite the French law of 1905 separating church and state.—A.H.

4. Kabyle is a mountainous region (up to 7,000 feet high) south of Algiers. The Kabyles are a Berber tribe, generally blond and blue-eyed, with a distinctive language and customs. They have maintained their ethnic solidarity since before the time of Augustine of Hippo (354-430), who was surely the Berber best known to history. Conquered by the Arabs, they have nevertheless been valiant guerrilla fighters against the French. Monotheists since the third century, they do not practice their Muslim faith as strictly as the Arabs. Very few have become Christian. Elisabeth Schmidt refers several times in the book to their anomalous situation in Algerian society.—A.H.

5. This refers to the night of August 24, 1572 when many prominent Protestants remained in Paris, celebrating the wedding (on August 18) of the Protestant king Henvy IV of Navarre (later Henry IV of France) to Marguerite of Valois—a marriage which was supposed to seal the end of the tragic civil wars. Catherine de Medici and her supporters suddenly decided on a general massacre, for which the Guise party and the fanatical people of Paris furnished abundant means. On August 24, St. Bartholomew's Day, the bloody work began. Coligny, the powerful Huguenot leader, was killed, and with him a number of victims that has been variously estimated, reaching not improbably 8,000 in Paris and several times that number in the whole of France. Henry of Navarre saved his life by abjuring Protestantism. For a fuller account of the complicated series of events leading to this tragic night see Williston Walker, *A History of the Christian Church* (rev. ed.; New York: Charles Scribners Sons, 1959), p. 384.—A.H.

6. See chapter 7, note 27.

9: The Deepening Rift

1. In an address on September 16, 1959, de Gaulle said, with his usual style and authority, "I consider it necessary that recourse to self-determination should be proclaimed today." Quoted in Elisabeth Schmidt, *J'Étais Pasteur en Algérie* (Paris: Les Éditions du Cerf, 1976), p. 100.

2. The putschists had an intricate scheme of parachuting to the airport in Toulouse and from there attacking Paris, enlisting support from opponents of de Gaulle in metropolitan France. —A.H.

3. In 1978, several years after Elisabeth Schmidt's retirement, Pastor Chevallier succeeded Pastor Marc Boegner and Pastor Jacques Maury as head of the French Reformed Church.—A.H.

4. Literally, "hairy." This was the term used for French soldiers in World War I. (Its companion pieces were the American "doughboy" and the British "Tommy.")—A.H.

10: Ministry in Nancy, 1963-72

1. We would say "senior minister." In France the designation relates also to the official board of the church, over which the chief pastor generally presides. The chief lay officer (for us, senior deacon, senior warden, etc.) is the vice-president of the council. —A.H.

2. The Blue Cross in France is roughly comparable to our Alcoholics Anonymous. In France it has a longer history and is more closely tied to the churches.—A.H.

3. The World Council had a "Department of Cooperation Between Men and Women in the Church, the Family, and Society." Madeleine Barot was its executive secretary.

4. The Third Republic style (1870-1940) was imitative, as in the great railroad stations of Paris and the Paris Opéra.—A.H.

5. Marianne is the emblem of the French Republic, a very French counterpart of "Uncle Sam" and "John Bull." In every city hall there is a bust of Marianne. From time to time a new face may be substituted for the old. At one time Brigitte Bardot's face looked down on the deliberations of the city fathers; at the time of the meeting of the regional synod to which Elisabeth Schmidt refers, it was a more matronly face which looked down.—A.H.

6. "Oeuvres et mouvements," literally "works and movements," hardly does justice to this important element in the life of

the French church. In broad-brush terms, the "societies and agencies" in France are the counterparts of our Boards, Commissions, and Instrumentalities. They cover missions, social action, and welfare work. In chapter 4 on Gurs, we saw CIMADE at work on a national level. In chapter 7 on Sète, we looked at the Lazaretto, a local institution which can help us to understand hundreds of others. If the National Synod were to invite a representative of each institution, its numbers would more than double. Hence a small selection of representatives is invited to each National Synod. By the peculiarities of French history (anticlericalism at the turn of the century in particular), these agencies are governed under a separate law (1901) and must be separately incorporated, even though they are run by the same people who govern and support the churches.—A.H.

7. A semimonthly magazine.

8. *Acts of the National Synod in Nantes, 1965*, p. 252.

9. This is the same Paul Keller who, professionally qualified both as an Alpine guide and as a pastor, now heads the practical phase of theological training, a new dimension to the ministry to which I alluded in chapter 7, note 22.—A.H.

10. *Acts of the National Synod in Nantes, 1965*, p. 39.

11. Ibid., p. 228.

12. Ibid., p. 31.

13. Ibid., p. 30.

14. *Acts of the National Synod in Paris, 1949*, p. 22.

15. *Acts of the National Synod in Nantes, 1965*, p. 247.

16. *Special Session at Clermont-Ferrand, 1966, Acts*, p. 27.

17. Decision VIII, *Acts of the National Synod at Clermont-Ferrand, 1966,* p. 29. The full text is as follows:
"The National Synod:
"1. Expresses the gratitude of the church toward the women who are already exercising ministries within it as parish assistants, deaconesses, etc. It affirms the eminent dignity of their ministries and hopes that these latter will be dignified by a better definition of

the responsibilities and functions which they carry with them. (Adopted unanimously.)

"2. Recognizing that Christ edifies his church through the unity, the diversity, and the complementarity of the different ministries which he gives, the Synod decides to welcome and ordain women as it does men, to the ministries of the Word, as well as to those of the Diaconate. (Adopted by 74 votes for, 7 against.)

"3. Henceforth it will belong to the competent commissions and councils (and not to the Synod in plenary session) to examine vocations, to grant to women as to men the authorization for consecration-ordination, and to consider and decide on assignments. (Adopted by 77 votes for, 3 against.)

"4. Knowing that it has become indispensable to define the content of the different ministries; and knowing that the participation of women, in particular, renews and broadens the conditions of the exercise of these ministries, the Synod expects from the common study decided upon by the councils and the four-church executive board: (a) that the study will allow a discrimination of the constitutive elements of the different ministries, beginning with the pastoral; and (b) that the study will clarify the way in which the exercise of these ministries may best be divided among several pastors, whether men only or men and women, whether in urban or in consistorial churches. (Adopted by 75 votes for, 5 against.)"

The four churches are: The French Reformed Church and its counterpart in Alsace-Lorraine, the Lutheran Church of the Confession of Augsburg in Alsace-Lorraine, and The Evangelical Lutheran Church of France. The two Lutheran bodies are in full communion with the Reformed, with free interchange of pastors, common programs of theological and continuing education, and sharing in chaplaincies and institutional ministries. The four churches collaborate both at the headquarters level and in the field. The highest unit of cooperation consists of the permanent national officers and is sometimes described as "The Four Executives," *Les Quatre Bureaux.*—A.H.

18. See chapter 7, pp. 129-30.

19. Elisabeth Schmidt has furnished this explanation: "Viscount

Charles de Foucauld was a French officer who explored Morocco, was converted in 1890, and left the army. He joined the Trappists, was ordained a priest in 1901, became a hermit at the oasis of Hoggar in the Sahara. He was assassinated in 1916 by a band of Muslims hostile to Christianity. At the time of the colonial conquests, he founded a whole school of Christian devotion along the lines of Francis of Assisi. In the years before World War I, in the incredible solitude of the Sahara desert, he proclaimed himself 'the brother of all men without exception or distinction.' Discounting their Roman Catholic stamp (invocation of the saints, etc.) I have found his writings helpful in my own devotions. 'Live as though you were going to die a martyr today.' He often put his symbol (a cross above a heart) at the beginning of his writings and wore that emblem outlined in red on his tunic. His followers, 'Little Brothers' and 'Little Sisters,' are at work in many parts of Africa. Small wonder, then, that with that portrait looking down at us, the Superior and I could start a dialogue!"—A.H.

20. This custom, which helps to account for the fraternal spirit among French pastors, goes hand in hand with the equalization of salaries. The only differentials are for cost of living in large cities like Paris, family allowances for the education of children, and a premium for seniority.—A.H.